YOU CAN LIVE IN
YOUR DREAM HOME!

YOUR ULTIMATE GUIDE TO RENOVATING YOUR EXISTING HOME OR BUILDING YOUR NEW CUSTOM HOME

By Dave Reagan

First Edition 2021
Copyright © 2021 by Reagan Homes, LLC

ISBN: 978-0-578-93570-6

Published by Reagan Homes, LLC
197 Long Wharf Road Mystic, CT 06355

Dave Reagan
www.ReaganHomes.com

Printed in the United States of America.

To my beautiful wife, Cheryl, and kids Michael, Thomas and Kate who always supported me. I will be forever grateful for all your love and support.

To my mother and father, Mel and Kathleen who always encouraged me to help others. Thank you!

To my brothers, Jeff and Scott, and other family members, thank you for all your inspiration.

To my clients who I have been blessed to work with over the years and trusted my knowledge and expertise to help them build or remodel their dream homes.

To the Reagan Homes Team who continue to serve our clients to the highest quality and help us live out our mission of helping families live in their dream homes.

To my mentors, coaches, peers, and friends who have helped and supported the Reagan Homes Team in fulfilling our mission.

To the readers of this book, who may just be thinking about building or remodeling your dream home, I hope this book helps give you ideas and guidance. Whether you are local to southeastern CT or afar, do not hesitate to reach out at www.ReaganHomes.com for further guidance. I also have a network of hundreds of quality builders and contractors throughout the country whom I mentor and have great relationships with. I am happy to help you in any way possible.

INSPIRATIONAL QUOTES

"

"Your life is like a movie and you are the
actor, director and writer so make it a blockbuster."
~ Dave Reagan

"If you think you can or you think you cannot you're right."
~ Henry Ford

"The past does not equal the future."
~ Tony Robbins

"If you do what you have always done you get what you've always gotten."
~ T. R.

"Your present circumstances don't determine where you can go;
they merely determine where you start."
~ Nido Qubein

"Whatever the mind of man can conceive and believe, it can achieve."
~ Napoleon Hill

"All our dreams can come true, if we have the courage to pursue them."
~ Walt Disney

"Talent wins games, but teamwork and intelligence wins championships."
~ Michael Jordan

"Don't be afraid to give up the good to go for the great."
~ John D. Rockefeller

"Great things are done by a series of small things brought together."
~ Vincent Van Gogh

TABLE OF CONTENTS

INTRODUCTION

Hi, I am Dave Reagan, owner and founder of Reagan Homes. I am so pleased that you are reading this book because that likely means you are considering building a new custom home or renovating your existing home.

I find many people feel like building their new custom home or renovating their existing home is not possible for them. At Reagan Homes, we understand that nearly every family can afford their dream home. Think of it this way: What you are investing in is bringing your family and friends together to create priceless memories that will last a lifetime.

Our website is full of great information including blog posts, white papers, articles, and more. I invite you to visit—to poke around, read some posts and blogs, learn a bit more about us and what it's like to build or renovate with us. I'm sure you have questions. We have answers.

I want you to know that we don't just care about home; we care about you. We will build your new custom home or renovate your existing home like it's our own. I assure you that our team will make the building or remodeling process as straightforward and rewarding as possible.

One of my favorite moments as a contractor is seeing happy families live in their dream homes, and my team and I pride ourselves on not only delivering top quality craftsmanship but also on guiding you every step of the way. From evaluating land to design to financing, and of course the construction, we have you covered.

We focus on a simple four-step process for building or renovating your dream home, and this simple set of steps truly makes the entire process easy.

STEP 1: We meet with you in person or virtually to learn about your goals and desires.
STEP 2: We help you design efficiently & budget cost effectively for your new project.
STEP 3: We will build your new custom home or remodel your existing home.
STEP 4: You and your family enjoy your new dream home!

Again, while I love the entire journey of remodeling or building your dream home, my favorite step is the fourth and final, during which you can create priceless memories.

I invite you to start the process by scheduling your complimentary, no-obligation consultation with me or one of our Reagan Homes team members. All you have to do is visit www.ReaganHomes.com or call (860) 962-6250 today.

We look forward to learning more about your goals, desires and what you have in mind for your dream home. Thank you!

~Dave Reagan

About Dave Reagan

I have always had a passion for helping people. I love helping people fulfill their dreams by creating fantastic home environments so they can share amazing memories with their friends, family and loved ones. During the 30+ years of building custom homes and transforming existing homes through renovations, I have learned so much which I am so excited to share some of my knowledge with you in this book.

I not only enjoy sharing my experience with our local clients and team members, but I also share my knowledge with other builders and contractors throughout the world by mentoring them. Furthermore, I love to help motivate kids. As a prominent business leader, I help empower our youth to dream big and help them fulfill their goals.

If I wasn't a builder, my close friends and family know that I'd be a songwriter! I love to play the guitar and sing. One of my favorite activities is to get everyone involved in karaoke at a party. I simply love music as it is great for the soul!

About Reagan Homes

On behalf of everyone at Reagan Homes, we look forward to learning more about your goal and desires as it relates to building or remodeling your dream home. A lot of people feel like building their new custom home or renovating their existing home is not possible. At Reagan Homes, we understand that nearly every family can afford their dream home. Really what you are investing in is bringing your family and friends together to create priceless memories that will last a lifetime.

Life is too short to live in an environment you are not thrilled with. Save time, avoid frustration and save a significant amount of money when you entrust Reagan Homes to build your new custom home or renovate your existing home.

Our expert, friendly and flexible team is here to guide you every step of the way. We strive to make the building or remodeling process as stress-free as possible. From brilliant designers to land surveyors to structural engineers to adept architects to our distinguished craftsmen, our team will help you build or remodel efficiently and cost effectively.

You will save time, avoid frustration and save a substantial amount of money when you entrust Reagan Homes to build your custom home or renovate your existing home. Our team is eager to intently listen to your ideas and help bring your desires to fruition.

We look forward to learning more about what you want in your dream home during your complimentary, no-obligation consultation. Visit www.ReaganHomes.com or call (860) 962-6250 today to schedule.

PART 1:

SHOULD YOU BUILD OR SHOULD YOU REMODEL?

Various situations could lead you to ask this question. You could be a newly wedded couple unsure if buying an existing home and remodeling it for your purpose would be better than buying land building from scratch.

Or maybe your family is already established and you're trying to decide whether remodeling your home would be more prudent than building another from the foundation up.

Is it better to build a new house or remodel an existing one?

There are advantages to both, but the deciding factors will come down to your desires and preferences. Of course, your budget will likely play a role in this decision as well.

We understand that each family's situation and preferences are unique. We strive to learn what is most important to you.

Our expert guidance can help you determine if it makes sense to build new, remodel, or expand at your current address. As a design-build firm we can present the most cost-effective solutions to you visually. Our clients find seeing 2D plans with 3D renderings allows them to decide which direction makes the most sense for them. We also provide ballpark costs to help guide decision-making throughout the process.

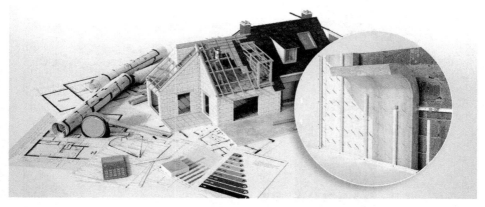

At Reagan Homes, we are eager to learn about your specific situation and what you want in a home. We can help guide you through the decision-making process and quickly provide you ballpark estimates and design options.

BUILDING A NEW CUSTOM HOME

The option of building a new custom home can be really attractive. When you build, you have all the freedom to shape and customize the house into whatever you want. This typically is a major advantage of building a new home.

Building a new home offers you the opportunity to choose the exact materials and finishes you want. You can also allocate spaces within the house as efficiently as possible without being constrained by existing layouts and rooms.

Furthermore, you have the chance of incorporating new technology into your building right from the onset.

If these are not attractive reasons enough, the planning of the house can be done with your entire family to fit all of your specifications and desires.

As attractive as these benefits are, you have to make many decisions throughout the process. As a full service design-build company we are here to guide you every step of the way should you want to build a new custom home.

From helping you find the perfect plot of land to helping you choose paint colors for your walls, we have you covered.

LAND
FOR SALE

RECENT NEW CUSTOM-HOME BUILD PROJECT SUCCESS STORY

This client wanted to build new. While they chose their land before meeting with us, we could have also helped them find land that would fit their lifestyle and the home environment their heart was set on. We shared multiple versions of virtual tours and plans like those below. We also provided different options and guidance based on cost-saving ways to build. When the job was finished, not only had we helped this client save thousands of dollars, but—most importantly—they got the house they wanted with the finishes and features they wanted.

Sample exterior rendering

Sample elevation drawing

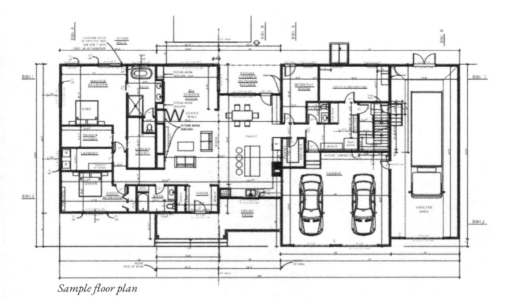

Sample floor plan

Samples of the virtual tour

RECENT NEW CUSTOM-HOME BUILD PROJECT SUCCESS STORY

Remodeling is a very broad concept. There is simple and light remodeling, which would involve changing some things within a building without massively affecting the structure and foundation of a home.

There is also more extensive remodeling and renovating, during which walls could be removed and bump outs or complete additions created to increase your living space.

If you love your current location and property, but desire more living space, we can help. When you renovate your existing home with an addition, you gain the advantages of building new with less expense than usually associated with building an entirely new home.

In some situations a complete teardown may make sense. Every situation is different and we can help you explore all of your options.

RECENT RENOVATION PROJECT SUCCESS STORY

One of our clients had a beautiful existing home and backyard but wanted to take their living environment to another whole level. They were not interested in moving or building new. We listened to the client's wants and wishlist. We put together a plan with multiple 3D renderings to provide the client with different options. Additionally, because of our more than 30 years of experience working with the town, we also knew what constraints could exist because of our 30+ years of experience and working with the town we also knew what constraints could exist in the permitting process. Not only did the client save thousands of dollars but, more importantly, they got what they wanted from their renovation.

Sample exterior renderings of the renovation

Sample interior kitchen rendering

Sample outdoor kitchen rendering

Sample game room rendering

In today's world there are so many options and variables to the building and remodeling process. You do not want to get taken advantage of and waste your valuable time and money. We can help inform you and direct you in your decision making process so in the end you get what you want.

One of the main keys to a successful remodel/ renovation or building a new custom home is proper planning and design. We have a team of experts from land surveyors, interior designers, landscape designers, architects, structural engineers, and, of course, our 30+ years of building experience help alleviate unneeded stress throughout your project. We make the process simple and rewarding.

PART 2:

10 WAYS OTHER CONTRACTORS WILL RIP YOU OFF

Working with a general contractor (GC), builder, or remodeling company isn't always easy. Even if he or she is highly rated or is recommended by someone you know well and respect, the experience can be rife with problems, leading to an incredible amount of frustration—not to mention the potential for lost time, lost money, and, ultimately, you may not get what you want.

Reagan Homes is different. Personally, I have been in the building and remodeling business for more than 30 years. I have built many deep relationships in Middlesex and New London counties. Our team consists of experienced professionals who help ensure the dream home you envision becomes a reality. There is not much we haven't done and not much we can't do. And nothing is out of bounds. Our team strives to deliver on time and on budget, and we won't rip you off like other contractors might.

We're not suggesting that ripping off clients is intentional. Sometimes it's the result of a lack of experience or bad business habits. Sometimes it comes with a too-busy schedule. Sometimes, though, ripping off clients—whether it's money, time, or energy—comes from negligence. And unfortunately, sometimes, the root cause is more sinister.

The following is a list of 10 red flags to be aware of. If you see, hear, or experience any of these issues while consulting with or working with a contractor, you may be in trouble.

1. THEY AREN'T EXPERIENCED IN OR THEY DOWNPLAY THE IMPORTANCE OF THE DESIGN-BUILD RELATIONSHIP.

Once upon a time, homebuilding generally included two separate contracts—one (usually with an architect or designer) for the design of a home and the second with a general contractor for the home's construction as per the architect's plans. Frequently, this arrangement can lead to trouble, finger-pointing, and hard feelings. And the homeowner is left to mediate and clean up the pieces.

Design-build construction, which has gained in popularity over the last decade, replaces the traditional homebuilding model. In the design-build model, everyone—from architects and designers to the general contractor and subcontractors to the homeowner—function as a team, working in concert and collaborating to diminish the likelihood of critical issues being missed. It also helps the building process to run more smoothly and quickly.

Two-dimensional plans are a necessity, but 3D renderings help you (and us) visualize your space more easily and accurately. We have a team of designers who provide 3D renderings, which allow us to build more efficiently and save you time, money—and most importantly—helps you achieve the end result you desire.

Sample 3D rendering of a new custom home

Sample 3D rendering of an open floor plan, from kitchen to living room, in for an addition that was to be used as an in-law apartment

Sample 3D rendering of a new custom home

If a contractor you are talking with is reluctant or flat-out refuses to work in a design-build environment, it's worth digging deeper to find out why. The answers may be disqualifying.

2. THEY WORK WITH A LIMITED GROUP OF SUBCONTRACTORS AND/OR SUPPLY YARDS

Working only with a select group of subcontractors—or having relationships with a limited number of lumberyards and suppliers—can cause multiple problems that, as a homeowner, you don't want to have to deal with.

First of all, there's time and the potential for blown timelines. What happens to the timeline of your build, for example, if your contractor's drywall crew is booked on another job with another builder when your job is ready and waiting for them? Your job is going to run late. NOBODY wants their home construction to run late for reasons so foreseeable and avoidable.

 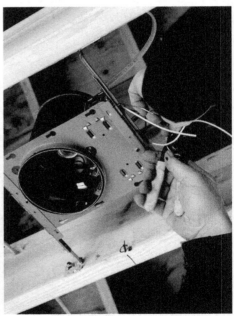

Additionally, having multiple relationships with a myriad of subcontractors allows us to help keep their pricing honest. And in the case of lumber yards, for example, prices (and lead times, for that matter) can vary significantly from yard to yard. Do you want to overrun your budget right out of the gate on materials and supplies that are critical to the construction of your new home? No, of course not.

Furthermore, following a year of shortages, pricing increases, and supply chain interruptions (thanks, global pandemic), good relationships with yards and suppliers help ensure we can secure the needed materials.

3. THEY ARE NOT UP-TO-DATE WITH THE MOST CURRENT AND INNOVATIVE BUILDING TRENDS

This is another area in which time and money—in both the short-term and the long-term—are at stake.

Two of the biggest trends right now are smart home integration and outdoor living spaces. You may decide you want at least one of these for your new custom home or renovation. Smart home integration can help homeowners save money on energy and utilities while also providing security and a sense of safety.

Outdoor living features speak to how a family lives and functions within their home and can expand the usable square footage of their living space.

Now, suppose the contractor you're consulting with doesn't know or understand all of what a smart home system can do for you. Or perhaps they fail to share in the belief that having outdoor kitchen and living spaces will benefit your family in untold ways for years to come. You could wait and have either of those features added later, but again, is it worth the time, money, and frustration not to get what you want upfront?

Or maybe they make assumptions and plan to install the kind of insulation or ventilation system they always do. They don't share with you new, more sustainable, eco-friendly options, options you would very much consider if only you knew about them. But they aren't experienced with them. So you don't know about them.

4. THEY DON'T HAVE PROPER INSURANCE

You're building a new home or renovating your existing home. Between financing and making thousands of decisions—while also carrying on with your life and job—should it be your responsibility to ensure your general contractor has the proper insurance? Well, maybe it shouldn't be, but if you want to know without a doubt that your contractor—and by extension, YOU—are covered in any of a myriad of possible scenarios, then you should do your homework

General contractors need to have workers' compensation, professional liability, general liability, property liability, and umbrella insurance. Together, such policies protect your contractor against employee injury, property damage, tool, equipment, and supply theft, and more. And if your GC doesn't have the proper insurance and someone is hurt on the job or a piece of rented equipment is stolen or damaged, you could be on the hook financially.

5. THEY HAVE POOR ACCOUNTING HABITS OR ARE NOT DETAIL-ORIENTED

Numerous models exist for how a GC charges clients for their work. Some general contractors charge labor plus materials–the **time and materials** model.

Others charge a single fee for all work and materials (billed at cost). They then add a fee on top of those charges to serve as their profit. This is called **cost-plus pricing**.

And then, there is **fixed-bid pricing**, which is very specific and detailed. Unless there are changes to the scope of the work, what is bid in such a scenario is what you will pay.

But all of these billing models are only as good as those keeping the records and handling invoicing. If the price of lumber goes down between the time your GC gives you a fixed bid and the time he orders it, you won't realize those savings yourself. On the flip side, if an equipment or supply invoice gets lost or misplaced, your GC could lose money if they don't realize and correct their mistake.

Surely, you want an accurate accounting of the cost to build your home. Discussing accounting practices–or speaking up when you suspect there's an issue–is critical for all involved. Better yet, choose only to work with a contractor who discusses accounting and billing practices as a part of their initial pitch to you.

6. THEY ARE DISORGANIZED

Would you describe yourself or someone you love or work with as disorganized? If so, what are the real-life ramifications of that disorganization? Lost time and money, right? How about frustration?

If you're paying someone by the hour, how keen are you to pay them for the excessive amount of time they spend searching for a particular small supply or tool on-site or in their vehicle? Or—pervasive, real-world example coming up—if they end up making four trips to the lumber yard in one day? Couldn't they have been better prepared and organized and purchased everything they bought during those four trips in just one trip? And what if they are late for a meeting or walk-through? Your time is valuable, too.

We wouldn't be keen on any of these matters, and you shouldn't be either. Speaking with previous clients is a good way to get a sense of how organized and professional your potential GC is.

Also, if you can, go to the jobsite of an existing project. Is the job site clean and organized. If the jobsite is messy, chances are the contractor is also disorganized. We invite you to visit any of our job sites and are happy to show you jobs in progress so you can see for yourself.

7. THEY DON'T HAVE A COHESIVE TEAM THAT SHARES THEIR CORE VALUES

We get it; hiring can be hard. Finding good people who will stick with you for the long haul can be challenging. But that's hardly an excuse for a team that fails to demonstrate trust, commitment, accountability, and pride–not only in the finished job but also in finishing the job.

Sure, some of it is in the pre-hire vetting and knowing what is wanted and needed in team members. Some potential hires are able and willing to grow and adapt. Some are incapable of doing so.

But as in any other work environment, the attitudes and performance of a team are reflective of that team's leader–in this case, the general contractor. It's in how he treats team members and speaks to them, how willing he is to collaborate and consider their suggestions, and in how he rewards them for a job well done. A cohesive team is built by how a GC communicates his or her expectations.

When a team doesn't feel like a team to its members, or when they fail to share core values, the impact on you and the building of your home may manifest as–you've got it–lost time and money and frustration. Sure, some of it is in the pre-hire vetting and knowing what is wanted and needed in team members. Some potential hires are able and willing to grow and adapt. Some are incapable of doing so.

8. THEY FAIL TO GUIDE YOU IN SELECTIONS FOR MATERIALS AND FINISHES

Selections of materials and finishes are critical for many reasons. Or better said, perhaps: Failure in selecting appropriate materials and finishes during the homebuilding process can lead to issues that may negatively impact safety, cost, usability, and various home systems. This is all knowledge your GC should be well experienced with. Their involvement in guiding you toward appropriate products and items is critical to so many other aspects of homebuilding.

The materials used in building and finishing your home, after all, are directly responsible for your comfort and safety. If your home is to be constructed in a windy area on the side of a mountain, you'll probably have better luck with insulation and windows manufactured to withstand those conditions. However, if your home will be in a river valley, it might perform better with materials selected for their ability to stand up to or even mitigate flooding.

From flooring to wall finishes and more, we will guide you in your selection of finishes. For example, we will direct you to more appropriate finishes for higher traffic areas. Furthermore, there is a wide variation of costs when it comes to materials and finishes. We will lead you through how different finishes and materials will impact your budget, whether you're building a new custom home or renovating your existing home. Our recommendations should save you money in the longer term, increase your comfort, and match your tolerance for maintenance.

9. THEY FAIL TO PRE-WIRE FOR YOUR FUTURE WANTS AND NEEDS

Let's say you have a toddler. Before you know it, he or she will be in school. And they'll need internet access and additional outlets in their room. Or maybe you don't need a fully wired home office right now. But what if, in a few years, you move into a home-based position? Perhaps an unfinished or semi-finished basement is fine for now. But might you want at some future time to convert it to a playroom, home theater, or home gym?

It's going to be a hassle—no doubt about it—to add or expand the systems you'll require later on. And yes, it will take longer to get such jobs done, and it will cost more, too. But while the electrical system is being built out, before the drywall goes up, that's the ideal time for your contractor to initiate a conversation about how your needs might change and what your future lifestyle could look like. It's about being intuitive and considering the realities of how you will use your space.

10. THEY DON'T DISCUSS YOUR POTENTIAL FUTURE NEEDS

If this home is to be your dream home, there's an expectation you'll live in it for a good, long time. In addition to considering matters like the number of outlets you may want to add or the easy expansion of wireless systems, it's also worthwhile for your contractor

to raise the issue of modifications that may be helpful as you age or if an aging parent may move in. The possibilities are endless. And your home surely can be retrofitted, remodeled, or renovated to meet future needs.

Preparing for tomorrow will never be easier or less expensive than it is today. And while you can't (and shouldn't) expect a general contractor to think of every future option, it should be a part of the conversation. And it likely will be if they understand and believe in the importance of the design-build model, is on top of the trends, pays attention to the little things, and provides logical and professional guidance to you throughout the building experience.

For example, you may be considering an addition down the road while you are building or renovating your existing home. Let us know so we can plan for another phase upfront to ultimately save you time and money in the long run.

The Reagan Homes team is the professional, experienced team you're looking for. I have been in the business for more than 30 years, building custom homes and executing major renovations for clients up and down the shoreline of Connecticut. I know the area, I know homebuilding, and I know (and live by) best practices.

I understand what your home means to you—that it's more than just the place you lay your head at night. There aren't many requests we haven't been able to fulfill. If you want something to be a part of your home, we want you to have it. We also want you to be sure you are not ripped off in the process.

Homes built by Reagan Homes

PART 3:

DESIGN

INVESTING IN DESIGN—THE LOGICAL APPROACH TO YOUR DREAM HOME

Design can help future-proof your plans. Investing in design before you begin your project can help you save thousands of dollars and help you get what you want.

Investing in design will allow you to modify your floor plans and make the most of 3D renderings. In fact, think of investing in design as a means to speed up the construction process and save on costs at the same time.

And in the end, when your project is finished, you will enjoy a beautiful space that will improve your mood and help you de-stress. With preferred design elements, you can create a brilliant home environment. A well-designed home structure fosters good health, comfort, and tranquility.

What Exactly Is a Predetermined Design Approach?

A pre-planned build approach refers to combining the construction and design aspects of a home remodeling or renovation project. If you want to renovate or construct a new project, Reagan Homes building expertise will ensure you have an efficient design and better flow to your new custom home or existing home renovation.

Essential Benefits of Home Design

When you heavily invest in design, you can expect the following benefits:

Get Superior Expertise

You don't necessarily have to outline every design element of the home renovation or remodeling project. Our team of expert designers will help you figure out how to maximize space and tie together different areas of your home.

Design Open Floor Plans

Open-floor design plans are an incredibly popular option. With an open floor plan, your home will feel more spacious, the flow of natural light will increase, and your indoor environment will be safely updated. Open floor plans allow you to create seamless indoor and outdoor spaces, and the smooth transition between the two can bring new life to your home.

Make Your Home Designs Aesthetically Pleasing

Just because you want to build an efficient and functional home doesn't mean you have to sacrifice visual appeal. Investing in design means you can embrace a more balanced approach to structuring space. With in-depth design preparation, you can add luxurious elements at an affordable cost.

Enjoy Continuity and Total Accountability

By investing in design upfront, you can ensure the continuity of construction and introduce design elements that will increase the efficiency of the construction process.

With the design-and build-approach, you should expect more accountability. When the design is at the forefront of a home renovation or remodeling project, there is more accountability in meeting deadlines and completing the entire project within budget.

More Collaboration, More Customization

When you invest in design upfront, the need to "control" and "obsess" over everything is eliminated. When you are not rushed to make a decision, as a homeowner, you feel more empowered to collaborate with us.

Designing upfront allows you the added flexibility to readjust, restructure, and redesign various aspects of the project. For instance, if you want to renovate or remodel the home to raise a new family, you can repurpose shared spaces.

Save on Costs and Time

The most significant advantage of investing in design is arguably the high cost-benefit ratio. With a heightened design approach, you can significantly bring down construction costs. With a condensed design process, you will also have lower engineering and architectural costs.

With an intuitive design approach, you will also learn more about how much each part of your home renovation or new custom home will cost. Furthermore, investing in design allows you to establish a more definitive construction schedule.

Throughout the construction process, you will also be able to revisit the design decisions you've already made and make minor changes that shouldn't incur additional costs. As a result, you're likely to utilize your home's space better.

Become More Involved in the Project

Another benefit of focusing on design is that you become more involved in the project. As an active participant in the design and construction of your home, you will begin to come up with better ideas and processes for accomplishing goals. In fact, your personal involvement in the design and construction processes will cause you to feel even more proud of your newly custom home or renovation.

Why You Should Prioritize Design

It is vital to take some time and invest in the design aspects of your home. It's a win-win strategy that serves as a continued evolution of your home. After all, your house reflects your personality, and you should opt for a space that offers the most comfort and relaxation.

Once you treat design as equal to construction, you eliminate the instinct to rush the project. Instead, you will have more time to finish the home's construction and get the details you want regardless of your budget.

Prioritizing design means you are prioritizing a more authentic feel for your house. Your house becomes a home with a blend of exciting design elements that will appeal to you and the people close to you.

When it comes to modern floor plans, you can imbue new life into our home by adding doorway-free rooms and increasing the flow of the air and space. Ultimately, investing in design allows you to create more vibrant spaces. Your space serves as the place that will bring people together and inspire others.

Because we are a design-build firm and have expert designers on our team, we can help you efficiently design your new custom home or existing-home renovation.

*To learn more, call the Reagan Homes team at (860) 962-6250
to learn more or visit www.ReaganHomes.com
to schedule a complimentary, no-obligation consultation.*

25 HOME FEATURES TO CONSIDER

With a renovation of your existing home or building of your new custom home come endless possibilities. Rest assured, the team at Reagan Homes is here to guide you throughout the process.

Custom Closets

Custom closets keep your home organized and provide a spacious ambiance. From walk-in closets to a pantry off the kitchen, each closet design is important to help keep your house (and your life) uncluttered. From installing custom shelving and custom cabinets to more simple ventilated shelving, we can help you determine which materials and layouts makes the most sense for you.

Creative Storage Spaces

Having extra storage is always a good idea. For example, we can create extra storage space under a staircase. We can also build storage space in higher, less accessible areas where you can store season clothing or items that are infrequently used.

Power Outlets in Your Closets

Whether you need to charge a vacuum or dust buster in your utility closet or plug in a watch-winder in your walk-in closet, extra outlets are a great feature to add; we suggest the addition of at least one outlet in each of your closets.

Storage and Closets in Each Room

Having a place to store books or other items in a built-in,closet, or other storage space in your study or home office is a great way to keep your workspace clutter-free. In fact, it is prudent to consider closets and storage in every room to help keep your home organized and looking great!

Lighting

From under-the-cabinet lighting to exterior landscaping lighting, from lighting fixtures to simple recessed lighting, there are many options when it comes to lighting your home. We have relationships with lighting designers who can guide you in what lighting will work best for you.

Mudroom

A mud room (off the entrance from the garage or front-door entrance area) is a place where you can store shoes, jackets, backpacks, and more. A mud room can also be a place for guests to stash some of their belongings when they come to visit. Whether you're building a new custom home or renovating your existing home, you may wish to consider adding a mudroom to help keep your home clutter-free and clean.

Outdoor Kitchen

More and more families want to enjoy outdoor living spaces. An outdoor kitchen can provide you a secondary environment in which to cook and entertain your guests while making additional memories with loved ones.

Double Ovens

If you are embarking on a kitchen remodel or building a new home, I'd strongly recommend that you consider double ovens. One can be a convection oven (which will help you cook your food faster), while the other can be a standard oven. Double ovens allow you to cook multiple dishes simultaneously at different temperatures, and they're especially helpful if you entertain often or enjoy hosting holiday meals.

Larger Cooktop

A 36" cooktop or range typically includes a fifth burner. Some appliance manufacturers with 36" versions accommodate griddles or grill attachments and still provide at least three additional burners for cooking. If you enjoy cooking or expect to do a lot of entertaining, you might even decide you need two cooktops.

Pot Filler

Not only does a pot filler look great behind a cooktop or range, you will love the convenience of not having to lug a pot full of water across the kitchen when you need to boil water.

Overflow Refrigerators

An overflow refrigerator located in a nearby mudroom, garage, or other room is a great option, especially for entertaining (and your holiday meals will be much less stressful) as guests often bring a dish that needs to be refrigerated. Planning for an overflow refrigerator also helps if your kitchen has a built-in refrigerator in which you lose a good amount of storage space compared to a traditional refrigerator.

Cabinetry That Hides Appliances

From panels that disguise the dishwasher, refrigerator, and ice maker to pop-up shelving from a base cabinet that can hide a mixer or toaster oven, there are many ways cabinetry can hide or disguise your appliances, making your kitchen looker cleaner, sleeker, and more organized.

Multiple Dishwashers

If you love to entertain or have a large family, you may want to consider having multiple dishwashers, which makes it easy to clean all of your dishes at once.

Hidden Safe Room

A safe room is a place to keep your valuables and other items that matter the most to you. A safe room can also serve as a place of refuge for you and your loved ones in times of danger, natural disasters, and emergencies.

Home Automation

Home automation can help increase safety, security, and peace of mind while also making your life easier and saving you money.

Hose Faucets on Second Floor Balconies

Decks and balconies on second floors are wonderful features. Making sure you have a hose faucet on a second floor balcony is a must to help keep such spaces clean.

Deep Sink in the Laundry Room

Having a deep sink in your laundry room is more beneficial than you might expect.

Dutch Door in the Laundry Room

Especially during the summer, many pets love the cool tile floors of a laundry room. Adding a Dutch door is much more aesthetically pleasing than using a baby gate to keep your pets in or out of the laundry room while still allowing air and light in.

Toy or Play Room on Each Level

If you have children, you will find that it is particularly convenient to have a playroom on each level—or at the very least, a dedicated area for kids to play in.

Inevitably, you will utilize each level of your home. Having a dedicated area on each is a way for your children to play safely while you are attending to whatever you need to attend to.

Barn or Other Detached Building

Perhaps you want to have a workshop or studio, a shed to store lawn equipment, or a pool house. Building a detached building while you are renovating or building a new home is a surefire way to add usable storage or living space. You can even connect the detached structure to the main house via a porch or breezeway.

Rain-Style Showerheads and Body Shower Jets

More people than ever are opting for rain-style showerheads and body shower jets in addition to handheld sprayers in their showers. These features deliver a spa-like environment. Consider these features especially for your master bathroom.

Finishing Your Garage

Having garage floor tiles or an epoxy-finished garage floor gives your garage a major upgrade in looks and functionality. (These kinds of garage floors are much easier to clean.) Storage space in the garage—often in the form of cabinetry—can also help keep you organized.

Ceiling Fans

Adding a ceiling fan to a room helps circulate air (cool air in the summer and heat in the winter), and with the wide range of ceiling fans available, a ceiling fan can also add to the aesthetics of a room.

Fireplaces

Today, there are many fireplace options, from electric to water vapor, from propane or natural gas to, of course, wood-burning. A fireplace can serve as a focal point in a room and help it feel warmer (literally and figuratively). Fireplaces and fire pits are also a great addition to your outdoor living spaces.

Patio

Extending your outdoor living space to include a patio that is covered with a porch, pergola, powered pergola, or that isn't covered at all is a great way to enjoy outdoor time with family, friends, and loved ones.

Maximize the potential of a new custom-built home or a major renovation by considering functional and essential features like those mentioned in this chapter.

At Reagan Homes, we are excited to have the opportunity to help make your dreams a reality at your current residence with a renovation or to help build your new custom home. We are here to guide you in deciding which features are must-haves and more.

To learn more, call the Reagan Homes team at (860) 962-6250
to learn more or visit www.ReaganHomes.com
to schedule a complimentary, no-obligation consultation.

5 BENEFITS OF
MINIMALIST HOME DESIGN

Your home should be a place of tranquility and peace. It should be a place to escape the hustle and bustle of everyday life. But if it is cluttered and cramped, you may have to seek refuge elsewhere. This is why adopting a minimalist design may be beneficial.

The concept of a clean, simple, and uncluttered space is the basis of minimalism. Minimalism is about embracing beauty, simplicity, and functionality in one place. In other words, you define the function of an item, know its necessity, then deploy it in your space; that way, you can focus on what is essential and let go of what is not.

Here is a question for you: What can a minimalist design do for you? And how can it impact your home's outlook? No idea? Not to worry. We have you covered.

1. Minimalist Design Can Influence your Mood

Minimalist design can have an impact on mood. Life feels different when you switch from a cramped and crowded home to a spacious one. Minimalist designs are usually simple and provide a spacious and aligned layout that makes you feel happier, calmer, and well-organized.

The effect this has on your life, in general, cannot be overemphasized because when you feel happier, better organized (and not stressed out), you may find you are more motivated and more productive.

2. More Space

Minimalist design is about focusing on that which is essential, functional, and necessary. It also means you may need to let go of any extra baggage, literally and figuratively, that you don't need and keep only essential items in your home.

By doing so, you will have more free space to move, work, and explore your creativity in the best ways possible.

3. Minimalist Design Makes Cleaning Easier

If you are looking for an easier, faster way to clean your home, you should consider a minimalist design. It's much easier to clean a house that isn't cluttered or cramped. More so, your house is likely to stay clean longer than if it's cluttered or cramped. When you're living with only essential items, you'll encounter a minimum of dust.

4. Cost-Effective

Minimalist design means buying less and saving more. With this design approach and as mentioned previously, you should concern yourself only with what is essential and functional in the home.

5. Luxurious Outlook

"There is elegance in simplicity" and "less is more" are two terms you might find cliché, but they are relevant to minimalist design. The thought of purchasing many expensive items to achieve a luxurious ambiance for your home is outdated. Try opting instead for simple, functional designs that demonstrate a contemporary and sophisticated outlook.

Adopting a minimalist design philosophy is an excellent choice if you would like to free up space and live in a simple, cleaner environment. A minimalist design style can also contribute to a calmer, more organized, and more productive lifestyle.

Experience great home designs and learn how they can positively impact your life. At Reagan Homes, we put you at the center of it all whether you want to have a minimalist design or not.

To help us bring your ideas to life, call the Reagan Homes team at (860) 962-6250 to learn more or visit www.ReaganHomes.com to schedule a complimentary, no-obligation consultation.

FOUNDATION OPTIONS

Basement, Crawlspace, or Slab: Which Foundation Type is Right for You?

Foundations are forever, and a solid, well-built foundation is a necessity, whether you're building a new home or adding on to an existing home. Sure, the foundation is the base upon which your home is built, but it also is responsible for so much more.

Your home's foundation is tasked with insulating against the cold, keeping moisture at bay, and resisting the movement of the surrounding earth. And–legitimately–a foundation should last forever. If you or anyone you know has ever had to contend with foundation issues, you know about the mental and financial stress that may result.

So yes, your foundation is critical to the functioning and longevity of your home. And of course, like everything else to do with building and remodeling or renovating, you will have a decision to make: slab, crawlspace, or basement. Which is the right choice for your project?

Our team has been building homes and additions for more than 30 years, and we have vast experience with all three foundation types. We know the pros and cons of each and will be happy to discuss the options with you in greater detail and help determine which is right for your home and family.

Slab on Grade

A slab on grade is likely the easiest, fastest and the least expensive foundation option. Once the home site is leveled out—or brought to grade—a simple wood form is built and concrete is poured. The result is a solid slab of concrete, between 4 and 8 inches thick, upon which a home is built. Slab foundations are reinforced with steel rods, and the home's drainage pipes are laid out in a grid before the concrete is poured. Overall, slab foundations are the most common type of foundations in the United States.

Aside from how quick and easy it is to pour a slab foundation, since there is no space for air to exist between it and the house, houses built on slabs are impervious to mold and termites. Both are potential issues in warmer climates and that's why you very seldom see anything but slab foundations in places like Florida.

That same lack of airflow, however, means that slab-based homes can warm up quickly and uncomfortably. Slab foundations offer little to no protection against flooding, and repairing damaged pipes embedded in the concrete can be expensive and messy. They also lack the storage and living spaces provided by other foundation types.

Crawlspace

Crawlspaces are another popular option, especially in areas with soil that is difficult to move and work. The space between the ground and the home built above it is usually no more than 3 to 4 feet. It is technically the concrete pillars (or footings) at the perimeter of the crawlspace upon which a house is built.

Crawlspaces do an apt job at protecting a home from floodwaters and shifting earth, and they can help cool a home in the summer months. They also provide limited storage space best dedicated to outdoor items.

But the ventilation that helps cool a home in summer can make winter heating more expensive. Trapped moisture can lead to mold, and there's plenty of room for critters, including termites. Crawlspaces should be insulated and sealed, which may add extra time to your building schedule and additional costs to your budget.

Full Basement

Basements come with lots of benefits—although they may take longer to excavate, pour, and cure. basements are the most expensive foundation option, but they provide extra storage space and usable square footage. The open underground area of a basement also helps cool homes during hot summers.

In addition to being considerably more expensive than crawlspaces or slabs, they are prone to flooding, moisture, and mold, especially in certain climates and geographies.

Our team can help you weigh the options, examining both your property and the needs of your family, to arrive at the best possible solution.

ROOF CONSTRUCTION: STICK FRAMING VS. TRUSSES

The next time you're out and about, look up at the roofs of the homes around you. Do you think more are stick-framed or trussed? Would you even be able to tell the difference? For that matter, do you even know what the difference is between the two?

Let's start by defining each. When a builder stick-frames a roof, that roof is being built—or assembled—on location, one piece of lumber at a time. "Ridge and valley" beams are hoisted into place first, followed by rafters and then ceiling joists. Each piece of lumber is cut to fit on the ground and then lifted to a framer who installs the "sticks," one at a time. Stick framing has been around practically forever. If you live in an older neighborhood, every house likely has a stick-framed roof.

A wood truss is a manufactured product built off-site to the specifications required by a builder. Trusses include sloping and ceiling joists in a single structural piece. Once constructed, trusses are shipped to the home site, lifted with a crane, and installed directly above the house's exterior walls. Trussing is a newer technology that has gained in popularity over the last few decades.

Benefits and drawbacks exist for each of these styles of roof construction. Reagan Homes is experienced with both, and our team would be happy to discuss the options with you, helping you decide which is better for the construction of your custom home, renovation, or addition.

Stick Framing: The Pros and Cons

Stick framing has a lot of support among builders of all stripes and in all locations throughout the United States.

The pros for using stick framing include:

- With stick framing, all roof construction is done on-site, which is beneficial especially for building done in remote areas where it may be challenging to ship and receive prefabricated trusses.

- Since every stick framing job is, by definition, a custom job, it's much easier to accommodate plan changes or make adjustments.

- Since all construction is performed on-site, no ordering lead time is required.

- Stick framing is a better option for complicated roofs with multiple gables or particularly steep pitches.

- Stick framing allows for vaulted ceilings, dormers, and attic space.

The flip side of many of the benefits of stick framing, however, can be drawbacks to this type of construction:

- When you are limited to building on-site, you're often at the mercy of the weather. Bad weather can cause timeline delays and can jeopardize the integrity of your lumber.

- With on-site, custom stick framing, a more significant opportunity for accidents and injuries exists.

- Some municipalities may require stick-framed roofs to be inspected by a structural engineer to ensure they are safe and securely built.

- Costs—labor costs, especially—can be higher since all work is completed on-site.

- Craftsmanship: It can be difficult for even the most experienced and talented builders to precisely duplicate dozens of identical boards and rafters.

*To learn more, call the Reagan Homes team at (860) 962-6250
to learn more or visit www.ReaganHomes.com
to schedule a complimentary, no-obligation consultation.*

Roofing Trusses: The Pros and Cons

Roof trusses have their place and have been gaining in popularity steadily over the last 50 years.

The pros for using trusses include:

- Easy construction. The prefabricated trusses are assembled similar to a numbered puzzle with pieces that fasten to the main house and connect easily.

- This is a less labor-intensive method of roof construction; the potential upside in cost savings is significant.

- A trussed roof is solidly constructed, providing excellent support for roofing materials and protection from wind and storms.

- The elements of each truss are identical, and measurements are precise since they are factory built.

- It takes considerably less time to install a trussed roof than a stick-framed roof.

- Few, if any, weather-related concerns exist due to off-site construction.

However, trusses are not always the best option for every building project. Among the drawbacks:

- Homeowners and builders generally have less creative input into the size and style of roofs that can be built using trusses.

- Trussed homes typically provide less (if any) opportunity for attic space (whether for living or storage).

- More complicated roof styles and those with steep pitches or vaulted ceilings are less appropriate for trusses.

- It can be challenging to have trusses delivered to remote areas.

- Lead time is required for ordering and manufacture.

- It is impossible, from a practical standpoint, to accommodate plan changes and adjustments.

Stick-framing and trussed roofs are viable options with their own sets of benefits and drawbacks. Homeowners seeking to build, renovate, or add onto an existing home should talk with us to determine which option better meets your needs, timeline, and budget.

FROM MODERN TO CLASSICAL TO RUSTIC: ROOFING MATERIALS TO COMPLEMENT YOUR HOME

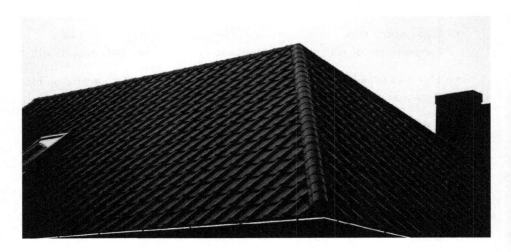

Your roof will protect you from the elements and is a defining feature of your home. While roofing may seem easy to overlook, doing so and "settling" on roofing materials for your new custom home or as a part of a renovation is a mistake. With the styles popular today—from a modern skillion to gabled, New England-dormered to salt-box, shed to bonnet—your roof can enhance the appearance of your home, as can your choice of roofing materials.

With over 30 years of experience building and renovating homes in Connecticut's southeastern corridor, the Reagan Homes team knows which materials are best for local weather conditions, which meet local codes or require specialized installation, and how certain materials can enhance the look of your home, expressing personal style and making the statement you want to make about the place you call home.

Asphalt Shingles

Currently, about 75% of all residential homes in the United States are roofed with asphalt shingles. A relatively affordable option, asphalt shingles are available in myriad colors and styles. You can expect such a roof to last for at least 10 years and as many as 30. (And, in fact, many are guaranteed to last for 30 years.)

Asphalt shingles may be made of fiberglass or, less commonly, organic materials that include recycled paper (referred to as felt shingles). The organic version has mostly been phased out as they are considered inferior to fiberglass shingles.

In addition to being affordable and attractive, fiberglass shingles provide consistent protection from the elements, are waterproof, and protect from UV rays and fire. Theoretically, they can be recycled into paving materials, but the reality is that most end up in landfills.

The average cost for asphalt shingle roofing is $200 to $400 per square installed (in roofing terms, a square is equal to 100 square feet).

Clay and Concrete Tiles

An ancient form of roofing material, clay and concrete tiles date back centuries. They are durable and attractive, but also very heavy. Fiber cement roofing tiles, composed of a clay and wood composite, are a lighter-weight alternative. Tiles often come in a half-barrel shape (like what you might expect to see on a Spanish villa) and interlock for easy, secure installation. Life expectancy is 50 or more years, and such tiles are waterproof, fire and insect resistant, sun-reflective, and recyclable.

However, they are quite expensive and breakable, and due to their weight, a structural engineer needs to be consulted before installation to ensure your roof framing can support them.

You can expect concrete tiles to cost between $200 and $800 per square installed, while clay tiles will set you back $500 to $1,000 per square installed.

Metal Roofing

Metal roofing is having a moment, and we're not talking about your grandparents' metal roofing or the kind on the barn down the road.

Today's metal roofing is super stylish and more durable and protective than any other roofing material widely available. It comes in colors and styles to complement any home. Metal roofs may last 100 years (warranties typically offer 30 to 50 years of guaranteed use) and are eco-friendly. In addition to rigid sheets, metal roofing materials may mimic the style of shingles, shakes, and tiles.

Most are made of recycled materials and are surprisingly lightweight. Solar radiant, metal roofing helps keep your home cooler in hot weather, thus keeping energy costs down. They can be installed quickly, shed rain and snow better than most other options, and have high fire ratings. They look great with almost every style of home. They can be louder, amplifying the sounds of the elements, but for some, this is welcome.

And while metal roofs are more expensive, the cost over the long term is similar or less than that of other options when you take durability and longevity into consideration.

You can expect a metal roof to cost between $300 and $700 per square, installed.

Slate

Slate is a statement-making roofing material, conjuring images of Tudor cottages and quaint country villages. It also happens to be durable and tough, able to stand up to the harshest elements. Available in numerous colors and sizes, slate tiles are virtually maintenance-free, will last 40 to 60 years, and are waterproof and non-combustible.

In addition to natural stone, composite and vinyl options are also available and deliver the same qualities and longevity as quarried slate, with the added benefits of being lighter in weight and less expensive. Slate roofing should only be installed by contractors who are well-experienced with the material, and extra care must be taken since slate is breakable.

A slate roof could cost anywhere from $600 to $1,500 per square installed.

Wood Shingles and Shakes

Wood shingles are machine-cut, while shakes are hand-split and more rustic in appearance. They are especially popular for traditional and historical-style homes and can be seen throughout New England and the Mid-Atlantic.

Both are commonly available in cedar, cypress, pine, and redwood. Cedar and redwood, in particular, are moisture and insect-resistant. While more expensive (and possibly less practical) than asphalt, wood roofing will likely last 5 to 10 years longer than asphalt, making the cost competitive.

Wood roofing is more insulating than asphalt, and both shingles and shakes are frequently made from salvaged trees. If untreated, wood roofing can be high maintenance, requiring frequent cleaning to avoid algae or moss issues and to allow the wood to breathe. Staining and discoloration may occur over several years, and repairs are relatively expensive.

If you're interested in wood shingle or shake roofing, you can expect to pay $400 to $900 per square installed.

A leader in custom home building and the renovation and remodeling of existing homes throughout southeast Connecticut, our team has experience installing roofing of all kinds. We know the ins, outs, and nuances of asphalt, metal, clay, slate, and wood roofing and can help guide you to a choice that will both enhance the appearance of your home and provide the durability you need.

*To learn more, call the Reagan Homes team at (860) 962-6250
to learn more or visit www.ReaganHomes.com
to schedule a complimentary, no-obligation consultation.*

DAVE REAGAN

GUTTER OPTIONS

Gutters are a trusty and necessary element for every home. Gutters are purposeful as they are tasked with keeping our homes clean, safe, and in working order. They ensure that any rain that falls against your home is directed away from your home and its foundation. This helps prevent damage to your foundation and siding. Gutters also help protect against flooding.

The type of gutters you choose and the materials with which they are manufactured can impact effectiveness and aesthetics. There are a few options you should consider before you build or remodel.

Types of Gutters

Gutters come in a variety of shapes, each having a different purpose when it comes to protecting your home. Some shapes will catch more debris than others, and if you live in an area with frequent high winds or heavy rains, your best approach will be to choose the style of gutter that best suits that climate. Certain materials will ensure your gutters don't become weathered or break due to the elements.

Half Round

Half-round gutters are the most traditional and standard style used today. They're likely what you imagine when you think of gutters. They are shaped like tubes cut in half lengthwise. The half-round design allows them to capture leaves and more without leaking. Half-round gutters don't require much maintenance, and they can typically be installed seamlessly. If your region experiences a lot of rainfall, half-rounds are an excellent option.

If you live in an older home, half-round gutters will also hold up well and keep your home safe from the effects of too much rain or snow. They are durable and lined to prevent corrosion. They don't need frequent cleaning as the half-round design helps flush out anything that may be stuck in them. The half-round design also prevents collection overrun.

K-Style

K-style gutters are a less traditional and more modern option for anyone who doesn't like the look of the more typical gutter styles, such as half-round gutters. The benefit of k-style gutters is that their sides are flat and can be directly attached to your house's fascia, making installation easier. They also require fewer parts. While they are easier to install and have a more attractive look than traditional half-round gutters, k-style gutters are not always the best option for every home.

If your home is older or more traditional, k-style gutters will not serve you as well as half-round; they lack the kind of weather protection a vintage home is likely to need.

Custom Fascia Gutters

Many modern homeowners choose custom fascia gutters for their ability to blend in with the rest of the home seamlessly. Gutters can protrude from a house at angles that make your architecture's overall appearance slightly less attractive. Designed to hug the borders of your roof so they still get the job done, fascia gutters blend in and are effectively invisible.

Custom fascia gutters often come with durability benefits, too, as they are usually made from galvanized steel. They won't rust, nor will they bend or tear away due to heavy rain, high winds, or excessive snowfall. Fascia gutters can also be made from recycled materials, which is a terrific option for anyone concerned with sustainability.

Materials

While the shape of your gutters is important, so are the materials from which they're manufactured. In certain climates, you may find that some materials will withstand the elements better than others: this is important because you don't want your gutters to rust or break down due to weather. Some materials may also be more durable and require less maintenance over time, saving you time and money.

Aluminum

Most gutters you'll see on traditional homes are made of aluminum. Aluminum has been a popular option for the last several decades and is durable, non-rusting, and affordable. Aluminum gutters can easily be customized (with different colors, for example) to suit the exterior aesthetic of your home. Aluminum gutters are a reliable and easy-to-install option for any home.

Vinyl

Vinyl is already incredibly affordable, and that's what makes it a popular option for gutters. Vinyl gutters can be finicky, however. They work best in climates that are more temperate, and they are unable to withstand heavy rain and snow. They aren't ideal for climates that are excessively sunny either. But if your home is located in an area that matches the ideal environment for vinyl gutters, they can be customized to match or coordinate with your home's aesthetic.

Zinc

Zinc gutters offer a unique benefit. Zinc is incredibly durable and forms a protective seal when exposed to dampness and open air. This quality essentially adds a barrier to your gutters that is weatherproof and resistant to scratches and blemishes. Zinc is also antimicrobial, so mold, mildew, and fungus growth will never be an issue. Zinc gutters are also easily customizable and can be finished in almost any color. Their life expectancy is very long.

Steel

Steel gutters are a very affordable option. They are easy to access and install, but they aren't the most durable. If you coat them properly, they can withstand the elements and remain rust-free, but even that coating can fail. Steel gutters are also prone to sagging, which can lead to damage if they fall and hit your home. There are ways to make these gutters more durable, but steel gutters aren't as popular as they once were.

Copper

If you're someone who prioritizes your home's appearance over functionality, copper gutters may be an attractive option. Copper gutters evolve in appearance the longer you have them, developing an oxidation layer that makes them look even better. If you don't like the patina that comes with oxidation, it can easily be prevented with regularly scheduled cleaning and maintenance.

Copper is incredibly durable and can withstand all weather conditions with ease. Copper gutters, though, are not available in any other colors.

The Benefits of Gutter Guards

If you're especially concerned about debris and leaves clogging your gutters, investing in gutter guards may be of interest. Especially if your property has a lot of trees, it might be beneficial to get guards, so you don't have to clean your gutters as frequently. Gutter guards minimize all issues related to clogging. The lack of clogging reduces the potential for sagging otherwise caused by the added weight of debris and leaves.

Let Us Help You Choose The Best Gutters For Your Home

At Reagan Homes, we know that keeping your home clean and orderly is critical. That's why we help you choose the best gutters for your needs as part of your existing home renovation or new custom home. With so many options to choose from, it can be challenging to understand which gutters will be optimal for you and your home.

To learn more, call the Reagan Homes team at (860) 962-6250
to learn more or visit www.ReaganHomes.com
to schedule a complimentary, no-obligation consultation.

EXTERIOR SIDING OPTIONS

At Reagan Homes, building dream homes is our business. Paying attention to defining details through a lens of world-class engineering, design, and craftsmanship is our specialty. We've been proudly serving our satisfied clients in New London and Middlesex counties since 1987.

With every passing year, we continue to expand our design horizons, but our commitment to excellence and quality remain unwavering. Clients come to us with ideas for their dream home, and we're here to make sure to guide them through every important aspect of construction with care.

Reagan Homes is the best choice when you're looking to partner with a custom build-and-design company that caters to your every need. We work closely with clients through every step of the process, even down to deciding which exterior siding to select!

There numerous options when it comes to exterior siding. Knowing which material will work best with your home is important. Bringing your vision to life requires a commitment to quality materials that fit cohesively into a top-of-the-line design.

Siding sets the aesthetic tone for a home but it also protects the structure against the elements and can influence the resale value of your property over time.

Here are some of the most common exterior siding materials that you can choose from.

Vinyl

Durable and reasonably priced, vinyl is one of the most popular exterior siding options on the market. It's available in a variety of shapes, colors, and styles. Best of all, it doesn't require a ton of cleaning or maintenance.

One of the big benefits of having vinyl siding installed on a home is that it doesn't easily fade over time. However, people who prefer the look of natural materials don't always love the synthetic appearance of vinyl.

The closest that you can get to a natural-looking vinyl siding would be cedar impression shingles. These are more expensive than traditional vinyl clapboards, but they mimic the look of natural wood with meticulous ridge-inspired patterns and designs.

Many homeowners go with clapboard vinyl siding, which allows for full coverage of a home using narrow vinyl panels that are nailed horizontally to the exterior. Clapboard vinyl panels are lightweight and can be customized to include insulation, making it possible to create a more energy-efficient home through your siding selection.

When it comes to environmental considerations, people looking to "go green" may want to avoid vinyl. The elements that make it so durable also allow it to last longer in a landfill. In general, vinyl siding costs anywhere from $2 to $7 per square foot to install.

Wood

People who long for their home to embody a natural aesthetic often fall in love with the idea of wood siding. This traditional material is very versatile and easy to customize.

Whether you go with cedar, redwood, pine, or spruce varieties, wood can be left in its natural state or painted in a finish and hue that fits homeowner preferences. When left natural, many of these species will turn gray, which is a common choice for many of the homes we have built on the shoreline. Wood stains are also a popular choice for siding.

Wood siding can be added as a set of jointed panels or shingles across a home's exterior and gives a structure a more rustic-chic appeal. Of course, some might opt for interlocking wood logs, instead.

While standard wood siding options are relatively inexpensive to install, maintenance costs should always be factored into the equation. Wood siding is generally more susceptible to weather damage and pest interference than synthetic alternatives.

It's true that wood is a highly-sustainable siding option, but depending on your desired finish it may require a full coat of clear finish to protect the surface of the siding every couple of years. People who choose wood siding can expect to pay anywhere from $5 to $9 per square foot, depending on the style selected.

Fiber Cement

This unique and durable exterior siding option is created from a mix of cement, clay, sand, and wood pulp. The combination leads to a long-lasting finish that's both pest-proof and fire-resistant.

Homeowners who select fiber cement siding will find that it's easy to paint or finish in a style that fits their ideal aesthetic. It also stands up well against humidity and fluctuating temperatures that might cause other siding materials to crack or break down.

Typically, homeowners can expect fiber cement siding to last upwards of 30 years after installation. However, the installation process is meticulous and requires specialized equipment and training that our craftsmen have.

Fiber cement siding is very heavy and can't be placed over any existing siding materials. It usually costs between $5 and $9 per square foot to install.

Stucco

There's something endlessly intriguing about a home's exterior that showcases a south-western flair. Nothing captures the essence of this aesthetic better than stucco siding.

Known for its durability and designer quality, stucco is a great choice for people who are designing a home built around the concept of unique textures and styles. It's a selection that seamlessly incorporates other exterior materials, as well.

Stucco siding is often done alongside eye-catching brick or ceramic tiles. It's a material that can easily be customized through a variety of tones to create naturally appealing, one-of-a-kind hues.

Many homeowners choose stucco for its fire-resistant qualities and low maintenance needs. However, it's important to keep in mind that installation is anything but simple.

Properly installed stucco siding requires a significant amount of prep-work and a professional team with the right installation equipment already in place. Stucco also needs to be mixed with epoxy to guarantee a chip-free finish. This exterior siding material is available at a price point generally ranging from $6 to $9 per square foot.

Engineered Wood Siding

People who love the look of wood siding or fiber cement options but who want to pay a bit less will often find that engineered wood siding provides a similar aesthetic at a lower price point. Fabricated from a combination of exterior-grade resins and wood fibers, engineered wood siding is durable and eye-catching, while it also holds up well in severe weather climates.

Engineered wood siding can last upward of 50 years after installation. The vast majority of homeowners who select engineered wood siding are drawn to this option because it's available in such a wide variety of styles and colors.

Engineered wood siding can easily be painted and finished according to preference, but it can also be installed as shingles or clapboards that are designed to resemble natural wood finishes. At only $3 to $5 per square foot, engineered wood siding is a cost-effective alternative to more natural options.

Aluminum

When durability, cost-effectiveness, and eco-friendly solutions are priorities for your home's siding selection, aluminum is a good choice. Its lightweight nature makes it simple to install and it's created using recycled materials.

Aluminum is a relatively low-maintenance siding solution that's adaptable to all kinds of weather. It's both fire-resistant and pest-proof, which many homeowners love.

The only downside to aluminum is that it tends to be noisy when severe weather strikes and it is susceptible to denting caused by hail. That said, it's incredibly heat-efficient and provides homes with insulation standards that can help cut down on energy bills.

Adding a rust-resistant coating to aluminum siding is always a good option for people who don't want the hassle with regular maintenance. Aluminum siding costs anywhere from $2 to $5 per square foot.

Brick

The traditional appeal of a brick-sided home is undeniable. People who want to finish their home in this durable material will find that it's available at a price point ranging from $6 to $12 per square foot.

Brick has a way of evoking a sense of elegance, but the installation process can be time-consuming. Much of the cost associated with a brick exterior stems from the labor-intensive process it requires.

While some homes are constructed with brick for the exterior finish and supporting walls, other homeowners opt to install a brick veneer that is exclusively a siding finish—it does not support the home's structure in any way. Both options are wonderfully durable and long-lasting.

When it comes to maintenance, brick doesn't require much. A pressure wash every once in a while is all it takes to keep brick looking its best.

Synthetic Stone

Homeowners who want to lean towards a natural-appearing finish will find synthetic stone to be a delightful choice. While it's not recommended for full exterior coverage, it's often used as accent siding.

Created from a mix of sand, aggregate, and cement, synthetic stone siding looks very much like its natural counterpart. Unlike real stone, synthetic stone provides a lightweight alternative that makes for a more efficient installation process.

Synthetic stone siding is often installed along the bottom portion of a home or on the chimney. Its fire and pest-resistant qualities are appealing, but its price point is worth keeping in mind. Synthetic stone siding is available for about $12 to $25 per square foot.

Whether you're considering building a new custom home or renovating an existing home, Reagan Homes would love to help. We have both the knowledge and experience to guide you through all of the available exterior siding options.

To learn more, call the Reagan Homes team at (860) 962-6250 to learn more or visit www.ReaganHomes.com to schedule a complimentary, no-obligation consultation.

EXTERIOR DOOR OPTIONS

Exterior doors aren't just functional; they add charm and a specific aesthetic to your home. The front door is often the first part of your home that visitors see. Your entrance door must have at least three qualities: durability, reliability, and a beautiful appearance. By choosing your exterior door designs wisely, you'll make an impression you can be proud of.

What are the differences between interior and exterior doors?

The doors of a house can be classified, basically, into two types: interior and exterior.

Generally speaking, interior doors are narrower than the exterior doors of a house. Interior doors are not exposed to humidity, sun, rain, or other weather elements. Interior doors can be made of any material, but in most cases, wood with or without glass is the best choice for interior doors.

Exterior doors tend to be wider than interior doors and require more care and maintenance. Exterior doors are constantly exposed to the elements, including: exposure to the sun, rain, snow, and humidity. Exterior doors are made of more weather-resistant materials, such as fiberglass, aluminum, steel, glass, and iron.

External Door Material Types

There are several types of doors you need to know about when you're designing your home. Each has its own significance in your home. When it comes to door types according to material, it is possible to find a huge variety of materials, such as wood, metal, aluminum, and iron, among others. To help you make the best choice, we are explaining in detail the primary types of doors you may need.

Wooden Doors

Wooden doors used to be installed in apartments. Today, they are mainly installed in private houses. Wooden doors are a classic, primarily because of their versatility; they are typically available in numerous styles, ready to serve a variety of purposes.

By design, wooden entrance doors are divided into three main types: solid wood, panel, and panel doors.

Solid wood doors are the most durable of all because they are made of one piece of wood. However, the craft of glued solid wood is more often used: individual wooden parts are glued together using special fasteners that give the doors even greater strength. When choosing, choose solid wood doors if possible, as they offer good durability and resistance to outside environment factors.

The most expensive wooden doors are made of oak, and their strength is close to that of metal doors. But even these cannot be compared in terms of burglary resistance to metal doors. Doors made of beech, cherry, walnut, and ash are also common. The least expensive wooden doors are made of pine. But, despite their relative cheapness, their strength is sufficient for them to suit many homeowners. Today most people of average income prefer to have entrance doors made of pine in their homes.

Metal Doors

Metal is used in door structure solely to provide maximum strength. The aesthetic qualities of metal doors are not often taken into account, since their aesthetic qualities are rather low. Metal doors are usually additionally sheathed with wood or plastic.

From the inside, metal doors have voids that are filled with insulation and soundproofing material. Mineral wool and various types of foam are most often used for these purposes. A steel door usually comes with at least two mortise locks, but some homeowners use even more. The weakest point of a metal door is door hinges; therefore, the best option will be a hinge made on support bearings. Such hinges can be adjusted in accordance with a variety of door operating conditions.

The main quality of a metal door is maximum burglary resistance, with durability also a consideration.

Glass Doors

The glass doors are perfect for entrances to offices and commercial buildings. For those who are daring, a glass door can also be used as a home entry door. Most who opt for glass entryway doors in the residential environment opt for matte glass models so as not to leave the interior of the residence on display for anyone who passes by. However, glass entrance doors are not the most popular as they are not the best option for security.

Aluminum Doors

Aluminum doors are a great option for the entrances of a house as they can have elegant visual characteristics. They harmonize very well with both bright and matte colors as well as glass. Aluminum doors are also high durability and, therefore, do not rust.

Door Types Based on Use/Location

Entry Doors

Your entry (or front) door's aesthetic is important, but it also has a job to do when it comes to energy efficiency. You'll want to choose a door or set of doors that can prevent cooled air or heat leaks from escaping between the gaps. When you're shopping for doors, though, you're likely to see a few material choices, including wood, fiberglass, and metal.

Wooden doors are what you likely think of most often when thinking of a front door. Wood is a popular option as you can choose different species, grains, and even stains to customize. You'll want to keep up with the staining or painting regularly because entry doors are exposed to the elements and are subject to peeling, chipping, fading, and rotting. Wooden doors are also more expensive than most door options and a bit more challenging to maintain. They are sturdy, but repairs and installation can be pricey.

If you want something that looks like wood but can withstand the elements better, you should consider fiberglass. Fiberglass entry doors aren't susceptible to the same weather-related issues as wood. They can be finished the same way as wood, so you can choose from various stains or paints to achieve the same style you might opt for with a wooden door. The best part about fiberglass is that it doesn't allow air or heat to get through, so they can help you save money on energy bills.

Metals like steel do an even better job of resisting the elements and keeping your cooling and heat from escaping. They are impervious to dents, dings, and unwanted pests, and with a metal front door, you can feel safe and secure in your home. Metal entry doors can be customized to look like wood, so you can have all the aesthetic benefits of a wood or fiberglass door without the hassle of maintenance.

Patio Doors

Your typical patio door is a sliding door–essentially two large windows, one of which slides on a track, allowing it to open and close. You can go with a more elaborate, decorative style, or a more secure option made of glass and wood or fiberglass. The most common patio door option, however, is made primarily of glass. These doors can be reinforced with metal, thicker glass, or other supports to ensure they do not break.

Vinyl, which is more durable and will better keep in heating and air conditioning, is another option. And vinyl isn't prone to cracking or other damage from the elements, as wood is.

Storm Doors

You may not think a storm door is a necessity, but depending on where your home is located, they can be incredibly helpful. Storm doors consist of three layers, and some of those layers can be removed when the weather is amenable. Storm doors protect against the elements and ensure that air and light can enter while keeping out insects, snow, rain, dust, and debris.

Storm doors can also be customized with different types of glass, metal, fiberglass, and wood grains to suit the aesthetics of your home without detracting away from it. They should be made of sturdy materials and not compromise on style.

French Doors

French doors add a touch of romance and elegance to any home, either as entry doors or patio doors. They are a charming addition to any home and feature stylish glass and your choice of wood color and finish. If you're looking for a simple but elegant accent to your home that is functional and fashionable, French doors can be a wonderful addition to your architecture.

French doors are also available in steel and fiberglass; they can easily be customized to match or complement your home while providing weather-resistance. Because durability is as important as appearance, you don't want to invest in flimsy French doors that will require maintenance in the coming years.

Bifold Doors

Bifold doors can add a certain charm to your home by opening up additional space for backyard entertaining. Typically made of glass, bi-folds are movable and fold upon opening. They usually come in sets of four panels, which leaves the space they occupied open and accessible and convenient for coming and going from the backyard into the house.

Bifold doors are a modern and charming accent that can be customized with colors, stains, and different materials to best suit your home's look and style.

Leaf Doors

Leaf doors are among the most traditional door styles on the market. Leaf doors usually have traditional measures and fit almost anywhere. In addition to being easy to install, they are much more affordable compared to other models.

Two-leaf doors are ideal for those looking for something elegant for an entrance hall. (They look somewhat like French doors.) Double-leaf doors offer a wider passage and are, therefore, recommended for larger houses.

Pivoting doors are a modern and elegant door design. Pivoting doors are stand-outs in architectural projects. They are widely used in high-end homes, usually as gateways.

Because they are large and heavy, the material they are made from should be robust, since these doors have an axis that needs to be supported. More often than not, pivoting doors are made to measure, and, therefore, are considerably more expensive than more common types of doors.

Shrimp Holder Doors

A shrimp holder door is ideal for dividing two environments when there is a lack of space. Installation is more laborious than with some other door types, as shrimp holders require customized materials such as latches, handles, and rails. Their unique installation may end up raising their overall price a bit.

Folding Doors

The folding door is one of the least expensive options on the market and is named after the accordion; this is because it bends as it runs on the rail. They are usually made of plastic or PVC and are most often recommended for damp environments.

Sliding Doors

Without a doubt, the sliding door is the best choice for projects where space optimization is sought; sliding doors maintain the integrity of their environment with a modern and elegant air. For home plans with limited space, sliding doors are an option that can be worked using rails, embedded in walls, and other applications.

The important thing to keep in mind when choosing exterior doors is to take into account the style of your decor, the space available, and your budget.

To learn more, call the Reagan Homes team at (860) 962-6250
to learn more or visit www.ReaganHomes.com
to schedule a complimentary, no-obligation consultation.

HOW TO MAKE YOUR FRONT DOOR STAND OUT AND WELCOME YOUR GUESTS

You may think your front door is of little importance when it comes to the overall aesthetic of your house, but it can actually make quite the first impression. Your front door is essentially the first indicator of what your home is like and gives guests a hint of what to expect even before they have stepped through it. Some people will always remember "the house with the red door" or "the house that had the ironwork on the door" and that can become your home's identifier.

So how can you make something as simple as the entrance to your house so memorable and enticing? Well, there are a few ways to go about it.

Color

Modern homeowners are taking steps to accent their otherwise neutral exteriors with bright and bold identifying colors. A house that is gray or white may benefit from cool or sunny colors to set its doorways apart from the neighbor's house. You'll always remember passing by the house with the bright green door when driving by a row of otherwise similar brickwork houses.

Some Realtors will even suggest staging homes for sale by painting entryways with clever accents—including doorways—as a way to set your home apart. Potential buyers will remember your home even after their seventh viewing of the day.

Not into bold, bright colors? You can also use custom stain colors for a front door that is traditional yet elegant and a little bit different than what everyone else has.

Interesting Door Knobs

Rather than your industry-standard metal knob, many homeowners are opting for more creative door knobs and handles. Bronze or burnished knobs may add an elegant accent to your entryway, whereas modern homes may opt for a minimalist handle to achieve a specific mood or feeling. If you're a little old fashioned or you're someone who likes historical architecture, you might decide on a knob or handle with designs or accents pressed into it.

Accessories

You might think the idea of accessorizing your doorway sounds silly, but that too can set your home apart from the other houses on your block or in your neighborhood. Simple welcome signs, wreaths, or any other identifying piece of decor can add a bit of flair to your home.

So, whether you're decorating for every day or just a special occasion, little accents can do wonders to make guests feel welcomed as soon as they step onto your front porch. Such touches don't need to be fancy. A welcome mat and some flowers in a planter beside the door can do wonders in setting your home apart and making it more inviting.

Door Size

Depending on the overall look of your home, a bigger front door might make the most sense. French doors are also an option to help your front door stand out.

*To learn more, call the Reagan Homes team at (860) 962-6250
to learn more or visit www.ReaganHomes.com
to schedule a complimentary, no-obligation consultation.*

GARAGE DOOR OPTIONS

Your garage door is something you see nearly every day, and it's a gateway of sorts that most families use to enter their homes. It's also one of the very first things visitors see when they visit.

When it comes to garage doors, plenty of options exist—including many that add style and performance to an area of the home that is too often overlooked. If you think it might be time to upgrade your garage door as you embark on an existing home renovation or if you're beginning to consider garage door options for your custom-built home, finding one that is suitable for your purpose and that adds to the attractiveness of your home is easily in reach.

The following is a sampling of the best options for modern, attractive, and high-quality residential garage door styles.

Sectional Garage Doors

Sectional garage doors are the most common garage doors used in the United States for residential homes. Panel sections that are connected with hinges make up the sectional garage door. As the door opens and closes, wheels at the edge of each panel roll inside a vertical track on each side of the door opening.

The hinges between each panel section bend over a curved portion of the track. This feature allows the door to sit parallel to the ceiling when completely open or in line with the walls when completely closed.

A pair of high-tension springs above the opening are attached to cables that operate the door and hold it from drifting down when only partially open.

These doors are typically made from steel, are low maintenance, and can be customized to include window inserts, hardware, textures, and colors. They come in both insulated and non-insulated models.

Carriage-Style Doors

The carriage-style garage door was influenced by the elites of the 19th century who needed a place to keep their horses after exhausting daytime rides. Those carriage doors featured large wooden doors that swung open to allow an estate owner's horses and carriage to enter. Obviously, we do not need to keep horses anymore, at least not typically and not at home.

The carriage-door design, however, has been ingrained in many modern designs. While traditional carriage doors were made with woods or steel and hinges to allow the doors to swing outward, today, the construction of carriage doors includes modern features that permit the doors to be rolled up. Modern carriage doors are frequently constructed with wood or steel overlays to mimic a traditional look.

Tilt-Up

Moving forward from 19th-century garage door style to that of the 20th century: Tilt-up garage doors gained prominence in the 1960s and 1970s. Despite being somewhat out of vogue, many homeowners still prefer tilt-up garage doors.

It should be noted that as design tastes evolve, many older garage-door styles become more dangerous and less appealing.

Tilt-up garage door options include over the canopy garage doors and the tilt-up over retractable garage doors. They extend beyond the front of the house when they are open.

Roll-Up Garage Doors

Roll-up garage doors are more often used in commercial applications than residential, but they are a well-constructed design option for areas with limited ceiling space.

This garage door style is made with steel slats that measure 2 to 3 inches each and roll around a drum above the door opening. Roll-up (or coiling doors as they are sometimes called) can withstand heavy usage. They are often built without springs or with an enclosure the protects the mechanicals. Both of these options result in a better functioning, longer-lasting garage door,

Sliding Garage Doors

Sliding garage doors may also be called slide to the side garage doors. They are relatively fashionable and unique, and they can be constructed exclusively of glass. They do not need balancing springs, and they often include an automated control system for opening and closing. Sliding garage doors bend to one side of the wall and are positioned parallel to the wall when controlled.

Canopy Garage Door

Canopy garage doors are a creative option that utilizes more common garage door mechanicals. An adaptation of a fully opened garage door panel, this style protrudes about a third of the way forward from the subframe to form a canopy. It provides the maximum width possible to drive through when open, and it is the easiest of all garage doors to install.

Your home's garage door matters—as much as what is in the garage. When you need a new garage door as part of an existing home renovation, or if you are choosing garage doors for your new custom home, together we can determine which option is best for your home and your needs.

To learn more, call the Reagan Homes team at (860) 962-6250 to learn more or visit www.ReaganHomes.com to schedule a complimentary, no-obligation consultation.

GARAGE FLOOR OPTIONS

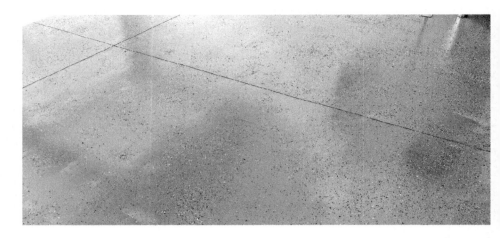

 If you're someone who spends a lot of time in your garage, whether working on your car or using it as you're an office or workshop space, the flooring in your garage is more important than you might think.

Different materials options will provide different amounts of coverage and better meet your needs depending on how you use your garage.

Interlocking Tiles

If you're someone who spends a lot of time working on your car in your garage, interlocking tiles might be the best option for you. Interlocking tiles are made of a rubber-based material, so they are nearly impervious to oil spills, gasoline, and other dirt and grime that might get on them. They are easy to clean and will ensure you don't have to fight tough stains.

If you want to cover up cracks or blemishes in your garage floor, interlocking tiles can be arranged to achieve a specific design that covers most damage.

Roll-Out Vinyl Flooring

If you're looking for easy installation, this is the flooring for you. The name says it all, as this flooring option can easily be rolled out to cover any pesky stains or damage. Once you cut it and secure it, it will remain in place with little effort. However, if the vinyl itself gets damaged, it can be a bit more challenging to repair; you'll have to pull up all the flooring rather than just removing the affected pieces.

Roll-out vinyl flooring is incredibly affordable and is durable enough to be considered a good option.

Peel and Stick Tiles

If you're looking to cover up a garage floor that has seen better days, you might also want to consider peel and stick tiles. They are incredibly forgiving and can cover up all sorts of damages with little effort. Such tiles are made from a vinyl that is durable enough to withstand the work you'll be doing on top of it yet are not easily damaged.

Because you can easily peel and stick them, it is easy to create your own patterns and designs with minimal effort.

Paint

If you want a simple and affordable option, painting the garage floor is a great option. You can use any color of paint or stain, and you can create patterns. The only downside is that paint can be disturbed, damaged, and even peel if subjected to enough wear and tear. A garage floor can require a lot of maintenance and effort to paint and seal properly.

Epoxy

If you're looking for something durable and long-lasting, epoxy is a solid option. The floor must first be adequately prepared. The epoxy and hardener then need to be mixed and poured within a specific amount of time or the mixture will not set-up correctly.

With an epoxy garage floor, you'll have a moisture- and grime-resistant floor that will be easy to clean.

Stained Concrete

Just like staining a piece of furniture, you can stain the concrete floor in your garage. Doing so won't impact your floor's durability, but it can help seal cracks and add visual interest. If you often work with oil or other dark fluids in your garage, a decorative stain can hide minor stains and flaws that might otherwise be obvious.

Concrete Sealer

If you're worried about damage or staining, but you don't want to shell out too much for garage flooring, you can seal your concrete flooring. Doing so will help with cracks, damages, and stubborn stains that you might not be able to protect against otherwise. While it isn't going to help you as effectively as other options, a concrete sealer is an affordable option.

To learn more, call the Reagan Homes team at (860) 962-6250
to learn more or visit www.ReaganHomes.com
to schedule a complimentary, no-obligation consultation.

DRIVEWAY OPTIONS

The exterior appearance of your home is just as important as the interior. When you drive up, you should be happy with what you see, and that includes your driveway.

Whatever your tastes might be, there is a driveway option to suit your style. Whether you're looking for something modern, traditional, or a little creative, there are several options for materials and driveway shapes to consider that can be customized for you.

Materials

Driveways can be made from many different materials, which allows homeowners to have considerable control over the exterior appearance of their homes. There are natural materials, eco-friendly materials, and more traditional or elegant options that can add a touch of sophistication to your home. Whichever you choose, you'll be able to find exactly what you're looking for and customize everything to your liking.

Asphalt

You'll find that most driveways in North America are asphalt. They hold heat well, which means snow won't stick as easily. Asphalt is an affordable and practical option. Asphalt driveways may need to be sealed and resealed every few years, however. Even with this drawback, it is still a relatively common option and has remained so throughout the years.

Brick

Brick driveways ooze elegance and may remind one of pulling up to a manor in the British countryside. If your house is also made of brick, you can either have the driveway match the color and type of brick, or you can vary it by using a style that will complement your architecture. This option is pricier than most, but it does add a beautiful touch to your home, one that will make it attractive to potential buyers should you want to sell in the future.

Brick driveways are highly customizable and will be durable enough to withstand a multitude of conditions.

Gravel

A loose gravel driveway is another popular option that brings with it a rustic charm and practicality that many find appealing. Especially if you live somewhere where ice and snow are an inevitable part of every winter season, gravel is a practical option—snow and ice won't stick to it. Gravel is a durable material that can be customized based on the type of gravel you select. You can choose to use varying sizes, colors, and textures. Gravel driveways create a no-slip surface, so you can be sure your car will be safe when pulling up to your house during inclement weather.

Gravel is an excellent option for those who favor durability and affordability.

Permeable Pavers

Like brick, permeable pavers are certainly a more expensive option but one that adds a lot of charm and potential resale value to your home. Pavers can be customized by type, shape, or color, and they require very little maintenance to keep them in tip-top shape. Pavers add a touch of elegance to your home's exterior and can be a charming accent, especially when lined with foliage.

All in all, permeable pavers are a wonderful option if you're looking for a modern and sophisticated touch to add to your home.

Stamped Concrete

Stamped concrete driveways have become increasingly popular in recent years due to the customizability of concrete. The appearance of the exterior of your home can easily be altered by adding a custom stamped-concrete pattern to your driveway. Some people may opt for a simple marbling effect, while others may prefer designs like longhorns or seashells to personalize their home. Stamped concrete driveways are easy to seal and more affordable than their brick or paver counterparts.

While this style of driveway doesn't require much maintenance, excessive cold can be damaging and cause cracking. Stamped concrete driveways are still a viable option, however, if this look is what you're seeking.

Concrete

Poured concrete driveways are another standard option that doesn't require a lot of extra work or maintenance. Concrete driveways can be customized, but a concrete driveway's simplicity can be incredibly appealing. They are appropriate for any part of the U.S. and homeowners never need to worry about their concrete driveways cracking or needing frequent resealing.

Poured concrete is a basic but still excellent option for any homeowner to consider.

Dirt

A dirt driveway evokes images of country roads and cozy cabins, so if you're looking for a more rustic look, you'll find it with this option. Dirt driveways, however, can be a bit problematic, so keep in mind that you get what you pay for. While highly affordable, dirt driveways are prone to damage caused by the elements.

Dirt driveways can be fickle, but if this style is what you want, they can easily be constructed to suit your needs.

Cobblestone

Cobblestones evoke a feeling of fantasy. When you imagine a cobblestone driveway, you probably imagine something fanciful, like the drive up to a castle or an estate out in the country. But you, too, can have a cobblestone driveway if you'd like. While cobblestone may be on the pricier side, it is a charming feature that adds a more natural element to your home's exterior architecture. While to some, cobblestone may seem a little old-fashioned and not worth the effort, cobblestone driveways are surprisingly durable and will withstand the elements well.

If you want a touch of the fanciful without detracting from the rest of your home's aesthetic, this is a great way to go.

Crushed Basalt

Crushed basalt driveways are essentially gravel driveways but with higher-quality materials than your average crushed rock. Crushed basalt provides better drainage, so it is especially appropriate for rainy and icy locations. It is also a beautiful dark black color, so you can add a bit of an elegant touch to your driveway with minimal maintenance or effort.

Crushed basalt is also a reasonably affordable option, so you can upgrade from regular gravel with a minimal increase in costs.

Recycled Glass

Recycled glass has become a fairly common driveway material option in recent years. With the push toward using eco-friendly materials, recycled glass has become a fantastic alternative to traditional poured or gravel driveways. Such driveways will also add a bit of visual interest to your driveway as many are speckled with colored fragments of glass.

Recycled glass is both eco-friendly and affordable, making it a great option for the modern homeowner.

Shapes

The shape of your driveway can have a significant effect on the aesthetic of your home's exterior. You can go traditional or get a little bit creative with it, but either way, your choices have both aesthetic and practical impacts. If you're planning on entertaining often or you want to keep your vehicles parked in your driveway, some shapes may be more appropriate than others.

Straight

A straight driveway is what you likely think of when you envision a traditional driveway. Straight driveways are straightforward and simple and don't offer any bells or whistles. This driveway style is practical if it will lead to a garage as there won't be any inclines or twists and turns that your car will need to contend with. Straight driveways also don't need to be planned out as meticulously as other driveway shapes.

If you have a modest design or a smaller house, a straight driveway will make the most of your space without detracting from it.

Curved

A curved driveway is a good option for properties that aren't modular. They provide both practicality and a touch of visual interest to your landscape. Especially if you've planted flowers, trees, or other foliage along the driveway, a curved driveway can make the drive more enjoyable. Curved driveways are relatively simple to install and can make a property more attractive without too much effort.

A curved driveway is a simple feature that can be even more interesting when designed by a professional.

U-Shaped

A U-shaped driveway may be the right choice for properties on an incline as they provide cars with a bit of space, so they aren't hugging the road. They also allow for creative landscaping in the front of the home.

Circular

If you're looking for something to amp up the elegance in your home in a simple way, a circular drive can be an attractive focal point for the exterior of your home. It's also the perfect option if you entertain often and don't want your guests to park on the street. Landscaping that uses and highlights plants or sculptures can make a circular driveway appear especially sophisticated.

Y-Shape

Y-shaped driveways are the perfect option for someone with a creatively shaped home that includes more than one garage. They are a helpful option spatially and provide your space with a truly modern look. Y-shaped driveways can create a transition, so the front of your house isn't cluttered and instead has a clear, well-defined entrance.

You can and should have the perfect driveway for your home. Whether that is a circular cobblestone driveway or a simple straight dirt path, your aesthetic and personal needs are the most relevant factors to consider.

To learn more, call the Reagan Homes team at (860) 962-6250
to learn more or visit www.ReaganHomes.com
to schedule a complimentary, no-obligation consultation.

DECKING & RAILING OPTIONS

Ah, summers on the deck. Conjures up images of images of cold, refreshing beverages, grilling, and fun with friends and family, right? There's nothing like a good deck for entertaining or just sitting and reading, enjoying the sunshine and fresh air.

A deck on the back of your house is a must—especially if you don't already have a porch or patio. A deck can also be a valuable selling point when the time comes and a point of pride for you as a homeowner until that time comes.

The Reagan Homes team has built more decks than we can count. Big decks, little decks, decks on new homes, decks on existing homes. We can help you design your deck—including all the amenities you want and need. As part of your new custom home or existing home renovation, we will build it for you, taking the financial, time, and potential legal concerns off your shoulders. When we're finished, all you will need to do is kick back and relax.

To ensure you are well informed on everything that goes into building a deck, let's review the parts and types of decking to consider.

What size should my deck be?

There are two basic guidelines we typically follow when we plan decks for our clients:

1. No deck should be more than 20% of the total square footage of the home itself. That means, for example, that if your home is 3,500 square feet, your deck should not exceed 750 square feet.

2. No part or section of your deck (if you want a multi-level deck, for example) should be larger than the largest room in your house.

Of course there are exceptions to these guidelines.

As we do for the rest of your custom home build or existing home renovation, we will suggest a number of deck plans that meet your goals and desires, and then to ensure the deck meets your expectations and that you can realistically imagine the end product, we will produce 3D rendering of the designs you are interested in.

Parts of a Deck

Flashing

Deck flashing is absolutely a necessity but one an amateur or inexperienced builder may not think of. Deck flashing is essentially a beam that attaches the deck to the house. The beam, or ledger is attached horizontally along a home's framing. The flashing is a rubber- stainless steel, copper, or vinyl-based, tape-like material that helps the deck shed water and prevents moisture from seeping through wood planking and from entering the house itself. Without flashing, your deck—and even your home's framing— may experience rot.

Ledger Attachment

Your deck's ledger is the beam that physically attaches a deck to the overall structure of your home. The ledger is a critical element of your deck and must be attached to the house via half-inch bolts or lag screws. Nails are neither acceptable or safe.

Guardrails

Deck railings, it should seem obvious, prevent people from falling off your deck. In most towns, guardrails are required when your deck is 30" or more off the ground. The minimum acceptable guardrail height is 36 inches (but they may be taller based on your needs or wants). And you can use a little creativity when it comes time to choose which railing style to use as there are numerous types and styles to choose from. (FYI, guardrails and handrails are not the same thing. A guardrail includes the structural rails, posts, and infill (often balusters) that prevent falling. Handrails are considered something one can grasp onto to steady themselves when climbing up or down stairs.)

In addition to guardrails around the perimeter of your deck, you also need handrails for any stairs that may be a part of your deck.

Guardrails may be made of the following materials:

- Decking Materials: Pressure-treated lumber that matches deck flooring is the most common and popular guardrail material along with other types of wood, including cedar, mahogany, and redwood. If your deck floor is built with a composite product (like Moisture Shield Vision composite decking), you may opt for guardrails also built with this material.

- Vinyl Railing: Vinyl is another option that is growing in popularity. Vinyl railing is extremely strong and durable and can be used regardless of which material you choose for your deck flooring. Among its other benefits: it is much easier to clean than wood, and it is resistant to blistering, decomposing, rusting, peeling, pests, rotting, and rusting.

- Glass Railing: If aesthetics are a priority for you, you may want to consider glass railing for your deck. It's a beautiful, high-end looking option that provides a solid barrier without obstructing views. The glass railing helps block wind. And believe it or not, glass railing is very durable; it is made from quarter-inch thick tempered glass. Glass is among the most expensive railing options, and requires more cleaning and maintenance than other options as well.

- Cable Railing: Stainless steel cable railing provides a fresh, modern look and feel for your deck. Another durable option, they are installed to and between wood, vinyl, or stainless steel posts at intervals of about 4 inches. More affordable than glass railings, cable railings are easier to install than some other options, require very little maintenance, and their life expectancy is quite long.

Stairways and Handrails

Stairs will likely be a critical element of your deck, and before the deck building is even begun, we need to assess likely entrance and exit points from the deck and carefully and meticulously plan for any stairs and handrails (if required). Stairs can also help you define specific areas on your deck for specific purposes.

In addition to the math and geometry that goes into building stairs, building codes require specific riser and tread widths and depths as well as height and load requirements.

Regarding handrails, not all decks require them; requirements are dependent on a number of factors, including vertical rise. In most towns, if your deck is more than 30 inches above the ground (or below grade), you will need two handrails.

Framing

Framing a deck is similar to framing a house—it's just on a much smaller scale. The deck framing process includes creating the necessary connections between beams, joists, and support posts that will yield a code compliant structure. Typically, when building a deck, the structure is begun against the house with the ledger board acting as a stationary surface and length to pull measurements from and attach joists to.

Posts and Footings

These parts of a deck are similar to the foundation of a house. They keep the structure stable and hold it up. A deck post footing is a poured concrete pad that measures 20-inch or more in diameter. The concrete is poured into a hole that is dug into the ground, and the hole needs to be deep enough that the bottom is below the local frost level. Once poured, a deck post is inserted in the hole and the concrete cures around it. Posts and footings and spaced in a way that permits the deck built on top will meet code for how much the weight per square foot the deck can support and so on.

Deck Flooring

There are a handful of materials with which a deck flooring may be built, and ultimately, there are four factors homeowners will consider in their decision-making: aesthetic, budget, climate, and maintenance. **Natural wood**, like cedar, redwood, or tropical hardwoods make for beautiful deck flooring that resists both pests and rot.

- Pressure-Treated Lumber: A more budget friendly option. Typically southern pine, the lumber is chemically treated to resist rotting and insect damage. In fact, the majority of home decks in the U.S. are made with pressure treated lumber, which isn't a terrible voice aesthetically and that is very durable. Pressure treated lumber decks will need to be pressure washed annually.

- Plastic Decking: Durable and easy to clean. It won't crack, split, or warp (even over time), and it's impervious to decay, insects, and moisture. Like composite decking, plastic decking can get very hot, mold and mildew can grow in cool, damp areas, and the surface of composite decking can become slick when wet. Furthermore, as it ages, it can develop an unattractive chalky appearance.

- Composite Decking: (such as Moisture Shield Vision composite decking) is an excellent option. Such products are made from a combination of recycled plastic and wood fibers. A durable synthetic material, composite decking resists warping, is unlikely to rot or suffer insect infestations. It is also available in a large variety of colors and styles, including looks that mimic natural wood. Composite decking does not require any sanding, or sealing—ever. On the other hand, dark-colored composite decking gets extremely hot in direct sunlight, mold and mildew can grow in cool, damp areas, and the surface of composite decking can become slick when wet. Moisture Shield Vision composite decking is the exception to composites that share many of these drawbacks. It stays cool even in the hottest climates, and is frequently used as a flooring material for decks that surround swimming pools.

- Aluminum Decking: The last to the common materials used in deck flooring. While its appearance is very industrial, it is long-lasting and requires minimal maintenance. When used in decking, aluminum typically features a powder-coated finish. Aluminum is resistant to mildew, mold, and staining, and it will not crack, peel, rot, or rust. Perhaps surprisingly, it remains cool to the touch, even on the hottest days. Aluminum decking is a more expensive option. If you are looking for an industrial look for your deck, aluminum decking is a great choice.

If you want or need help planning and building a deck, whether as a part of a new home build or a part of an existing home renovation, we would love to share our knowledge and experience with you.

To learn more, call the Reagan Homes team at (860) 962-6250 to learn more or visit www.ReaganHomes.com to schedule a complimentary, no-obligation consultation.

PATIO OPTIONS

How would you describe the patio of your dreams? Is it neat and formal? Flanked by gardens? Casual with comfortable seating? Eclectic? Cozy? Rustic?

How will you, your family, and your friends spend your time on the patio?

How does the patio feel under your feet? Is it stable? Do the materials shift with each step? Do you feel a little wobble?

And how much effort do you want to put into cleaning and maintaining it? Do you want to spray it down with a hose and sweep off the leaves, and be done with it? Or are you OK with pulling a weed here and there?

These are just a few of the questions you'll want to answer before building a new patio.

Patios are typically made of one or more of six materials: brick, concrete, stone, gravel, pavers, or tile. It's what you do with your chosen materials that will set the mood and tone of all that time you'll spend outdoors. That's where our team of trusted professionals can help. Not only have we built hundreds of patios throughout southeast Connecticut, we are the experts to turn to for information on local building codes, setback requirements, and more.

Brick

Brick is one of the oldest building materials of all, and it's still a favorite after all these millennia. Fired in a kiln and made of clay and other materials, bricks are long-lasting and provide a classic and neat look that complements many home and landscape designs. In addition to patio flooring, bricks are often used for pathways, edging, walls, and decorative features. They can be sealed to keep them in pristine condition, but some prefer the weathered, mossy look natural, untreated bricks may take on.

Concrete

Concrete is an affordable patio material that is long-lasting and relatively easy to maintain. If poured, your concrete patio should include expansion joints to help avoid the cracking that can come with repeated freezing and thawing. Concrete slabs or tiles are additional options that allow homeowners to escape the negative impacts of the freeze and thaw cycles and that can be mixed with other materials to create a one-of-a-kind patio.

Stamped Concrete

If you're considering a concrete patio, you might want to take it a step further, adding pattern, texture, and even color to your concrete patio with stamping. You'll still benefit from the same features that come with concrete, including affordability, longevity, and low maintenance needs, and you'll have a patio that is more high-end looking than bare concrete. Popular patterns mimic stone, pavers, and even wood. You'll still need to take freeze and thaw cycles and the potential resultant cracks into consideration to protect your stamped concrete patio.

Flagstone

Flagstone refers not to a single type of stone but a variety of quarried stones used independently or together. Flagstone types include bluestone, limestone, quartzite, and sandstone. Each comes in rough slabs and may be laid in soil or sand or embedded in concrete or mortar to form a patio's flooring. Flagstone is prone to cracking if not laid in concrete or mortar. The flagstone is often pieced together like a puzzle.

Cut Stone

Cut stone isn't entirely different from flagstone, although it is cut into more geometric and standardized shapes and sizes. Cut stone is typically used in more formal patio designs and may be referred to as cobblestones, stone blocks, or Belgian blocks. They are most often cut from bluestone, granite, limestone, marble, phyllite, sandstone, slate, and travertine. Travertine is a great option for patios around pools as it is one of the coolest temperature stones available—it's great for bare feet.

Gravel

Gravel is an affordable patio option and can be the star or a supporting character. It provides excellent drainage and keeps weeds mostly at bay. But it's not super comfortable to walk on, and it's prone to shifting and moving, which can result in material erosion. To get around the comfort and erosion issues, gravel is sometimes used in conjunction with other materials, filling in the gaps, for example, between concrete slabs or tiles.

Pavers

Pavers are also assembled in a puzzle-like manner, and interlocking pavers require neither grout or mortar. While first-generation pavers were available in a limited selection of relatively unattractive colors and only a few styles or shapes, today they are available in a broader range of natural-looking colors, shapes, and textures. Many pavers mimic brick, cobblestone, and cut stone. Pavers are a versatile material that will yield an attractive patio.

Tile

Porcelain, quarry, and terracotta tiles—all unglazed—are an attractive option for patio flooring. Each is recommended for a specific climate or environment; terracotta, for example—which provides a lovely rustic look—happens to be highly porous and will function best in milder climates. Regardless of which tile one chooses for their patio, all tiles should be sealed to protect them from moisture, staining, and excessive wear. Tiled patios are pleasant to walk on and easy to clean.

To learn more, call the Reagan Homes team at (860) 962-6250 to learn more or visit www.ReaganHomes.com to schedule a complimentary, no-obligation consultation.

DAVE REAGAN

WALKWAY OPTIONS

Walkways are often overlooked and taken for granted, which is unfortunate since they serve as form, function, and even beauty. The main basic function of a walkway is to enhance the ease of a pedestrian to get from point A to point B. They are also used to protect landscaping from potential damage.

Functionality aside, walkways can be a direct reflection of one's style and taste, and they enhance the curb appeal of your home while adding value to your property.

You can choose from a wide variety of materials, colors, textures, and an unlimited number of designs to fit your style and budget. Walkways need not be boring!

How to Choose the Right Walkway for Your Home

You will want to ask yourself several basic questions that will help determine which type of walkway will fit your needs, budget, and lifestyle.

How much will your pathway be used?

Is it purely utilitarian for maintenance and daily use, or is your intention to connect outdoor spaces for recreational purposes, like going from the house to the pool or an outdoor kitchen? Or to showcase your stunning landscaping via an inviting, meandering path.

It is not uncommon for high-end custom homes to have several walkways to serve several different functions.

How narrow or wide should your walkway be?

Is it for the front entrance of your home or the side entrance? The front entrance will need a much wider path to accommodate guests or showcase a grand entryway. Generally, we recommend at least 6-foot wide or a pathway to your front door.

Narrower pathways can be used for pathways to the backyard or other sides of the house. Typically, a 24" pathway is needed for one person, so if you want a pathway to accommodate two people walking comfortably, at least a 48" pathway is needed.

Many builders will use a 36" pathway as a standard, but if your property allows, wider pathways make more sense.

Pathway compatibility to your home style is another factor to consider in choosing the right path, material mix, and finish to complement the home's architecture, style, and personal taste.

Types Of Walkways

There are a multitude of walkway materials available, and any of them can be mixed and matched to suit your needs, budget, and style.

Gravel

This is usually the most affordable material for residential walkways. Gravel is informal in style, easy to work with, and the least expensive to install. There are different types of gravel varieties, textures, and colors available.

Gravel costs will run from about 40 cents to $2 per square foot. You can choose from rock base, crushed limestone, rock pebbles, shells, crush and run, caliche, steel slag, and shale. These gravel choices are typically priced by the cubic yard or by the ton.

Pros:
- Typically the least expensive materials to purchase
- Low installation cost
- Quick installation
- Makes for a nice contrast between the light and dark
- Low maintenance
- Provides good drainage
- Flexibility in look to be formal or natural and wild

Cons:
- Needs to be raked and maintained to be kept tidy
- Requires a border to keep gravel contained
- Not friendly to sensitive pet paws or bare feet
- Not good to put furniture on
- Weeds can grow through the gravel and gravel can develop algae
- Can get dusty

Mulch

Mulch is also readily available and economical. People pay an average of $18 per yard for bulk delivery with premium mulch available, making it affordable to purchase and install. You can also combine mulch with gravel to create stunning looks.

Pros:
- Affordable material cost
- Low installation cost
- Quick installation
- Mulch is a natural weed blocker, just add more annually
- Low maintenance
- Saves water
- Suppresses weed growth

Cons:
- Annual replacement
- Not a pedestrian-friendly surface; needs to be combined with something study
- Needs a border to keep tidy
- Can cause pest issues

Stepping Stones

Stepping stones provide a casual, easy, affordable, and durable look when combined with gravel, sod, and/or mulch. This type of walkway allows for a more personal style that is reflective of your stone choice and that complements your home. We can offer you a choice of flagstone, ranging from 1 to 4 inches. We can provide or recommend other varieties of stone as additional options.

Flagstone, for instance, typically costs between $2 and $3 per square foot for 1.5" thick. Flagstone does, however, require additional labor to prep the soil, grass, or bed of sand that is needed.

Pros:
- Affordable and a step up from mulch and gravel
- Can lay high-end stones but maintain affordability
- Lifetime lifespan

Cons:
- Only for pedestrian use from Point A to B; not appropriate for utilitarian use
- Stones can get hot and retain heat
- Can be very slippery when wet
- Needs an even foundation or stones can break

Brick and Concrete Pavers

Brick and concrete pavers are machine-cut, flat bricks typically used for driveways, walkways, and patios. Which you might choose is merely a personal choice. Bricks are made out of clay and concrete pavers are made of cement. Paver materials cost usually between $3 and $10 per square foot.

These pavers are available in a wide variety of colors, designs, and patterns. Pavers beautifully accent any landscaping, give a pop of color to the grounds, and add elegance to historical homes—especially brick pavers.

Pros:
- Can withstand up to 8000 psi of pressure
- Durable
- Uniform
- 20 to 50 year lifespan
- Low maintenance
- Stronger than poured concrete
- Easy to remove and replace damaged pavers
- Adds a nice pop of color
- Unlimited design patterns

Cons:
- The surface can degrade over time if de-icing salts are used
- Labor intensive, time-consuming
- More expensive than stepping stones
- Weeds can grow in between the joints if not installed properly

Stamped Concrete

Also known as imprinted concrete, this material is a solid pour of cement that is embossed with a pattern and one or more color tints (if desired). The design options are numerous, and most finishes range in cost from about $8 to $25 or more per square foot (depending on the design). Stamped concrete can mimic brick, slate, flagstone or even wood! Typically, stamped concrete comes with a 25-year warranty since it's the same process as standard concrete.

Pros:
- Durable 25-year warranty
- Various designs, colors, textures, and patterns to choose from
- Can be less expensive to install than pavers
- No weed growth between joints
- No expansion/ contraction from seasonal changes

Cons:
- If sealed, you will need to re-seal every 2 to 5 years
- Will crack eventually
- Hard to color match in case of repair
- Colors can fade over time
- Some finishes can be slippery when wet

Flagstone, Limestone, Travertine, and Slate

These are the best premium walkway materials you can invest in. You can even purchase them in varying thicknesses, but for a walkway, a 1" to 1.5" thickness is preferred. Generally, the wider and larger the stone piece, the better.

Installation requires the craftsmanship of a stonemason to make sure the stones fit together perfectly. Thus, it's not surprising that these materials are usually the most expensive options with which to build a residential walkway because of how labor-intensive installation is. Flagstone costs approximately $15 to $20 per square foot installed. Limestone and travertine will cost between $13 and $30 per square foot installed, and slate will cost between $18 and $45 per square foot installed. These types of stone are also available as real stone pavers.

Pros:
- Long-lasting
- Low maintenance
- Resistant to chipping and cracking
- Pick from a variety of high-end stone colors, finishes, and natural beauty
- Boosts curb appeal and home value
- Travertine is great for pool decks and patios because travertine tends to stay cool enough in the hot sun to still walk barefoot
- If a stone cracks, it is easier to replace a single stone as compared to an entire stamped concrete pad

Cons:
- Expensive, labor-intensive
- Slate can be slippery
- Can grow moss or mold stains in areas that are particularly wet or humid

Rustic Wood or Recycled Pallet Wood

This is a great option for environmentalists. Recycled wood can often be purchased inexpensively or even procured for free (like pallet wood). Since wood is such a flexible material, as a walkway, it can be embedded in the ground or raised. It is also easily mixed with other mediums.

Pros:
- Environmentally friendly
- More flexible than stone
- Durable
- Can elevate a path away (from muddy areas, for example),
  and remains dry and solid year round
- Affordable or even extremely economical depending sourcing

Cons:
- Wood rot
- Can be slippery when wet depending on the finish
- Shortest useful life out of all hard surface options
- Requires seasonal maintenance to keep it looking fresh

There are no hard and fast rules for mixing and matching walkway materials and the various forms and functions you need to fulfill. Your new walkway is a blank canvas for your imagination.

When you are looking for a walkway that provides affordability, beauty, safety, and durability, we've got you covered. You will get beautiful, functional designs when you work with our expert specialists to align your desired goals with your budget.

While there are many walkway options to choose from, we are here to guide you in your selections and in determining the best walkway widths for your purposes.

Whether as part of an existing home renovation or a new custom-home build, Reagan Homes wants to help.

To learn more, call the Reagan Homes team at (860) 962-6250
to learn more or visit www.ReaganHomes.com
to schedule a complimentary, no-obligation consultation.

EXTERIOR LIGHTING OPTIONS

Lighting is just as important outside the home as it is inside. Ample lighting keeps pathways well-lit, backyards optimized for entertaining, and adds beauty and charm to the exterior of your home. Many great options exist to help you achieve such goals, but if you're not quite sure how to go about selecting and installing outdoor lighting, you're not alone.

The first step is to assess your outdoor lighting needs. Can you tell which areas are under-lighted or that need a bit of a boost? Quality, appropriate outdoor lighting not only adds ambiance but also provides significant security. Some people even choose to invest in motion sensor lighting to ensure they know if someone—or something— happens to be lurking about in the late hours of the evening.

You should feel happy, safe, and secure in your home, and exterior lighting is just another way to achieve those feelings. But what sort of lights do you need around your home?

Security Lighting

One of the most critical purposes of exterior lighting is security. If your home is not close to other houses or a main road, investing in security lights will help you feel safer and more secure. Motion sensor lights, triggered by movement, are an excellent option.

Depending on the type of motion sensor lighting you purchase, you might be able to set the sensors, so it doesn't trip when wildlife—small animals like squirrels and rabbits, for example—cross their paths. That way, you can be confident that you need to pay attention when the lights come on. Some may even come with cameras to capture whatever may be causing a sensor to go off.

Security floodlights, LED lights, and lights that sense when the sun has gone down and turn on and off automatically are also available.

Pathway or Walkway Lighting

Lighting up the path to your front door is a wise decision. It ensures that you, your family members, and visitors don't lose your/their footing and fall while approaching the house at night. Missteps can happen, and especially when weather conditions are less than optimal, you need to be able to see clearly to the door. Pathway lighting helps with safety by potentially preventing slips and falls while bringing in packages.

Pathway lighting can also help visitors find your house. Delivery drivers, friends, and neighbors will be able to see the way to your front door easily.

Path lighting can also add personality and in new, fun, and innovative ways. You might opt for solar lights, small lamps, glass bulb lights, colored lights, or any other of an almost infinite selection to suit your personality and the individual style of your home.

String Lighting

String lights add a touch of whimsy anywhere you put them. And, fortunately, they aren't just limited to holidays anymore. String lights can provide ambiance, warmth, and atmosphere to your backyard entertaining. String lights can also be wrapped around pillars, columns, and balconies for added character.

String lights are available with colored bulbs, white bulbs, and gold bulbs. The bulbs themselves come in many shapes, as well, including icicle-shaped, Edison bulbs, and globe-shaped.

If you're looking to add even more fun to your outdoor environment, consider using lights with fun shapes or twinkling effects.

Outdoor Wall Lighting (Sconces & Lanterns)

Wall lightings, like sconces and lanterns, can add charm and elegance to the exterior of your home while also providing reliable lighting to your porch and near your doors. They come in many different styles, and you won't have any trouble finding options that can work with the rest of your exterior decor. A few options include metal and glass lanterns as well as more modern options that will add to your home's appeal while reflecting your style and personality.

Whether you're looking for something more elegant or you want something industrial or modern, outdoor wall lights exist to meet every taste.

Deck Lighting

For lighting needs on your deck, you aren't limited only to lights that can be hung or mounted. One of the more popular options today is to light your deck flooring. You can have lighting built directly into the floorboards of your deck.

You can also go the more whimsical route and add string lights or even a light fixture (such as an outdoor chandelier) that hangs from a pergola. Deck lighting can be a simple way to add a bit of fun to your entertaining space.

Stair Lighting

Stair lighting not only provides an easy way to see where you're headed when you let out the dog at night or head into the backyard, but it is necessary for safety. Many accidents are caused by improperly or poorly lit stairwells. It's worth putting some lights along outdoor stairways. Even though this is mostly for safety reasons, this kind of lighting, too, can add some charm or fun to your home's exterior.

Get creative with different colors and shapes to customize your lighting to suit your home's style. Just because your house's exterior needs lighting for safety and security reasons doesn't mean you can't have fun with it.

Spot Lighting

Spot and floodlights are ideal for the backyard, for when you need to take the dogs out at night or when you just need a little extra lighting in darker areas, for example. They are good to have in front of your house as well—to light up bushes and over the top of any exterior walls. With spotlighting, you never need to worry about odd things (whether they are people or creatures) hiding in the bushes.

Pool Lighting

Traditionally, pool lighting is either on the sides or the bottom of a pool, and the lighting is usually built into or embedded in the pool. You could also choose to put pool lighting in the stone or brickwork of your pool's apron if you'd rather the lighting be on the exterior. Or, if you want to get creative, you can float lights in your pool. All sorts of LED lights and colorful lighted objects are available for just that purpose, and they provide a fun, mystical effect.

What Reagan Homes Can Do For You

Reagan Homes wants to help bring a little light into your life by helping you build an outdoor lighting plan. Whatever your style, whatever your home's aesthetic, our team can help you plan for all your outdoor lighting needs.

We would be happy to discuss outdoor lighting with you, and we have years worth of knowledge and experience to share.

To learn more, call the Reagan Homes team at (860) 962-6250
to learn more or visit www.ReaganHomes.com
to schedule a complimentary, no-obligation consultation.

FENCING OPTIONS

Many homeowners want the outside of their homes to signal the style and décor visitors will find when they enter. If your property requires a fence for a pool or you want a fence for your pets or just for aesthetic reasons, one of the first things a visitor will notice is fencing.

Fencing is available in various shapes, patterns, and sizes. Fences serve many purposes for the homeowner, and including one in a new home plan or renovation plan is something all homeowners should consider.

Types of Fences

Wood Fencing

Classic wood is a style of fencing that has been around practically forever and that is still widely loved and appreciated today. Wood fencing is also one of the most affordable fencing options.

Perhaps the best quality of wood fencing is its durability. The wood used for fencing is typically high quality, and with proper maintenance, a wood fence can last for many years.

Aluminum Fencing

What aluminum fencing lacks in durability, it more than makes up for in attractiveness. Aluminum fences are some of the most sophisticated fencings available. They are also easy to find in stock, and installation is typically easy as well. Ease of maintenance is also a strong suit for aluminum fences. However, they may not provide the security that other kinds of fencing do. If you're considering aluminum, you'll have to decide if you're willing to sacrifice security for a beautiful appearance and easy care.

Vinyl Fencing

Vinyl fencing has grown in popularity over the last several years, thanks to some noteworthy features. According to many reliable sources, vinyl fences are stronger, more durable, and as effective as almost any other type of fence. They are also easy to maintain, exude class, and are resistant to damage and vandalism. The upfront costs associated with vinyl fencing are higher, but homeowners typically find the expense worth the benefits. Today, vinyl fencing is also available in many colors beyond white.

Electric Fencing

Most people who use electric fencing do so to keep their dog or dogs within the bounds of their own property. A battery-powered collar receives a signal from the electrical unit that powers the fencing. Maintaining such a fence is pretty simple, as long as the wiring doesn't get tangled and any digging or lawn work neither interferes with nor cuts through the usually buried wiring.

Gate Options

Sliding Gate

Particularly popular in upscale neighborhoods, sliding fence gates represent class, poise, and style. They're the perfect way to welcome visitors to your home. Unlike conventional gates, sliding gates open from the middle, with panels that move to the left and right. Some sliding gates can also be opened and closed automatically—with the touch of a button.

Vertical Pivot Gate

The most expensive gate option of all is the vertical pivot gate. This type of gate opens in a way that is vastly different from other fence gates. A vertical pivot gate has electronic sensors that lift automatically lift the gate open any time the sensors are tripped by an approaching vehicle.

Automatic Gate

Just like sliding gates, an automatic gate is one of the most frequently purchased, and many people prefer it to the former. Automatic gates are used in just about every business you can think of, and that's because they're pretty easy to maintain and control, and they get the job done. While automatic gates are usually attached to a main power source, they typically come up with back-up batteries and work 24/7—even when the power is out.

Fencing options have grown exponentially in recent years, with numerous new types entering the market. The experienced professionals at Reagan Homes are familiar with all types of fences and can help you understand each option's nuances. If you'd like to discuss your fencing needs, maintenance requirements, and design choices for a new custom home or the renovation of your existing home, our team would love to help.

To learn more, call the Reagan Homes team at (860) 962-6250
to learn more or visit www.ReaganHomes.com
to schedule a complimentary, no-obligation consultation.

GRASS OPTIONS

Your home should sit upon something lush and green that will be the envy of the entire neighborhood. Grass not only makes the exterior of your home more attractive, but the vegetation is good for your community and will make your space look more natural. But you may be thinking, "Grass is grass," right?

How many options could there be to choose from, and how might each affect your home? With more than 30 years of experience, we will help guide you through the different options when it comes to grass.

Sod

If you don't want to wait for your grass to grow before you can see it become lush and beautiful, you'll want to opt for sod. Sod is an instantaneous addition that will have your lawn looking fresh and perfect almost as soon as it is installed. You'll have to wait to walk on it or put up lawn ornaments and furniture, but it will give you that perfect-lawn look without any wait.

Sod is grass that has already been grown. Technically, it is a mixture of grass and a layer of soil woven together using the grass's own roots or a netting material. You don't have to install it at any specific time, just during the growing season. You will, however, want to make sure the weather isn't too hot when it comes time to install.

Opting for sod will also help limit or eradicate weeds as sod is crafted without the seeds that develop into weeds in the first place. Once the roots extend into the soil in your yard, you'll be able to enjoy your lawn–lawn ornaments, furniture, games, and all. Once installed, watering the sod is critical for it to take root and continue to grow.

Hydroseeding

Sod can be expensive, which is why a lot of people opt for hydroseeding instead. You only need a small team of people to help get your hydroseeded lawn started. You'll use a mixture of seed, water, mulch, and fertilizer. Once laid down, your hydroseeded grass can get started sprouting. Growth should be apparent in a week or less. The quality of the grass that grows once it has begun sprouting will be better than many other options—as long as it is fed the proper nutrients to encourage thorough and proper growth.

Hydroseeding mixtures remain moist, so you don't have to worry about the grass drying out right away. And you'll be able to enjoy your lush, healthy lawn throughout the seasons. The efficiency of installation and the speed with which the method effectively grows grass will only make the outcome and your satisfaction that much better in the long run.

Traditional Grass Seed

The cost of traditional grass seed is significantly lower than sod and requires less effort to install. You can choose from a wide variety of grasses, such as Kentucky Blue or St. Augustine. Traditional seeding provides a unique look that will differ from neighbors.

With traditional seeding, however, you do need to seed your lawn during a specific timeframe. It will also take a while for the grass to grow and mature. You'll likely have to weed more often as well since traditional seed may carry weed seed with it.

Synthetic Grass

Synthetic grass is a good option for areas with high heat, heavy snow, or a poor growing season. Sometimes grass won't grow efficiently depending on climate, so synthetic might be your best option if you desire a full and lush-looking lawn. The installation of artificial grass is easy and instant, but it can be pricey.

Irrigation System Benefits

To keep your grass hydrated and growing well, you will definitely want to consider investing in an irrigation system. Many lawns need an extra bit of tender loving care to remain healthy. Dry, brown lawns can be a real killer when it comes to the visual appeal of your home and neighborhood.

Irrigation systems help your lawn be lush and green—even during the peak of summer—it's an investment worth looking into.

Reagan Homes Wants To Help You

We know how important it is for your home to have a beautiful, thick, green lawn. As part of your existing home renovation or new custom home, our trusted team of experts at Reagan Homes are here to help you determine precisely what your yard would benefit from based on your climate and the placement of your home. We will be happy to discuss your options so your home can be unique and beautiful.

WINDOW OPTIONS

Windows need to bring in enough light, suit the aesthetic of your home, and be functional. What you might not expect when you're choosing the windows for your new custom home or remodel is the vast array of options available to you.

There are more than a dozen different types of windows to suit every possible need you might have for your home. Our design team will help you find the right balance for your design. With so many windows to choose from, let's go through them so you can be more knowledgeable about all of your options.

Double Hung and Single Hung Windows

Single-hung and double-hung are terms that describe how the window moves when opened. If your window is single-hung, it will open up from the bottom sash while the top sash stays in place. With double-hung windows, on the other hand, the bottom and the top sashes will both open.

These two types are the most common types of windows you'll find in a modern house. They are practical, easy to clean, and relatively inexpensive to install. They have a very modern feel and a clean aesthetic. They let in a good amount of light without overwhelming you with too much sunshine. Due to their popularity, it isn't going to be difficult to source single- and double-hung windows or have them installed.

Casement Windows

These windows are incredibly popular in modular and modern architecture as they are very minimalist. Constructed mainly of glass, they open up to the sides so you can get a good amount of air and light into the room. They do have a modern aesthetic, but they also have an air of romance to them as they open up completely so you can enjoy the fresh air. Casement windows are relatively on par with the cost of double- and single-hung windows.

Picture Windows

If you've got a beautiful back or front yard view, a picture window may be the best option. Picture windows do not have bars or sashes, and they are fixed–they cannot be opened. They are essentially immovable slabs of glass that allow you to maximize your exposure to light and see the beauty of your landscape. Your view will remain entirely unobstructed so you can truly enjoy the natural appeal of your land or neighborhood.

Picture windows can be moderate to pricey depending on size. A picture window can easily be customized, and we can place a picture window at the right point in your home to ensure your view is picture perfect.

Bay Windows

Almost everyone loves a bay window. The aesthetic is one of those things that makes old fashioned Victorian homes (or any home for that matter) truly elegant and charming. They protrude windows from the exterior of a home, creating a pocket on the inside where you can opt for a window seat or perhaps place your desk for the best view in your house. Although not commonly used in kitchens, installing a bay window over the sink can provide a deep window sill while also adding architectural flair. Bay windows are highly sought after for the space, light, and atmosphere they provide.

Bay windows do tend to be more expensive than many other windows, and because they protrude from the home at a particular angle, your home needs to be constructed to suit the inclusion of such a window.

Awning Windows

Awning windows are especially beneficial for those who live in rainy climates as they open outward so rain simply slides off the glass. They are ideal for opening during thunderstorms to watch and listen while relaxing with a good book or a hot drink. The cost of awning windows in the middle ground of all window styles—they are not as expensive as bay windows but are pricier than the single-and double-hung windows.

Aside from being functional, awning windows add a charming modern feel to any home.

Slider Windows

The name says it all; these windows slide open from side to side rather than sliding up or down or opening out. One window will be stationary and then the one that slides will slide in front of or behind it. These really help open up spaces and allow more light and fresh air to enter the room. They are a really lovely and charming addition to any design and provide so much atmosphere in the form of natural light.

The prices on these vary a little bit, and they can either be in the middle range of expense or they can be more expensive depending on the size of the window.

Transom Windows

Transom windows aren't functional at all, but they are more for visual appeal. Transoms usually are a part of a design around or above a doorway or other areas of the home where you want to break up negative space and add visual interest. Transom windows are popular in master bedrooms over a bed or in a bathroom where you may desire light in but also want privacy. These windows are relatively inexpensive as they are generally quite small and are used exclusively for design purposes.

Depending on what designs you're looking for, transom windows are available in a variety of shapes, like half-moons, squares, or rectangles.

Arched Windows

These are named after what they represent, which are archways. The top of the pane is rounded off and they are usually floor to ceiling to allow in a lot of natural lighting. The beauty of these windows is what makes them an appealing choice as they do not open so they can't allow in any air. But mostly these are used as a lovely focal point for your home that will add charm and elegance.

They aren't as expensive as you would think they would be, as they don't need any mechanics for functionality.

Egress Windows

You won't see egress windows on most modern houses unless they have a basement. Egress windows are designed as a safety precaution for those on an underground floor or a basement in case of fire or other emergency. Some states may require homes with these underground floors to have egress windows or they will be fined.

Because they require digging out space for an escape route, they can be much pricier than you'd expect.

Garden Windows

These windows are a smaller version of a bay window, so they are structured to protrude from the house for the purpose of keeping plants. They provide the perfect place for your indoor plants to perch to get the optimal amount of sunlight and keep them out of the way of any pets who might otherwise knock them over. Garden windows are a beautiful addition to any home and are perfect if you've got a green thumb and want to grow some herbs or succulents on a windowsill.

They do come at a higher price since they protrude from the house. They can also come with additional bells and whistles; the sides of a garden window may open to allow fresh air to pass through.

Hopper Windows

These windows are a little bit old-fashioned and aren't typically found in modern home builds. They require a crank to be opened and they open into the house—the opposite functionality of awning windows. They are usually found in bathrooms or smaller spaces to let out steam or let in fresh air when you can't have a larger window in the space for reasons such as privacy.

They fall into the same price range as single or double-hung windows or casement windows; hopper windows are fairly compact and don't require any special installation.

Jalousie Windows

If you've ever seen slatted blinds, you're already familiar with the general style of a jalousie window. Instead of the blinds being what opens up to allow light in, the slats are the window itself and are made of glass and metal to open up the window that way. This allows for fresh air to enter the home without letting too much light in. They have a crank as well to help those slatted windows open, but they aren't as expensive as you'd assume. They can actually cost a bit less than your standard single or double-hung window.

Round Circle Windows

These windows are purely for stylistic purposes. You'll find them most often in a modern home build as they are more fashion than function and add a little whimsy and charm to your architecture. While they are seen mostly in modern homes, they are a bit of a charming homage to historical builds.

They can be fully circular, half-moon or even oval-shaped to suit whatever aesthetic you're going for in your home. They tend to fall in the same price range as casement or slider windows.

A round skylight, for example, is ideal if you want to give a certain room more natural light (if you don't have the wall space for windows in that room). They can suit an attic room or a bathroom and offer lovely light without taking up too much space. Typically, round or circle windows are fixed, but some designs may be able to open depending on how accessible the windows will be.

If you do want to open a skylight window, some models open manually, and higher priced models can open with a click of a button. Options that open tend to be pricier.

Storm Windows

Storm windows can be built like any other window but they have a specific function: they essentially provide extra layers of glass that help create a better seal so elements like rain and snow can't get into the home. Storm windows keep your heating or air conditioning in your home while also keeping out the harshness of winter cold and summer heat waves. In New England, storm windows might be beneficial.

They cost about the same as your standard single or double-hung windows since they are little more than layers of extra glass and sealing elements.

What Can Reagan Homes Do For You?

Windows are an essential element to any home build, our team at Reagan Homes can help you determine which windows will suit your needs the best. We are experts in the field of home building and remodeling, so you can be assured you're getting the best advice on your home build without compromising on quality. If you're looking to build your dream home or remodel the one you've got, we are here to help.

*To learn more, call the Reagan Homes team at (860) 962-6250
to learn more or visit www.ReaganHomes.com
to schedule a complimentary, no-obligation consultation.*

ADDING ADDITIONAL LIGHT BEYOND TRADITIONAL WINDOWS AND DOORS

Generally, homes are equipped with the usual traditional windows and doors. However, there are additional ways you can brighten your home. Unfortunately, few home-building businesses will give you information on how practical and appealing these options can be, let alone give examples or suggest such options. The two types of light in this category, solar tube and skylights, are so similar that it is hard to say there is much difference between them.

Skylights

Skylights need not be limited only to attic spaces. When you want to brighten a room that is too small to install a traditional window or that is simply lacking direct access to the roof to allow for conventional skylight installation, there remains another option to add natural light to your indoor environment.

Tubular skylights are installed through a shaft that starts on the roof and extends into your home. As it captures sunlight on the rooftop, the tube redirects that light down a highly reflective shaft and diffuses it throughout the interior space.

These skylights offer optional features, ideal for use in bathrooms and laundry rooms. Electric light kits can modify the unit, allowing you to use the tube at night as an additional light fixture. Or you may opt for a dimmer switch that allows you to adjust the level of daylight that enters through the tube. Upon installation, the entire unit is sealed to lock out dust, bugs, and moisture.

Solar Tubes

If you want to enjoy more natural light in your home but find skylights too big, expensive, or hard to maintain, solar tubes offer a simple alternative. Also known as tubular skylights or sun tunnels, solar tubes give you a discreet way to brighten the darker areas of your home with soft, natural light.

The standard solar tube is a polished sheet metal tube installed in the roof to channel sunlight into the house's interior. They're most commonly available in 10- and 14-inch-diameter sizes, which fit between standard 16-inch roof joists. On the roof end of the tube is a weather-resistant acrylic cap. On the ceiling side is a round window-like opening fit with a diffuser that helps distribute the light. When installing a tubular skylight, start by marking the location inside the room. Line up your preferred location with a flat area in the roof before cutting any holes.

Pros of Solar Tube Lighting

- <u>Free Lighting:</u> On a sunny day, one 10-inch solar tube provides about the same amount of light as three 100-watt bulbs. That's enough to illuminate a 200-square-foot. room well enough for office work, or light a 300 square-foot room enough for less visual activities, such as taking a shower or folding the laundry. With this much light, you'll no longer have to use electric lighting on sunny or even moderately cloudy days. You'll enjoy extra convenience while saving money. If you want or need extra light at night, too, choose a solar tube model that includes an electric light.

- <u>Design Flexibility:</u> Given their size, skylights are hard to miss when you walk into a room. On the other hand, solar tubes are subtle design elements that add light without calling attention to themselves. If you want to bring more light into your living room or bedroom without altering the room's architecture, solar tubes let you do so. They also fit into smaller spaces than traditional skylights, making them a practical way to brighten a dim hallway or pantry.

- <u>Lower Risk of Leaks:</u> Traditional skylights are well known for their tendency to leak. A significant reason for this is their tendency to collect debris, such as leaves, which prevents rainfall and snowmelt from draining off the roof. The built-up water then finds its way under the adjacent roofing material and then into your ceiling. Solar tubes are less likely to leak because their small, relatively flat domes allow water to drain around them.

- <u>Budget-Friendly Installation:</u> Solar tubes might look like a luxury feature, but they don't require a major investment. The tubes themselves cost less than skylights, and they're also less expensive to have installed because they don't require any changes to your drywall or framing.

Cons of Solar Tube Lighting

- <u>Less Control and Limited Design Impact:</u> Solar tubes give you fewer options for controlling the light entering the room, and their small size means they do little to enhance your home's architecture.

- <u>Fewer Options for Control:</u> Skylights give you more control over the quality of light you let in. Skylight shades work just like window shades, while the variety of skylight diffusers on the market offers plenty of options for distributing the light in the room. You can also add film to reduce UV light, which can fade your rugs and furniture.

  Vented skylights even allow you to bring fresh air into your home along with your sunlight just by opening the skylight as you would an awning window. With solar tubes, shades and venting aren't options. While you can use diffusers and window film, you'll have a more limited selection than what's available for skylights.

- <u>Little Design Improvement:</u> Skylights are an architectural design feature unto themselves, making rooms feel larger and airier and providing you with an ever-changing view of the passing clouds. They add both an ambiance of luxury and a feeling of connection to nature. Most solar tubes, however, are too small to affect the feel of a room beyond letting in light. They also don't offer much of a view of the outdoors.

- <u>Not Equally Suited to Every Home:</u> The type of roof you have might make it impractical to install solar tubes. Most solar tubes are designed for roofs with a slope between 15 and 60 degrees. If you have a flat roof, you'll need to look for tubular skylight models specifically designed for this type of roof. On a steeply pitched roof, such as an A-frame, installation might not be possible.

  In high-humidity climates, condensation on the inside of the tube can be a common problem. You can minimize this by wrapping the tube in R-15 batt insulation before you install it. If your home could use a little more daylight, particularly in smaller, darker spaces, but you don't want to spend a lot or change your rooms' overall look, solar tubes are a practical solution. On the other hand, if you want to make a significant impact on a room's appearance and you're willing to pay for it, you may want to stick to traditional skylights.

If you'd like more information about adding skylights or solar tube lighting to your home—whether as part of a custom build or a renovation or remodel of an existing home, our experienced Reagan Homes team would be happy to guide you through your decision-making.

CEILING OPTIONS

Ceilings are more important in your home than you likely even realize. They hide the electrical and plumbing work from view, and that's just for starters. Ceilings deliver the most extensive unobstructed views within our homes, and often they are usually one of the first parts of your home that guests see. A beautiful ceiling is indicative of the beauty of a house. The infrequently considered ceiling, it turns out, is essential to both your home's aesthetics and interior design. There are many ceiling styles that we can incorporate into your design. Let's review some of them.

Conventional Ceilings

Conventional is the most common ceiling type in the United States. Conventional ceilings feature a standard drywall finish and the materials used in making them are relatively inexpensive. The installation is an easy process. Conventional ceilings are plain and flat, and they are compatible with virtually any construction size. They are usually 8 to 10 feet from the floor.

Coffered Ceilings

Coffered ceilings are often found in upscale homes, hotels, churches, and other public/residential spaces. They reflect a classic and luxurious tone. Coffered ceilings are a preferable option to conventional ceilings, and specialists are required for installation. It features a flat ceiling just outside of a tray that surrounds the highest part of the ceiling, which is raised in the center.

Tray Ceilings

Tray ceilings are also known as penned ceilings. They add elegance and make a room feel taller. The height of a tray ceiling (from the floor) should be a minimum of eight feet. Tray ceilings are similar to coffered ceilings. While coffered ceilings have multiple recessed sections, a tray ceiling has just one larger, inverted area. If you want a beautiful ceiling to hide superfluous plumbing and wires in the house, tray ceilings are a good option.

Tray ceilings also provide a dynamic and luxury feeling. They aren't ideal for houses with lower ceiling heights, however, as the edges of the tray can make a house feel claustrophobic. Also, they may make kitchens appear smaller than they are because the edges may determine cabinet placement.

Beam Ceilings

Beam ceilings are gaining popularity in kitchens, living, and dining rooms. Beam ceilings are a traditional style made primarily from hardwoods. Beam ceilings provide a classic yet rustic look. They can be adapted to fit various interior design styles, and they produce beautiful effects. However, one has to be mindful of where beam ceilings are installed so smaller rooms aren't overwhelmed. The natural wood used for beam ceilings provides visual variety that is different from other rooms. The beams on a beam ceiling do not have to be structural; they can simply be aesthetic.

Cathedral Ceilings

Cathedral ceilings are shaped in a cathedral sequence. Frequently used in large living rooms, bedrooms, and sometimes master bathrooms, cathedral ceilings are also called vaulted ceilings. They are known for their inverted V shape in which the tip of the V is the highest point and the sides of the V slope down. They may be constructed from a variety of materials.

Suspended Ceiling

A suspended ceiling is often referred to as a drop ceiling. Drop ceilings hang from an existing, permanent ceiling. The benefit to such ceilings is that they create opportunities for designers to conceal mechanical, electrical, plumbing, and other wiring and piping. Drop ceilings are most often used in commercial buildings, offices, and retail spaces, as they provide designers remarkable flexibility. In residences, a suspended ceiling may be ideal in a finished basement.

Shed Ceiling

Shed—or single-slope—ceilings are used on the top story of a home. They have a distinct look and typically are painted to match the wall color. A shed ceiling will begin at a high point at one wall and slope down toward the opposite wall.

Sloped Ceilings

You're sure to find sloped ceilings in homes with pitched roofs. Sloped ceilings create some cozy corners in attics (and former attic spaces) directly below the roofline.

Coved Ceilings

Coved ceilings are dome-like in shape, with concave edges that feature soft, curved angles instead of sharp angles. They are generally built with curved molding or framing. In homes, rooms with coved ceilings often have a magical feeling to them. Apart from being used to enhance formal spaces, coved ceilings can serve as archways to separate rooms.

Dome Ceilings

A dome ceiling makes a house look like a spherical building with a spherical glass dome covering the roof. They range widely in sizing. Some dome ceilings may span a room's entirety, while others are smaller and adorn only a portion of a room. Dome ceilings are wonderfully dramatic and elegant.

Exposed Ceilings

This type of ceiling is purposely "unfinished," although exposed elements, such as ductwork and pipes, can be painted for a cohesive look. Exposed ceilings are an inexpensive option, but rooms with exposed ceilings are noisier and less insulated. With exposed ceilings, all structural, mechanical, electrical, and plumbing systems remain visible, unhidden by

drywall, plaster, or other building materials. In modern interior designs, the exposed systems can serve as decorative elements. Most exposed ceilings, however, will benefit from sound treatments since they cannot absorb sound like other ceiling styles. Exposed ceilings also require consistent maintenance, unlike other ceilings.

Groin Vault

Groin vault ceilings were first introduced by the Romans but they subsequently fell into relative obscurity. They are difficult to construct because of the angles and geometry necessary to cut and place the cross groins. Groin vault construction requires great skill to form the requisite neat intersections.

Barrel Vault

A barrel vault ceiling is also known as a tunnel vault or wagon vault. It features a half-cylinder to the total vault. There is an arch-based construction in a barrel vault. The barrel vault is primarily used in classical designs. Because the construction of a barrel vault ceiling is very difficult, there aren't many contractors who possess the required skill set. As a result, this ceiling is used infrequently in homes.

Vaulted Ceilings

Many vaulted ceilings designs exist, and all of them are architecturally self-supporting and usually built of stone and brick to cover a ceiling or roof. Generally speaking, vaulted ceilings offer grandeur and a feeling of spaciousness. They typically allow more natural light to enter the home. However, they are harder to maintain than more conventional ceilings.

Your ceilings may be the first impression a guest gets of the interior of your home, so they should be attractive. Ceilings are also integral to your lighting options. If you crave tons of natural light pouring in your windows, you'll want high ceilings.

Whether you are looking for a ceiling style that is tasteful, eccentric, or functional, our designers would be happy to work with you to align your goals with your budget.

HVAC OPTIONS: KEEPING YOUR HOME COMFORTABLE ALL YEAR LONG

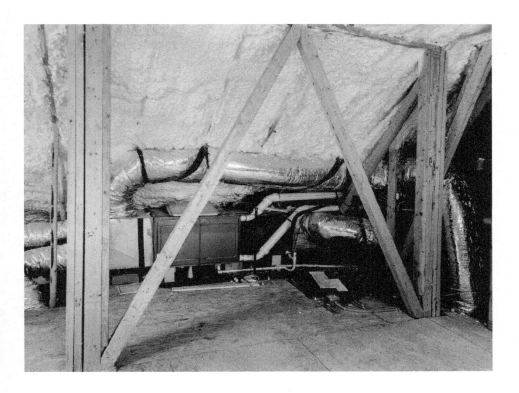

From air quality to energy efficiency, making the right choice in selecting your home's HVAC system is a decision not to be taken lightly.

A home's HVAC system is responsible for keeping residents warm in winter and cool in summer. It's something that, if you're building a house or renovating or remodeling, you want to get right. Aside from comfort levels, energy consumption is critical. According to the Department of Energy, a home's HVAC (or heating, ventilation, and air conditioning) system is responsible for as much as 48% of a home's energy consumption.

With decades of experience recommending and installing systems in new and existing homes, our team can guide you toward the system that will keep your toes toasty and your wallet full.

Boiler with Radiant Heat and AC

If you have ever lived in a home with radiators, this is the modern update of such a heating system. A boiler, which may run on electric, natural gas, or propane, heats water to a very high temperature and then forces the water through looped pipes embedded in your flooring. The heat produced is among the most comfortable—neither too dry nor too humid—and such heat is more evenly distributed as well. Since there is no air being moved, dust and allergens aren't an issue, which means indoor air quality is better with a radiant heating system than a forced-air system.

But it's an expensive system to install and can take more time than other options to heat up. Repairs may come with higher costs as well since the pipes are embedded. And a separate air conditioning system is required.

Electric Furnace and AC Split System

An electric furnace is one of several forced-air options and can be thought of most simply as a giant space heater. A practical HVAC system in many parts of the U.S., especially warmer weather areas, with an electric furnace, a furnace blower fan pulls in untreated air, heats or cools it, and forces it through your home's ductwork.

Electric furnace and AC split systems are often used in vacation and second homes, which makes up for the system's overall relatively poor energy efficiency.

Geothermal Heat Pump System

An extremely energy-efficient option, a geothermal heat pump system uses the earth's natural heat to warm or cool water circulating through a network of underground pipes. It's a popular system with those seeking to limit their environmental footprints and who are conscious of their energy usage. Geothermal systems should last for several decades before needing major repair or replacement. Homeowners can save as much as 65% on their energy bills, and such systems are multi-functional; they may also supply hot water.

But they are the most expensive of all currently available HVAC systems and are particularly pricey to add to an existing home. Repair costs are also higher than with many other systems.

Mini Split Heat Pump System

A system growing in popularity in the United States, the mini-split offers efficiency, lower energy costs (with savings of $1000 to $2000 per year possible), and is ductless! The system relies on several smaller heating and cooling units located strategically throughout and outside the home—zones controlled independently of one another. A multi-split is an excellent option for remodels and renovations and can be electric-, gas-, oil-, or propane-powered.

A mini-split heat pump system is an expensive system to install, however, due to its relative newness on the scene, and repairs can be costly because of the difficulty in tracking down replacement parts. Furthermore, in regions that experience sub-zero temperatures, mini-split technology may not be enough to heat a home consistently.

Standard AC and Furnace Split System

A dominant HVAC system throughout the U.S., a standard split system is another forced-air option that heats by pulling in air, warming it, and then forcing it through ductwork to heat the home. Such systems are prevalent in regions where air conditioning isn't necessary, and newly installed systems powered by natural gas are extremely energy-efficient, saving homeowners money. They are also environmentally friendly.

However, standard split systems may develop leaks, especially in the ductwork, introducing carbon monoxide as a serious health risk. And forced air systems may negatively impact anyone who suffers from severe allergies, as dust and other allergens are quickly spread.

Standard Heat Pump and Air Handler Split System

A standard heat pump system can be an excellent all-in-one option. When heat is needed, the system forces cold air out of the home, and when cooling is needed, it pulls warm air out. An indoor circulating air handler ensures a consistently comfortable temperature.

Standard heat pump systems are more affordable and more energy-efficient than many other options, but they require ductwork and can spread allergens. They also aren't the best choice for regions that routinely experience sub-zero winter temperatures

Oil vs. Propane/Natural Gas for Your Home's Heating

If you're building a custom home or renovating an existing home, consider your heating options carefully. One option may work better for your home type or the area you live in than another. Home heating isn't a decision to be made lightly.

Oil

Oil isn't the best option if you want high energy efficiency, and most oil heat systems become less efficient as they age. However, oil heating systems are typically easiest to repair because parts are more readily available. With oil, you'll likely use a boiler or a furnace that will require a permanent place of its own. You'll also have to store extra oil in a tank, which will require additional dedicated space. But oil-burning heating systems can be the right choice in certain circumstances. Furthermore, newer model systems are more efficient than ever before.

- Furnaces: The gas from furnaces is released through a chimney. Older model furnaces not only lose efficiency as they age, but they also lose efficiency as their internal temperature increases, which is a flaw (albeit a necessary flaw) in their functionality. Modern furnaces use a fan to transfer exhaust and convert it into heat. Furnaces also produce a lot of condensation. But they do warm spaces effectively.

- Boilers: Boilers work by boiling water. The water then moves through the home, and the heat exits through heating elements like baseboard heaters, radiators, or radiant flooring. Once the water has cooled, it returns to the boiler, where it is reheated and the process repeated.

The oil heating is produced via a combustion chamber. The oil is ignited, and the energy from the burning oil warms and circulates the air or boils the water that the furnace or boiler uses to heat. Furnaces and boilers need to be cleaned and refreshed with new oil routinely.

To learn more, call the Reagan Homes team at (860) 962-6250 to learn more or visit www.ReaganHomes.com to schedule a complimentary, no-obligation consultation.

Natural Gas/Propane Heating

More commonly installed today than oil heat is natural gas and propane-fired heating systems. They work more efficiently and are cleaner to run. They also do not require as much maintenance since they use natural gas or propane as their fuel source. If you opt for propane, you'll need to replace the tanks occasionally, but propane is a clean-burning fuel source that doesn't cause emissions like oil does.

A few different types of gas and propane-fueled heating systems are available:

- <u>Forced Air:</u> Most modern homes use forced air heating and cooling systems. Air enters the system and is then heated or cooled based on your preferences. When the gas combusts, however, the system will shed CO_2 and condensation. Because of this, natural gas and propane heating systems should not be vented into the home. Instead, off-gassing must be released outside of the house so that inhabitants aren't poisoned by a build-up of CO_2. or carbon monoxide, which can be deadly.

- <u>Hydronic:</u> As with boilers, hydronic heaters use water to deliver heat through the home, but they do so in addition to heating with forced air. Hydronic heating uses heated water that travels through the home, heating the space. That water is then cooled by a fan and repurposed to be heated once more.

- <u>Space Heaters:</u> Space heaters take up less space than traditional units. They are typically used to heat individual rooms rather than an entire house. They are energy efficient since, in addition to using natural gas, they heat smaller spaces.

Natural gas-fired heating systems are highly efficient. They typically cost much less to operate than oil, and the units are usually much smaller and require less maintenance.

Propane-fired units function similarly, the main difference being that they use an igniter to light the propane. Once ignited, the flame is distributed through the system and sends heat waves throughout the space.

While they shouldn't be used in enclosed spaces because, again, they need to off-gas to the outdoors to avoid CO_2 poisoning, the energy efficiency and general functionality of natural gas and propane-fired heat is suitable for most modern homes.

There's no question about it. You want heating and air conditioning that is comfortable, efficient, reliable, and cost-effective. Our team can help you determine which HVAC option is right for your family and home.

BRING CLEAN AIR INTO YOUR HOME WITH AN HRV OR ERV

You can have both clean, unpolluted air and energy efficiency. Reagan Homes can help.

Energy efficiency is something we all aspire to in our homes. It keeps us warm in winter, cool in summer, and it saves us money. But is there such a thing as a home that is too energy efficient? And if so, what would that look like?

Surprisingly, there is a downside to having a well-insulated home, and it can negatively impact your health and that of your family. It's poor Indoor Air Quality or IAQ. The sorry truth is that the more tightly zipped up our homes are, the less opportunity air has to move. The less air moves, the more pollutants may linger in the air and make that air less healthy to breathe.

According to the Environmental Protection Agency, our best efforts to insulate our homes have led to significant build-ups of airborne pollutants that would have found their way outside only a couple of decades ago. In fact, it's not unusual for indoor air pollution in our homes to now measure at 2 to 5 times higher than outdoors.

That means that substances like cooking gases, household chemicals, mold, pet dander, and smoke can be found in higher levels in our homes than ever before. That's a concern for everyone but especially those who suffer from severe allergies or asthma.

Fortunately, there are options that allow us to maintain efficiency while also ensuring cleaner, safer IAQ–ventilation systems that help us expel stale, polluted air and pull in clean air.

Monitoring Indoor Air Quality

If you have reason to suspect the IAQ of your home is a problem, air quality monitors are an inexpensive first step to take. There are literally hundreds of options available that measure humidity, temperature, volatile organic compounds (present, for example, in paint and carpeting), and particulates (dust), as well as carbon monoxide, carbon dioxide, and radon.

Such monitors are or can be a part of a smart home system or can be individual stations. Upon measuring for all of these elements, a monitor will provide an air quality index.

Along with determining an air quality index, it may be prudent to note any health symptoms (like a runny nose or persistent sneezing) that may be related to air quality. Factors to consider include time of day and room or area of the house, both of which can provide insight into problem areas and systems. Our team has experience with ventilation systems meant to improve IAQ. We can help you decipher your air quality index. If such a system is recommended, there are two types to choose from: energy recovery ventilators and heat recovery ventilators.

Heat Recovery Ventilation

Heat recovery ventilation systems (HRVs) use the heat in your home's stale air to heat the air it draws from outside. In this system, stale air and fresh air pass without mixing.

The most significant benefit of such a system is that the energy required to heat outside air is minimized, saving money on heating bills. Established brands and manufacturers boast of efficiency rates between 55% and 93% (55% to 75% is typical).

Energy Recovery Ventilation

Energy recovery ventilators (ERVs) go a step further than HRVs by impacting the humidity in both outgoing and incoming air sources. That means your house will retain its relative humidity levels year-round and maintain a comfortable indoor ambient humidity level.

By impacting temperature and humidity, ERVs reduce the energy used by air conditioning and dehumidifier units

Which is Right for You?

Which system to choose depends on several factors, including your home comfort preferences and the environment or geography in which your home rests.

A home with high winter humidity will benefit from an HRV, which will eliminate some of that humidity. If your home is too dry in the winter, an ERV will help retain humidity. Overall, an ERV is likely a better choice in hot, dry climates, although an HRV paired with a dehumidifier is yet another option.

Ultimately, having one or the other is better than neither and ensures the air you breathe is clean and healthy. And having the guidance from our team who know the ins and outs of southeastern Connecticut's climate and its nuances, is the best bet of all. Our team has installed countless ERVs and HRVs in custom-built and renovated homes throughout the region. We can help you make this seemingly confusing decision much more manageable.

To learn more, call the Reagan Homes team at (860) 962-6250
to learn more or visit www.ReaganHomes.com
to schedule a complimentary, no-obligation consultation.

HOT WATER OPTIONS

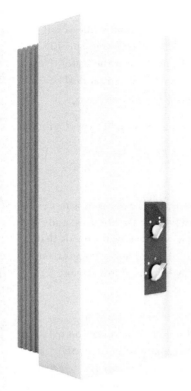

Today, more options exist for how we heat our water for everyday use than ever before. While we used to be limited to options that use a ton of energy, we can now reduce energy consumption while still taking those long hot showers you may have come to love.

But how does water get heated without a traditional water heater to do it?

Conventional Storage-Tank Water Heater

A conventional storage-tank water heater is the tried and true option that we've been using for decades. Such units consist of an insulated tank in which water is heated and stored, so it is available when it is needed. Many houses use electric water heaters, but natural gas or gas-fueled water heaters are also options.

Natural gas or propane water heaters are incredibly energy efficient, so if you want to go the traditional route while also reducing your energy consumption, these are a great option. They may be more expensive when it comes to the initial purchase, but they will save money in the long run. The storage of hot water comes at a higher price as well since there needs to be a constant flow of energy to keep the water hot.

Tankless (On-Demand) Water Heater

This water heater system does not store any water, but it can still supply a steady flow. Tankless water heaters can be an excellent choice if you're trying to be more energy-efficient since they can use natural gas or propane to heat the water.

If you want an electric tankless water heater, you may have to spend a bit more money to upgrade your home's electrical system. Tankless models will ultimately save you money, though, as there is no need to keep stores of water heated for future use.

Heat Pump Water Heater (Hybrid)

If you really want to focus on energy efficiency, a hybrid pump water heater is the way to go. They use 60 percent less energy than typical water heaters, and while you'll invest more upfront, they pay for themselves in no time. They need a very specific space set aside for them, though, as they use heat from the air to heat the water. Heat pump water heaters can't be kept somewhere cold. They also need a great deal of space as the pump itself takes up a lot of room.

A heat pump water heater will also need a place to drain, as you should expect a lot of condensation leakage.

Condensing Water Heater

This type of water heater runs on gas and can hold more than 55 gallons of water at a time. A condensing water heater might be ideal for rural homes, farmhouses, and rustic cabins. While not very energy-efficient, they are useful if you have water needs that tankless can't meet. If you're in a colder climate or most of your energy comes from unconventional resources, a condensing water heater may be a good investment.

Which Should You Choose?

At Reagan Homes, we want to ensure that your needs are met. Wherever you live, your home should have the right water heater to help your home run efficiently. It can be difficult to know which will work best for your home, but our trusted team of professionals can help you make the right decision for your new custom home or as part of your existing home renovation.

To learn more, call the Reagan Homes team at (860) 962-6250
to learn more or visit www.ReaganHomes.com
to schedule a complimentary, no-obligation consultation.

INTERIOR DOOR OPTIONS FOR EVERY SPACE IN YOUR HOME

If you need help understanding the differences between door types and styles, our team is a resource with decades of design and installation experience. We would love to help you determine which doors will best suit your needs

Perhaps you have never browsed the doors department of your local home improvement store or supply house. Obviously, doors are a necessary part of the interior of your home. They divide spaces, provide and protect privacy, and welcome guests. A beautiful, stylish door can even enhance the appearance of your home and increase its value.

When it comes time to choose the doors for your new custom home or your remodel or renovation, the first thing you'll want to decide on is what type of doors you want. Are solid wood doors the right choice for you? Or maybe a solid or hollow core door might be better for your budget.

Then it's time to move onto the style of door. If you have a beautiful, large first floor and intend to do a lot of entertaining, maybe something like French doors or pocket doors might do the trick. Or perhaps you have kids who will undoubtedly be in and out of your kitchen 1,000 times a day. If so, saloon doors might be appropriate.

In any event, we would love to share our knowledge and experience with you.

Door Construction

Wood

Wood doors are constructed of solid wood. They have a warm appearance, and their grain patterns add interest and detail. Wood doors are available in almost any species and can be stained and finished to complement any interior design. Wood doors are especially appropriate in places where you want to limit or shut out noise.

Solid Core

Solid core doors are comprised of engineered wood fiber that looks and feels like wood and is as durable as wood. Solid core doors, however, are more affordable than real wood doors. While they, too, can block noise, they aren't as effective in doing so as wood.

Hollow Core

Hollow core doors are the least expensive type of door. They are also lightweight and easy to move and handle. They are made of two boards that "sandwich" a core of honey-combed or grid worked wood material between them to achieve a desired thickness.

Molded

A molded door has a hollow core and is flush in style. This type of door's interior frame is made from softwood, and the outer part is formed from layered battens. Only a small amount of the door can be trimmed to fit a uniquely sized opening, meaning their use and application is limited. Molded doors are inexpensive and incredibly lightweight.

Door Styles

Barn Doors

Barn doors are trendy right now and can fit in with many home styles, as the number of colors and finishes available for barn doors has exploded. Unlike other doors hinged on the side, barn doors are hung from a top rail that sits above the door's opening. They slide back and forth to open and close. They are frequently used for bedrooms, closets, and pantries. They do require a bit more space than other doors.

Bi-Fold Doors

You've probably seen bi-fold doors used for closets, laundry rooms, pantries, and other small spaces. They contain multiple panels that fold into each other, accordion-style, allowing one to pass through the opening created.

Double Doors

This one is exactly what it says; no surprises here! A double door consists of two separate smaller doors that meet in the middle when closed. They are frequently used for bedrooms and as entryways to larger rooms within the home.

Flush Doors

A flush door is minimalist in style, with both sides usually devoid of any raised decoration. Functional in nature, flush doors are often used in areas where space is at a premium since they take up a little less room than other doors. Flush doors may be solid or hollow core, but the interior is usually filled with particle board or foam rather than wood.

French Doors

French doors, it seems, are a classic and as popular today as ever. Comprising two separate doors that open in the same direction (inward, for example), they typically feature several glass panes that allow you to see through them and for light to flow through them as well. They are on the more expensive end of interior door costs, but they are statement-making and stand the test of time. They may be used as doors that lead to a patio, bedroom, living room, or dining room. There is no limit to where French doors may be used.

Louvered Doors

The louvers (similar to those on a shutter) on a louvered door—often used as closet doors—allow air to pass through. They are generally a less expensive style of door with limited applications in the home.

Pocket Doors

Pocket doors are unique and beautiful and were often included in older, more historic homes. When pocket doors are open, they are hidden or stored within a wall. While they aren't particularly difficult to install, they require that the room you will use them for has enough wall space on either side of the door opening to accommodate the doors while they are open. Pocket doors are used to separate living or dining areas from the rest of a home's first-floor space.

Pre-Hung Doors

If your doorways are of standard sizing, pre-hung doors, which come with hinges already attached and holes drilled for the doorknob, may be a feasible option for you. They are available in solid and hollow-core versions, and you may choose from flush or slab options.

Saloon Doors

Saloon doors, sometimes referred to as café doors, are swinging doors that frequently only fill part of a doorway as they don't usually go all the way to the floor, for example. They allow for easy flow between rooms and provide a degree of privacy when a fully shut or open door isn't wanted or isn't practical.

Slab Doors

Slab doors are the most decorative and stylish of all doors. Also known as panel doors, they usually have between 2 and 6 raised panels, which may be squares, rectangles, or some combination of the two

Knobs

Some doors need to blend in, and some are designed to stand out. The doorknobs you choose for your interior doors should also abide by this principle.

Popular styles of interior door knobs include:

- keyed entry
- passage
- privacy
- antique
- modern
- dummy

Levers are also an option that many clients are attracted to. They offer a sleek, modern look that works well with most interior doors.

Common Finishes

Whether you choose levers or knobs for your interior doors, you will also have an enormous variety of colors and finishes from which to choose. The Reagan Homes team is here for you, and our expert team of designers would be happy to guide you in choosing the right finishes for your interior door hardware.

Some of the most common finishes for interior door hardware are:

- gold tones
- bright brass
- antique brass
- silver tones
- bright chrome
- polished nickel
- satin nickel
- distressed nickel

Other options are bronze to black tones, oil-rubbed bronze, aged bronze, and matte black.

Our team at Reagan Homes will help guide you in the process of your door selection. Our team has plenty of knowledge and even more experience in selecting and installing doors and designing the spaces in which they'll be used.

KITCHEN DESIGNS SPACE GUIDELINES

What is that one room everyone in the house cannot do without? Let us give you a hint; everyone would go hungry without that room. Yes, you guessed right, the kitchen. The kitchen is an indispensable part of the home. Today's kitchen is no longer just a place for cooking meals; it also doubles as dining, an activity center, and a lot of times family bonding takes place within the kitchen space. Guests tend to gravitate towards the kitchen.

Knowing the importance of the kitchen to the house, attention should be paid to the dimension of the kitchen during the planning of your new custom home or when remodeling your existing home. There are several guidelines on how a kitchen should be designed and built to look great and function smoothly. These guidelines cover working spaces or zones in the kitchen, walkway width, work aisle width for single and multiple cooks, and other important details for keeping your kitchen organized.

Spacing Tips for Your Kitchen

There are basic guidelines that should be followed when planning your kitchen. Some of the most important are

1. Doorways should be at least 32 inches wide; swinging doors are best, and doorways should be designed in such a way as not to interfere with the appliances in the kitchen.

2. Passageways through the kitchen should be at least 36 inches wide.

3. Walkways in working areas of the kitchen should be at least 42 inches wide for a single cook, and at least 48 inches for multiple cooks.

4. There should be proper ventilation systems especially in work areas that involve cooking.

5. If you want seating at an island, you should plan on at least 30 inches in width per bar stool.

6. If your kitchen is less than 13 feet wide, we do not recommend adding an island at all.

7. You should have at least 42 to 48 inches between an island or counter and a dining table

8. Flank any sink with a countertop of 24 inches on one side and at least 18 inches on the other.

9. Have your dishwasher be within 36 inches of your sink.

10. Leave at least 21 inches between your dishwasher and other appliances.

11. Remember to include trash and recycling bins within your cabinets if you want to keep your garbage bins out of sight.

12. Plan for at least 15 inches of countertop on the handle side of refrigerator

13. Don't place a cooking surface under an operable window.

14. Never use flammable window treatments above a stovetop or oven.

15. For corners, consider a lazy susan or pull out shelving for efficient storage.

The Kitchen Work Triangle

The Kitchen work triangle is not a new concept; it was originally developed in the early twentieth century. Its functionality is still spectacular today even with modern kitchen layouts. Also known as the golden triangle, the kitchen triangle is a rule that states that in a kitchen there are to be three working spaces. These spaces should be independent but close in proximity. According to its foundations, each leg of the triangle should be between four and nine feet of the others. The sum distance of the triangle should be between the 13 and 26 feet depending on the overall size of your kitchen. The three working spaces that makeup the kitchen work triangle are the refrigerator for food storage, the sink for cleaning food, and the stove for cooking your food.

Islands and Counters

Islands and counters are usually placed at the center of the kitchen, and they sometimes double as sitting and sink areas. Experts advise that there should be at least 158 inches of usable linear countertop space, including islands, that counters and islands be at least 24 inches deep with at least 15 inches of clearance above.

In summary, there should be a proper flow within the kitchen, and work areas should not have elements interfering with each other. At Reagan Homes, we have a team of interior and kitchen designers who can help design your dream kitchen as part of your existing home renovation or new custom home.

To learn more, call the Reagan Homes team at (860) 962-6250 to learn more or visit www.ReaganHomes.com to schedule a complimentary, no-obligation consultation.

CABINET HARDWARE OPTIONS

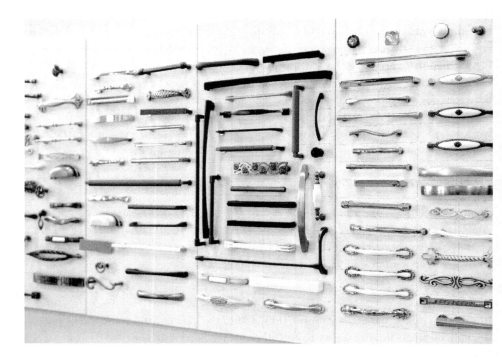

Cabinetry is one of the most important features inside a home. Most Realtors, rental agents, and homebuilders prioritize cabinets as a critical aesthetic and functional component in any home. But there is more than just the material, style, and finish to think about when it comes to your cabinets' look and functionality.

It may not seem like it, but there is an almost innumerable number of options to choose from when it comes to cabinet hardware. Do you want to go with a handle or a knob? Do you want a metallic finish or something matte? We will help guide you through some of the most common options when it comes to cabinet hardware.

Types

Cabinet hardware is essentially the device with which you open your cabinets. When we talk about cabinet hardware, we're usually talking about pulls or knobs, which come in such a variety you'll never need to worry about them looking generic. While cabinet hardware may seem like a trivial aesthetic decision, such options can significantly impact your cabinets' functionality and can tie a room together or cause a clash.

Knobs

Knobs come in all shapes and sizes, so it is up to you to decide which one is right for you. A traditional knob might feature a rounded knob or a flat circular design. Such designs are tried and true and have been used by homeowners for decades in various colors and materials to suit the aesthetic of any kitchen or bathroom.

If you want to spice it up a little bit, specialty designs like the T-style European knobs, ceramic, glass, and pressed metals are now available and are sure to make an impression. You may also be able to order custom knobs with different patterns, colors, or shapes. If your home is near the shore, you might like a knob with a coastal design—shaped like a seashell, anchor, or starfish, for example. If you live on a farm or in the country, you might be partial to a horseshoe, star, or rooster-shaped knob.

Knobs are easily customized to your tastes and preferences and are easy to install.

Pulls

Maybe you'd like to go for something a little more modern. If so, pulls and handles might be a better option for you. Drawer and cabinet pulls can be straight or curved, brushed metal or wrought-iron. They are easily customized for the modern kitchen or bathroom and are easy to sanitize. Some pulls may even be "invisible," hidden within the build of the cabinet, like a thin metal bar that runs along the bottom for a seamless look.

Pulls are easy to install and maintain. Most are likely made of metal and provide a simple but modern aesthetic. They may also be accented with colors or designs along the side if you wish for them to stand out against more simplistic decor choices.

Common Finishes

As most cabinet hardware is made from metal, pulls and knobs are available in all sorts of different styles. Whether you have a lighter kitchen and want to accent your cabinets with something darker or you desire a more sophisticated look, there are options to please every taste.

Chrome

Chrome is popular due to its classic look, which has been around for decades. Chrome cabinet hardware is most often found in traditional or farmhouse-style homes. It adds a bit of shine without detracting from the other kitchen accents. Chrome is a relatively inexpensive finish, and while it can be somewhat challenging to keep clean, it can be a charming addition to your space. Chrome's mirror-like surface makes cabinet hardware genuinely stand out and shine.

Polished Brass

Another traditional option for your home, commonly used in older or vintage houses, is polished brass. Many people who enjoy a more traditional look for their cabinets might find satisfaction in polished brass. Like chrome, it retains a shiny appearance, but it has a warmer tone that offsets darker cabinetry nicely. It also adds contrast to lighter wood or painted cabinets. Though brass may currently be considered a little outdated, it can be a charming addition that is less expensive or of a less intricate design.

Polished Nickel

Polished nickel is an attractive option that can be best described as having some of the traits of both chrome and polished brass. It has the shine and light of chrome but a bit of a warmer tone, like polished brass—an almost rose-gold hue that has made it popular in modern homes. It has that touch of traditional with a new modern twist.

Satin Nickel

If you want something a little less shiny but that will work well with stainless steel appliances, satin nickel might do the trick. It doesn't quite have the warmth that other finishes have, but it has a more homey look than the sometimes overwhelming shine of chrome. Satin nickel is less susceptible to grime and stains, and it doesn't need to be cleaned as often as some other options.

Brushed Nickel

Brushed finishes have become more commonplace in recent years because of their simple sophistication and ability to hide unsightly fingerprints, dust, and dirt. They add charm to your cabinets without being too difficult to clean or maintain. Brushed nickel has a lovely silver appearance but isn't too shiny.

Brushed Stainless

Stainless knobs and pulls are an especially good option for busy kitchens and bathrooms. If you have children, brushed stainless may be the perfect choice. With stainless, you'll find you won't need to contend with fingerprints and dirt perpetually. Brushed stainless knobs and pulls are easy to clean, and the brushed appearance helps minimize the appearance of any stains you've yet to clean.

Antique Brass

An antique brass finish will add vintage elegance to your space without compromising on functionality. The old-time feel of this option can be accented with inlaid designs and darker appliances, resulting in a kitchen that has a relaxed and almost romantic aesthetic. Don't let vintage scare you into thinking your kitchen will look dated because antique brass certainly has its place in the modern century.

Aged Bronze/Oil-Rubbed Bronze

Aged and oil-rubbed bronze can give your kitchen or bathroom a more rustic feel. Because the oil and the aging process both oxidize and tarnish the bronze, hardware with this finish will work particularly well with vintage pieces while also adding a modern flair to your farmhouse kitchen. Aged and oil-rubbed bronze is a unique finish gaining popularity because of the visual interest it imparts.

Black

Black is sleek and modern. Black will give your kitchen or bathroom a clean and understated look without making your cabinetry a focal point. Black knobs and pulls are a wonderful and affordable option that isn't flashy.

Consider Comfort and Usefulness

Your knobs and pulls should be chosen for their usefulness and functionality. You don't want hardware that will make it more difficult for you to open cabinets and drawers. Whatever you choose should be reliable and comfortable.

How We Can Help

At Reagan Homes, we value your opinion and want to help you build the home of your dreams. That includes everything from the shape of your driveway to your cabinet hardware and everything in between. You should never have to compromise on style or taste, and we can help you design and execute whatever aesthetic you desire. Our team of experts has your needs and wants in mind always, so don't hesitate to bring all of your ideas to the table.

*To learn more, call the Reagan Homes team at (860) 962-6250
to learn more or visit www.ReaganHomes.com
to schedule a complimentary, no-obligation consultation.*

TOP TIPS FOR CHOOSING THE PERFECT WALL TILE FOR YOUR BATHROOM

Wall tiles are an essential part of any beautiful bathroom. They not only add aesthetic value to your home, but they also help the functionality of an easy-to-clean bathroom. Here are six tips to help you select the perfect wall tiles for your bathroom.

Your Budget

There are a lot of options for you to choose from when picking wall tiles. Ceramic tiles tend to be the most affordable and natural stones the most expensive. At Reagan Homes, we have extensive relationships with local tile vendors that can help guide you in choosing tiles within your budget.

To learn more, call the Reagan Homes team at (860) 962-6250
to learn more or visit www.ReaganHomes.com
to schedule a complimentary, no-obligation consultation.

Style & Color

Your choice of style is dependent on several factors: your taste, environment, and budget too. You could go with a classical approach or a more modern choice. In addition to visiting our recommended tile showroom vendors to see tile samples first hand, our design team will build out 3D renderings so you can visualize how your tile will look with your vanity and other components of your bathroom. We can present multiple options so you are confident in your tile selection.

Material

Picking the right material for your bathroom tiles is very important. There are four main types of materials you can choose from:

- <u>Ceramic</u> is easily the most affordable of materials and they make beautiful bathroom tiles.

- <u>Porcelain</u> is more durable than ceramic because it is denser. It is a bit more expensive than ceramic. Porcelain is available in a wider array of bright colors.

- <u>Glass</u> is appealing to the eyes, lightweight, and typically easier to install

- <u>Natural stone</u> as the name implies includes natural materials such as marble, limestone, and travertine. Natural stone is the material with the best grip.

Tile Size

While smaller tile sizes were in vogue, newer bathroom tile sizes tend to be bigger due to the evolving nature of the design. Today, many designers consider a tile as big as 12"x24" to be a great size for your bathroom wall.

Grout

There are many color options when it comes to grout. Our designers will help guide you in choosing complementary grout colors based on the tile color.

Other Considerations

Keep in mind you do not have to have floor to ceiling wall tile. Perhaps you will want sheetrock with a glossy paint to help keep the wall easier to clean. Some people opt for wallpaper. Some for shiplap. Again, with our team of designers, we can build out 3D models so you can easily envision how your selected tile will look as part of your bathroom along with the other materials used.

In summary, whether you are building a new home or renovating your existing home, our team is here to guide you in the wall tile selection process.

WHAT TO CONSIDER WHEN DESIGNING YOUR MASTER SUITE

Your master suite can be your sanctuary, a place where you can exercise, work from home, relax, and get a good night's sleep. Budget and size do not necessarily determine a master suite's value to a homeowner as long as the master suite is designed to meet your needs. Our design team at Reagan Homes can help guide you in designing the master suite your desire. We are able to design and build the master suite of your dreams.

Here some basic matters you should consider when planning a master suite.

Define the Available Space

There can be a big difference between what you think will fit in your bedroom and the space that is available. For instance, the bed is sometimes forgotten about even though it is the central piece of furniture in your bedroom. Beds are oblong and they can take up a lot of space. Our design team knows how best to utilize space to meet your needs and provide you with the most comfortable master suite possible.

It is important to consider how, besides sleeping, you will spend your time doing in your master suite. If you plan to have an exercise nook or a home office within your master suite, we can help you define each area as if they were separate even though they are in the same room. Or perhaps your new custom home or remodel will have a dedicated space for exercise or a home office. Based on your overall design, layout and desires, we can help guide you in what makes the most sense for you.

You should not sacrifice important space just so you can fit everything you want in your master suite. Choosing built-in storage for clothes and bedding can save space where a chest might otherwise go. Then, you can take that saved space and apply it somewhere else, like choosing to put your television above the built-in storage or a fireplace if you desire. You also want to plan for any changes or updates you may make in the future such as buying a bigger bed or creating a place to work from home.

Natural vs Artificial Light?

We find our clients typically want their bedrooms to be full of natural light during the daylight hours and then dark at night when they are sleeping. Depending on your preferences, the location of the master suite is important. If you like waking up to a room full of sunlight, then your master suite should face east. If you prefer waking up to a dark room without much natural light filtering through, then your master suite should face west. Again, we can help you determine the location of your master suite based on your unique plans.

Certainly, we can design windows and treatments that will give you more control over the amount of light in your master suite. With smart-home technology, you can have blackout curtains installed on your windows that will be easily controllable from your phone, with the touch of a button, or that raise automatically based on a predefined number of minutes before or after sunrise.

Artificial lighting can also be designed and installed based on your specifications. Depending on the size of the room, you may want to be able to control which areas are lit at specific times. For instance, we can configure the lighting in the room to respect a sleeping partner while you get ready for work or use the restroom in the middle of the night. We will help you pay attention to details like this, which will maximize your enjoyment of your master suite for years to come.

Add Luxury to Your Bathroom

Always remember that this is your home and you deserve to get exactly what you want. We are happy to make suggestions based on our extensive experience. We suggest that you consider reserving part of your budget to add luxury to your master suite bathroom. Additions like heated floors, high-end shower heads and spa-like amenities will make your bathroom feel extra special.

We can also help you match the colors and fixtures of your bathroom to the colors and feel of the rest of the master suite. This will help "blend" your bathroom and master suite.

Privacy is the key to a great bathroom in your master suite. If you are sharing this room with a partner, we can help you design a bathroom that can be used in complete privacy while someone else is in another part of the room. In fact, we can also design your master bathroom to provide a sense of privacy for you, even when it is occupied by two people.

Assess Your Storage Needs

You really don't realize how important adequate storage is until you may need some that doesn't exist. We can help you design your potential storage needs while we are designing your master suite with you.

Walk-in closets are a luxury that should not be overlooked. They should be designed to fit your needs, or you risk having wasted space in your master suite. If you have enough room for a walk-in closet but no place for your partner to get ready while you use it, then consider installing a vanity mirror outside your walk-in closet.

Perhaps your layout will allow for his and hers walk-in closets and even a separate dressing room.

Reagan Homes will provide solutions and options for each of these necessary design considerations for your master suite. We have seen it all in both new construction and renovations, and we will be able to make your master suite design dreams come true.

To learn more, call the Reagan Homes team at (860) 962-6250 to learn more or visit www.ReaganHomes.com to schedule a complimentary, no-obligation consultation.

INTERIOR LIGHTING OPTIONS

Your attraction to your home depends heavily on the quality of its illumination. Lighting does not just help us see; it also reflects our moods and provides positive energy. So, if you're building new or remodeling a home, do not underestimate the role of lighting.

Light has psychological effects. Emotions have more intensity when lights are bright. Good lighting is essential to nearly every part of your life. When you wake-up in the morning, the bright lights of your home shining along with the sun makes you look forward to the day ahead. On the other hand, when it's late at night, and you are retiring to bed, you might prefer a darkness lit only by dim lights that evoke candlelight to cool your nerves and relax.

There is no cookie-cutter approach to interior lighting. Every home has its own unique lighting needs. Moreover, color can have a significant effect on a person's psychological and physiological states. The color of your room and the color of the lighting in that room may determine whether you feel energetic or sluggish when you. Rest assured that we will help with your lighting needs. The following types of lighting fixtures are among your options.

Recessed Lighting

With recessed lighting, fixtures are hidden away, usually in the ceiling, making it difficult to see the light source. This type of lighting is often described as "pot lighting or downlights." Recessed lighting is effective and can be comfortably used in several rooms in a house. It brightens the ceiling area and can fully illuminate a home. It is also ideal for a home with lower ceilings.

Wall Sconces

A wall sconce is a feature that can add both an accent and light to your home. Wall sconces are a perfect addition for bedrooms, bathrooms, kitchens, dining rooms, and hallways. Sconces are a beautiful way to illuminate your space, and they come in numerous styles. They serve to complement almost every design element in your home.

Chandeliers

Chandeliers can be pure works of art. Today, you'll find an almost infinite selection of chandeliers from which to choose. Crystal, downlight, transitional, tiered, and rustic are just a few of the available styles.

Furthermore, chandeliers are available in different sizes appropriate for various rooms and purposes. Depending on your needs, you may opt for any of the following chandelier sizes: mini, small, medium, large, entryway, living room, dining room, and bathroom. A chandelier is different from other lighting options as it usually has a tree pattern. Chandeliers may be branched, canopied, central body-style, chain, or bulb fixtures.

When choosing a chandelier, getting the proportions right is essential. A chandelier that is too small or too large can draw unwanted attention when its purpose is to complement the room it is in.

Pendant Lighting

A pendant light is another interior lighting decorative style available in many forms. Before choosing pendant lights, it's important to determine the function they will serve. Pendant lights typically hang from the ceiling of a room. They are, however, much lighter and less bulky than the average chandelier. Pendant lights are a popular option in kitchens and laundry rooms. They are also an excellent option for brightening dark spots and corners.

Track Lighting

Track light is a type of Interior lighting homeowners frequently use when they do not want to cut into their ceilings or walls to run wires.

Under-Cabinet Lighting

When it comes to kitchen lighting, more is more. It helps you better see what you are chopping and stirring and allows you more quickly to find those infrequently used tools that may be hiding in upper cabinets or dark drawers. The usefulness of under-cabinet lighting is often underestimated.

Under-cabinet lighting usually serves as additional illumination. It helps prevent accidents and injuries in the room of the house with the most potential for cuts, burns, and falls. Under-cabinet lighting eliminates shadowy spaces. It can add ambiance to a kitchen, especially in the evening.

Vanity Lights

A vanity light, also called a vanity bar, is a long light fixture mounted above a bathroom mirror. The counter and mirror are the de-facto focal points of a bathroom, and vanity lighting draws attention to this vital spot. Vanity lights and vanity bars come in a range of shapes, sizes, and colors. And since not all bathrooms look the same, not all vanity-style lights belong in all bathrooms. Deciding on the suitable material, color, shape, and size for your vanity lighting helps establish a bathroom's look and mood.

Lamps

Lamps play more of a psychological role in lighting than other types of lighting. When choosing lamps, consider the mood you want to create and the tasks you will perform in the room. Then select the appropriate lamps in a style that complements the room and its furnishings. Most rooms are multi-purpose, and the right lamps can help you define zones. In a family room, for example, a reading lamp with an opaque shade placed next to a chair targets light for someone reading while keeping the rest of the room dark for watching television. Lamplight helps to set the mood for particular activities performed in multi-use spaces. Lamps typically are low-energy consumers. Lamps add to the aesthetics of any location in which they are placed.

Lighting is not something to take lightly when remodeling or building a new house. Lighting impacts moods and mindset. It's helpful to make lighting choices that are flexible and can be used in many ways. Your lighting choices may also directly impact your utility bills. That said, if it comes down to it, quality lighting should be a priority since it can express a lot about the quality of your home.

If you're considering new lighting or a lighting upgrade as part of your existing home renovation or new custom home build, the Reagan Homes team would love to share our knowledge and help guide you toward making the best decisions for your home.

FLOORING OPTIONS

From engineered hardwood to laminate, hardwood to luxury vinyl,
our team has the answers to your flooring questions.

Flooring is what you'll stand on while cooking dinner and while entertaining. It's what your bare feet will touch when you get out of bed in the morning or step out of the shower.

Just because you like hardwood, doesn't mean it's the best choice for a bathroom. And you probably won't enjoy tile in your bedroom or in a child's playroom.

We will take a look at several of the most popular options in residential flooring, and we'll review the pros and cons of each.

Our team is an excellent partner in this arena, with decades of experience helping homeowners select the right materials for their custom homes and remodels. Our team is knowledgeable, friendly, and courteous and is always available to collaborate or educate.

Some of the considerations our team will work through with you and that will help you decide which flooring options are right for your home include:

- Which room are we talking about? Some materials are ideal for certain rooms while others are not.

- Do you have children or pets?

- What's your budget?

- Did you know flooring may require special installation that can drive up costs or add time to a building or renovation schedule?

- What aesthetic are you hoping to achieve? Being able to answer this question is a tremendous help in pointing you toward appropriate choices.

- Are you looking for a return on investment? And if so, long-term or shorter-term?

Engineered Hardwood

Engineered hardwood flooring sure looks like hardwood and is usually installed similarly. So what exactly is it?

A manufactured product, engineered hardwood was created to serve as a less expensive option to popular hardwood flooring. It consists of a layer of high-quality plywood topped with a thin layer or veneer of hardwood. In addition to versions that can be glued or nailed down, some engineered hardwood floors can be "clicked together" for what is referred to as a "floating floor" installation.

Most engineered hardwood floors will last for 25 to 30 years, but one caveat: This flooring type, because of the thin layer of real wood, is typically only suitable for sanding and refinishing once.

Hardwood

Long-lasting, solid hardwood flooring is a perennial favorite for myriad reasons. It's beautiful and warm and available in many species, styles, colors, widths, and stains. Hardwood can last for centuries and can be sanded and refinished multiple times.

The most popular species for wood flooring in the U.S. is oak. Red, white, domestic, imported; if you want options, you can have them with oak. Other species commonly used in flooring include maple, walnut, and hickory.

Hardwood is a practical flooring solution for almost every part of the home. However, you should avoid using hardwood in areas that are likely to get wet frequently, like entryways, basements, bathrooms, and mud or laundry rooms, as hardwood does have the potential to warp when exposed to water.

Hardwood flooring may be purchased unfinished or pre-finished, and pre-finished is an excellent grab-and-go option that requires no onsite finishing.

There are drawbacks to hardwood flooring, of course, and those are cost and maintenance. All hardwood must be finished for moisture and scratch resistance and to protect against heavy wear and tear. They also need to be cleaned regularly to keep them looking their best.

Hardwood does offer long-term ROI, however; should you choose to sell your home at some point, hardwood flooring is always a valuable selling point.

Laminate

Today's laminate flooring is nothing like your grandma's laminate flooring. Sure, it's still an affordable alternative to hardwood as it's easy to install, it's durable, and it can be very attractive. Yet, since your grandparents installed it in their home, technology has aided manufacturers in improving laminate flooring with beveling, deeper, more precise texturing, and better graphic reproduction. Among the bestselling laminates are those that resemble hardwood flooring and function like engineered hardwood.

The life expectancy of laminate flooring can be anywhere from 10 to 25 years, depending on the product's quality and the traffic it experiences. It's relatively easy to clean and maintain, but some people have too hard a time moving past their own perceptions of the "fakeness" of the product to consider using it in their homes.

Laminate is prone to damage from moisture, so not the best bet for kitchens or bathrooms, and it isn't easy to repair.

Bamboo

Bamboo is a flooring option that is growing in popularity. Technically a kind of hardwood, bamboo has a look all its own. It is one of the most durable natural flooring materials you can use, and it is entirely sustainable and eco-friendly. It's scratch- and moisture-resistant, which makes it an excellent choice for kitchens and decks.

Carpet

Carpet can be made from several different materials, including acrylic and wool, for example. Carpet is available in many colors, textures, and styles. Aside from those matters, however, carpet needs no other introduction. Some people love it as it's cost-effective, soft, warm, and offers a degree of soundproofing. It also looks terrific when it's new and it's easy to install. Some people, on the other hand, loathe carpeting as it can be unsanitary, difficult to clean, absorbs odors, is a magnet for pet hair and stains, and should never be used in moisture-prone areas, like kitchens and bathrooms.

Cork

Cork is another material gaining popularity, especially among those who value renewable and sustainable building options.

Technically, the cork used in flooring is a composite product made from bark pressed into planks and installed similarly to hardwoods. Cork is also low VOC (which means it doesn't "off-gas" like other products might), fire-resistant, and sound-blocking.

Cork flooring is often used in quiet areas, like home offices and nurseries. But cork flooring is too soft and prone to scratches and damage for use in a home with pets or in high-traffic areas.

Linoleum

Sadly, linoleum gets a bad rap, with many people thinking of it as a low-quality product. The perception isn't wholly unearned; during its heyday, linoleum was churned out quickly, with substandard and faux linoleums damaging the product's reputation.

But did you know? Linoleum is a natural product made with renewal materials, including cork powder, jute, and linseed oil. It's antimicrobial, anti-static, colorfast, durable, and moisture-resistant. It's comfortable under the feet and easy to install.

Commonly thought of as coming in colorful and sometimes busy patterns, today's most popular linoleums mimic the appearance of both hardwood flooring and tile.

Linoleum is considered a mid- to high-end flooring option that is particularly well suited for use in kitchens and bathrooms. The lifespan of a linoleum floor is between 20 and 40 years.

Tile

It's hard to go wrong with a tiled floor. It's long been a favorite option for bathrooms, and some homeowners also prefer tile flooring in their dining areas, entryways, hallways, kitchens, laundry rooms, and mudrooms. Tile doesn't have to be expensive (although, on the high end, it certainly is), but installation is labor-intensive and requires both subflooring and a cement board or tile backer base.

There's a tile for everyone; the number of color and style options is almost infinite, from the availability of tiny mosaic tiles to large format floor tiles to tiles that look like hardwood but provide more durability. Glazed ceramic and porcelain tiles are the most durable of the bunch and require little maintenance. Sealing grout periodically is necessary to prevent staining.

Tile is hard and can be cold to the touch, so it is used less often in bedrooms, dining rooms, family rooms, and living rooms. Tile is also slippery in areas that are moisture prone, like bathrooms, entryways, and laundry rooms. Non-slip tile should be used in such areas. Tile flooring is waterproof, however, and great for high-traffic areas, but it is expensive and can chip or scratch. Tile costs vary widely, based primarily on the de type of tile chosen.

Vinyl

Vinyl flooring is a plastic product, usually made from PVC, acrylic, or similar polymers. It comes in many styles and a wide range of price points and qualities, from low-end to premium. It's another of the "everything old is new again" flooring options. It's available in sheets or tiles and is both easy to install and maintain. Like laminate and linoleum, popular vinyl patterns mimic ceramic tile, hardwood flooring, and even stone.

Even with the Renaissance vinyl flooring is experiencing, it continues to be an affordable and versatile option. It does have a lower return on investment than wood or laminate flooring, and like linoleum, some will not consider it at all due to preconceived notions.

There is a lot to know and even more about your lifestyle and family to consider when choosing flooring materials. Ultimately, your home should speak to your tastes and styles while incorporating building and décor materials that are durable, practical, and will last as long as you will live with them.

Whether you're building a new home or updating an existing home, our team has the experience to help you make the decisions that are right for you and your family especially when it comes to your flooring.

INSULATION OPTIONS

Do you want a home that's more comfortable, more efficient, and that will help you save your hard-earned cash? Insulation is the solution.

Insulation. It's not glamorous, and for many, it's something we don't want to have to even think about handing over a big, fat check for. It is, however, an essential part of your home or renovation. Insulation fills in spaces, like the cavities in walls and attics, where air might escape. Good insulation will save the average homeowner 15% on heating and cooling expenses and, as estimated by the Environmental Protection Agency's Energy Star program, 11% on overall energy expenses. That's an average of $200 for each homeowner every year.

So it's surprising that, considering the financial (and comfort) benefits of a well-insulated home, that the vast majority of U.S. homes are under-insulated (the North American Insulation Manufacturers Association pegs the number at 90%).

One thing you want to consider when choosing an insulation product is the R-value, a measure of the product's "resistance to heat flow." The higher the R-value, the more effective that insulation is at preventing energy loss. We can explain more about R-values as we have more than 30 years of working experience with homeowners in southeastern Connecticut. We can answer your questions you have about insulating your custom home or making insulation a part of your renovation or remodeling project.

While there are several insulation options available, most have specific uses, and not all will be appropriate for insulating your residence.

Blanket Batts and Rolls
R-value = 2.9 to 4.3 per inch of thickness

Fiberglass blanket batts and rolls are a popular form of home insulation (and may also be available in cotton, mineral wool, natural fiber, and plastic fiber versions). Manufactured to fit between standard-sized joists, rafters, and studs, installation is an easy job. Most feature vapor or air barriers. Some are available with flame-resistant facings.

Spray Foam
R-value = 3.7 to 6.2 per inch of thickness

Spray foam insulation is a liquid polyurethane-based product used to seal leaks and gaps in existing spaces (think window and door frames and plumbing and electrical entry points). It is available in two formulations, closed-cell (which provides the highest R-value of any commercially available insulation) and open-cell.

(Spray foam insulations with chlorofluorocarbons or hydrochlorofluorocarbons—both of which are damaging to the earth's ozone layer—are a thing of the past.)

While spray foam sounds like an easy DIY project and is frequently advertised as such, it can be complicated. Spray foam insulation is a job best left to the professionals.

Blown-In
R-value = 2.2 to 3.8 depending on contents

Blown-in insulation typically consists of fiberglass, reclaimed (or recycled) materials (like newspapers and cardboard), or rock wool. During the application, small particles capable of filling every nook and cranny are blown into open spaces and can conform to areas of any size or shape.

Reflective or Radiant Barrier

This type of insulation works by reflecting heat away from a home, preventing heat gain and transfer. Since it works so differently from other insulation products, its performance is not measured in R-values. It is used most often in warm climates and isn't recommended for cooler climates.

Foam Board or Rigid Foam Panels
R-value = 4.0 to 6.5 per inch of thickness

Foam boards and rigid panels are among the best insulating options available for reducing energy consumption. Not only can they be used to insulate every part of a home—from the foundation to the roof—they minimize the loss of heat that may occur through structural elements such as wood or steel. This kind of insulation is also used in exterior applications like sheathing.

FIREPLACE OPTIONS FOR YOUR HOME

There is nothing better when chilly weather comes knocking than curling up by the hearth of your home's fireplace. The hearth has been a gathering place for families, friends, and loved ones for centuries, and that hasn't changed over time. Whether you're in the market for a new custom home or considering a remodel/renovation of your existing home, if you want that cozy fireplace experience, there are more options to choose from than you may imagine.

Depending on the size of your space, your family, and your specific needs, the fireplace you choose may vary.

What To Do First

Before deciding on a fireplace, you'll want to figure out exactly what you're looking for. Fireplaces vary depending on fuel type, materials, sizes, and styles. You may be fantasizing about a wood-burning fireplace, but your space is more suited for a gas or electric unit. With so many options, it really comes down to evaluating your space and your needs to make the most informed choice.

Wood Burning Fireplace

When you picture a fireplace, a wood burning fireplace is typically what comes to mind. The crackling of a wood fireplace provides a cozy ambiance that adds warmth and comfort to your space. There are many benefits to adding a wood-burning unit to your home as it can be nostalgic and can make your space feel more inviting.

A wood-burning fireplace does require regular cleaning and maintenance to keep it functional and free of excessive ash. Wood and fire starters can add up a little bit in price and these hearths tend to take up a good bit of room, so it is recommended to take your space into account when considering this option.

Electric Fireplace

Currently, these units require even less maintenance and consideration than their gas-fueled counterparts. They are powered through heating coils that have been built into the unit and they don't require a fuel line or cleaning. Because they are entirely electric, they don't need logs or kindling and can be customized with different inserts to add interest to your room's aesthetic design.

They can often be controlled via remote so you can keep a fire burning as long as you like and don't need to be constantly watching it. Because there's no ventilation needed, you can install one of these beauties in any room of the house. They pose less of a safety hazard for your little ones as well.

Electric fireplaces have come a long way in aesthetics and there are even water vapor electric fireplaces to give a 3D realistic looking flame. There are models that do not put out any heat if you are looking for pure aesthetics. Such models allow for combustible materials such as wood or sheetrock to be near the electric fireplace with no problem.

If you are looking to have A/V components such as a TV or soundbar very close to the fireplace, an electric fireplace may be your best choice.

Gas Fireplace

These have been a popular option for several decades as they take the wood-burning aspect and turn it on its head. They are a lower-cost option that is ultimately safer as the fire is more contained. The ignition of the wood is through a gas line and the fire dies out as soon as the gas is turned off.

Gas fireplaces require less cleaning than wood burning fireplaces, and there is no need for wood or fire starters to a fire burning. They require simply a gas line that can be fueled by natural gas or propane. They do need a way to vent, such as a chimney but they can easily be customized for your space.

Additionally, gas fireplaces can be ignited with a click of a button from a remote or even your smartphone.

How We Can Help

Whichever fireplace will suit your needs, Reagan Homes can help. There are many sizes and shapes available—from linear fireplaces which are becoming more popular to more traditional fireplaces.

As part of your new custom home or existing home renovation/remodel we are happy to guide you in selecting the right fireplace or fireplaces for your home.

To learn more, call the Reagan Homes team at (860) 962-6250
to learn more or visit www.ReaganHomes.com
to schedule a complimentary, no-obligation consultation.

MOLDING AND
FINISHED TRIM OPTIONS

Trim is a general term for all molding in a home, like windows casings, baseboards, door casings, and more. Molding is a broad classification of millwork. Put another way, molding refers to the wood products made in mills and used for interior decoration or detail work in your home. Molding provides windows, doors, and baseboards with a finished look, an aesthetic effect, and prevents them from looking drab and boring.

There are several options available.

Our team of experts are available to help you make trim or molding decisions. Let's review the various applications of molding and trim as well as the possible materials.

Baseboards

Baseboards are the molding installed where the wall meets the floor. Baseboards are essential to give a properly finished look. The purpose of a baseboard is to provide a transition between the wall and the floor. Baseboards can be as simple or intricate as you desire.

Solid Wood Baseboards

Solid wood baseboards are a natural option for the home, and they are durable. Solid wood baseboards, moldings, and trim also allow you to work with a consistent color scheme throughout your home. If you want all of the finishing details in your home to be the same—and since solid wood adapts well to a variety of paints and wood stains—you can choose a stain or paint color that coordinates with the rest of your interior.

Jointed Pine Moldings

Jointed pine moldings provide the same natural feel as solid wood but at more cost-conscious prices. You won't have to worry about warping or knots because jointed pine moldings are treated and primed.

Medium Density Fiberboard (MDF) Baseboard

MDF baseboards are one of the most popular options for molding, trim, and baseboards. MDF is economical and very easy to use. Made from wood fibers, MDF is bound together with heat, pressure, and multiple types of resin binders. MDF baseboards are great to use when you are going to have painted baseboards.

Tropical Woods Baseboards

Tropical woods like teak, mahogany, ipe, red-balau, and several fine exotic hardwoods can also be used for baseboards. These woods present all of the advantages of using solid wood and add a touch of luxury to your home due to their unique coloring and grain textures.

PVC Baseboards

PVC is a synthetic baseboard, trim, and molding option. While we usually think of PVC as used in plumbing, you can now find PVC options for your home's finish work. PVC trim is often labeled as "vinyl trim," and it has the advantage of being resistant to the elements. You can safely use PVC trim in bathrooms and kitchens where water accumulation is probable, and you can even use it outside.

Window Trim Casings

Your windows are important for many reasons. They provide ventilation and allow you to see the world outside your home. Window casings are the moldings that go around your window frames. They are used to block cold air from entering and heated air from exiting the home. Casings are also the finishing touch to a window installation. Window casings may match the color of your baseboards and door moldings, providing a cohesive look to your home. Conventional homes tend to have just simple casings Victorian-style houses, on the other hand, may feature more elaborate designs and use thicker casings.

Complete Casings

Moldings that surround all sides of your windows are referred to as complete casings. They can consist of a simple layer of molding that trims out the windows to make them more appealing and decorative. Interior casings typically complement the interior moldings of your house.

Low Profile Casings

Low-profile casings are more practical than decorative, and they help visually tie the windows to other elements of the home. They also block cold air from entering the house, keeping it warm.

High Profile Casings

High-profile casings provide the most options. They can either surround the window or sit as a pediment above it. They suit homes that are classic or Victorian in style.

Modern Casings

Minimal and cleanly lined, modern casings often match the color of the wood or material of the rest of the window. With this molding, the window glass takes center stage rather than the molding.

Traditional Casings

Traditional casings are simple in style and similar to low-profile casings. They best suit older homes and can be made of a single layer of wood or composite material.

Door Trim Casings

A doorway casing is the trim around a door. It serves to make the door look more finished and appealing. Doorway casings conceal construction gaps between the door and the wall. In modern construction, a doorway casing consists of three construction casings: two long pieces for the sides and a shorter piece known as a head casing. Options range from simple to more elaborate trims. Primary considerations for choosing door casings include joint options and available sizes.

Door casings help beautify your doors, making them more visually interesting, polished, and defined. Here are examples of doorway casings types:

Paint-Grade Wood Casings

Perhaps considered the most popular molding option, paint-grade wood casings consist of wood that we can paint. Sometimes they are even primed. Painting the casings will hide the joints.

Hardwood Casings

Hardwood door casings are more expensive than paint-grade wood casings. They are, however, the best option for surfaces that may be exposed to moisture as they are unlikely to warp.

Multi-Density Fiberboard (MDF)

MDF casings are made from pressed sawdust and resin. MDF is a durable material that resembles paint-grade wood casings. They are usually primed, which makes them easy to paint.

Crown Molding

Crown molding is essentially the opposite of baseboard molding. It is installed where the top of a wall meets the ceiling. While not all rooms necessarily require crown molding, it is a beautiful touch to any room. Crown molding can be simple or elaborate or somewhere in between, depending on a homeowner's taste.

Chair Rail

A chair rail is a wall molding installed three feet above and parallel to the floor. They can be decorative in homes but can prevent scratches and marks on walls.

Picture Rail

A picture rail is a small molding, usually one and a half or two meters wide, installed horizontally on a wall just a couple of feet from the ceiling. Sometimes picture rails are installed quite close to the ceiling, just a few inches down, in fact, which can cause people to think it is a small kind of crown molding. A picture rail, however, is not just for decorative purposes. Rather, they are intended to accommodate hooks. Hooks are by far the best way to hang things on a wall without causing damage to the plaster or wallboard. If properly installed, a picture rail can support heavy loads, such as decorative mirrors.

Wainscoting

Wainscoting is a broad term that refers to any decorative panel nailed to the wall. Wainscoting was initially created to prevent damage to the wall, provide a decorative accent, and better insulate a room. Available in many styles, wainscoting is generally capped at the top with a chair rail. The most common types of wainscoting are beadboard, batten, flat-panel, and raised-panel. Wainscoting is used to cover the lower part of the wall, but some opt to cover entire walls with it.

Plate Rail

A plate rail is a rail or part of a wall used for displaying plates, ornaments, and collections. While they were originally used as a home for precious ceramics in the kitchen, today, they are also used to hold framed certificates, degrees, and awards in a home office or bedroom. Plate rails add a sense of distinction to a room.

The beauty of your home directly correlates with the beauty of your home's moldings. Our team has a lot of experience with molding and trim, and we can help you achieve the aesthetic by guiding you through all your options. Whether as part of a renovation or remodel of your existing home or the construction of a new custom home, we would love to consult with you.

*To learn more, call the Reagan Homes team at (860) 962-6250
to learn more or visit www.ReaganHomes.com
to schedule a complimentary, no-obligation consultation.*

INTERIOR WALL FINISHES

When it comes to finishing the walls in your new or to-be remodeled home, the options are abundant. Our team is here to help guide you toward the treatments that will help you express your style and individuality.

Your house is a home, of course, but what does it really say about you? In addition to the furniture and décor you bring in to customize your environment, the way you finish your home's interior walls is one of the most effective ways to express yourself. Whether paint or wallpaper is more your style, whether you add a feature wall of vintage barn wood planks or cool, modern wall panels, our team of professionals with decades of experience can help you find your style and create a personal oasis you're happy to live in and proud to share.

Decorative Stone

While decorative stone is available at several price points, all can be considered expensive. A high-end, status finish gaining in residential popularity, interior decorative stonework—whether in a kitchen, family room, bedroom, or bathroom—is a job better left to the professionals.

Decorative Plaster

If you want to warm up or cool down your space's mood or mimic a classic interior style like that of Mexican or Southwestern adobe architecture or a Tuscan villa, decorative plaster is the way to go.

Applying a decorative plaster finish is similar to adding a veneer—it's a light coat of material similar to stucco. An intriguing option, a variety of textures may be achieved depending on the brushstroke and pressure used.

While plastering isn't an especially difficult or skilled application, it is time-consuming and monotonous. To ensure a desired effect or color, pigment, mineral particles, or silicates can be added to the plaster.

Paint on Wallboard

Painted walls—paint on wallboard—is the No. 1 option for most American families. Not only does paint offer nearly infinite color options, specialty methods, tools, and add-ins can make something truly special of your home's interior. Paint is relatively inexpensive, and the process is simple.

For painted walls to deliver the look you desire, they must be in pristine condition; paint tends to highlight flaws and defects.

Reclaimed Wood

Wood is an old-school interior finish that is experiencing a resurgence in popularity. From the paneling of the 1960s and '70s to lodge-style interiors, we've seen it all and been through it all.

Today's wood interiors tend to feature reclaimed wood—especially barn wood and scrap wood. Wood seems to be gracing accent walls and partial spaces (similar in style to wainscoting, for example) rather than full rooms. Wood features can add both a rustic feel and a touch of elegance when done properly.

Wood walls are an affordable décor option. They should be sealed, however, once they are applied to the wall. Once sealed, they are, for the most part, maintenance-free.

Tile

Tiling walls or portions of walls can be expensive, and installation is a complex process. That said, tile is an excellent option for finishing walls in kitchens and bathrooms specifically. Tile is resistant to moisture, heating and cooling cycles, and myriad other potentially harmful issues. With the vast selection of tile types, styles, patterns, and colors available, there is something for every taste and home, and tile is a material worth the investment.

Wainscoting

Wainscoting has been around for centuries as a way to insulate walls, act as a decorative accent, and prevent or hide damage to walls. Usually made of wood, wainscoting is popular in more traditional and formal homes and is frequently used in relatively high traffic areas. Usually installed from the floor or baseboard up, it typically extends three to four feet up the wall and may be bordered or edged with a chair or picture rail.

There are several styles of wainscoting, including beadboard, board and batten, flat panel, and raised panel. Wainscoting is a durable and affordable interior option

Wall Panels

Wall panels got their start in the commercial and hospitality markets but are popping up more often on the residential scene. Wall panels are, essentially, three-dimensional decorative panels made from a wide variety of materials and available in a wide variety of styles. Many are peel and stick products, while others are applied like tile. They may be purchased ready to install, or they may be painted to suit individual tastes.

Ideal for accent walls in living, family, and dining rooms, it's not unusual for wall panels to require a bit more cleaning and maintenance than other finishes.

Wallpaper

Wallpaper can be a controversial topic. Most people either love it or hate it. But if you think you hate it, then you probably haven't seen the new styles, designs, and materials that have entered the market over the last few of years. Easy to clean vinyl wallpaper is perfect for a decorative touch in the kitchen, and a heavier, waterproof wallpaper can add visual interest to a bathroom. Also available are naturally textured wallpapers, textile and photo wallpapers, and three-dimensional wallpapers. One of the newer options is a peel and stick repositionable product—no long-term commitments necessary.

You'll find wallpaper everywhere, from the big box stores to Etsy. Like paint, when it comes to wallpaper, there is something for everyone, and all at a variety of price points.

Perhaps you have an idea of the wall treatments you'd like in your new home or as a part of your renovation or remodel. Maybe you're even considering a hybrid of multiple types of wall finishes. Whatever your thoughts, with more than 30 years of experience in home building and remodeling, our team of trusted professionals can help. We are in the know about the hottest trends and the most classic options. And we would love to discuss what we know with you.

To learn more, call the Reagan Homes team at (860) 962-6250
to learn more or visit www.ReaganHomes.com
to schedule a complimentary, no-obligation consultation.

CHOOSING PAINT COLORS
FOR YOUR INTERIOR ROOMS

Let the experts at Reagan Homes be your guide to choosing the perfect interior palette for YOU, your family, and your lifestyle.

What should be one of the most enjoyable, exciting parts of building your custom home or renovating and remodeling your existing home is often a time fraught with uncertainty, stress, and double-guessing. Yes, we are talking about painting your home's interior and selecting a color scheme that will complement your home, furnishings, and style.

The resources available to learn about choosing your home's color scheme are many (thanks to cable television and the internet). But we thought you might like to hear directly from the professionals, those people who have decades of experience helping homeowners make decisions just like this. Along Connecticut's southeast shore, the Reagan Homes team are those professionals. Our team can help guide and help you with your color selections.

When it comes to painting the inside of your home, there are no right or wrong colors to choose. What's important is that the colors you choose reflect your style and personality and say to visitors what you want. That may sound easy, but it isn't always. Color possesses the power to transform, and while "It's just paint," you don't want to be repainting year after year. You want a palette that is timeless within the bounds of your personal style and that you can live and grow with over many years.

Inspiration for your color choices can come from almost anywhere. We recommend you thoughtfully consider the art you will hang on the walls or a memorable décor piece that will live on an occasional table and pull colors from those items. You might then choose to work with tones—lights and darks of those initial colors. Keep a mood board or notebook where you place paint chips, fabric swatches, and pages cut from magazines to serve as inspiration and keep you organized.

And when in doubt, turn to the professionals. my designers, builders, contractors, and I build and renovate dozens of homes each year. We know the trends, and we know what the classics are too. We can help you set a mood or make a statement.

But first, here is a simple primer on all you need to know about interior paint and how to choose what's right for you.

Paint Finishes

Interior paints are available in various finishes, grouped by or referencing their reflectiveness. Depending on the finish, the appearance of a single color or shade can vary significantly. So, if after reading about different finishes, their durability, and common uses, you're still stuck, it's time to test them out.

Flat/Matte

Flat or matte paints have little to no reflective quality or shine. However, they provide excellent coverage and require the least number of coats to cover old paint and imperfections. Unfortunately, they are not particularly durable and are prone to staining, smudging, and bruising. They are best for low-traffic spaces like dining rooms, and they're a good option for ceilings.

Satin/Eggshell

These are the most popular paint finishes, with satin being the most popular and versatile of all finishes. Both satin and eggshell are more durable than flat finishes and deliver just the slightest hint of sheen. They don't cover as easily or hide imperfections quite as well, but their versatility can't be beaten. Builders and designers recommend satin and eggshell finishes for the highest traffic areas in any home—the kitchen and living room, family and bedrooms, and playrooms and bathrooms.

Semi-Gloss

A semi-gloss finish is shiny and reflective. Incredible durability and mildew-resistance make semi-gloss finishes perfect for kitchens and bathrooms as well as kids' rooms. They are also an excellent choice for trim, but be aware that semi-glosses are more likely to show imperfections when painted on walls.

High Gloss

Extremely durable and easy to clean, high-gloss finishes are, well, shiny. It's not a finish most people will choose for their walls, but doors, cabinetry, and trim all benefit from being painted with such an easy-to-maintain finish. Imperfections and even brush strokes are quite visible with this type of finish, however, so be sure you or your contractor apply high-gloss paint properly.

With more than 30 years of home building and remodeling experience, our team can help you make the right finish decision and will get your painting job done right the first time.

Match the Color to the Feeling You Want to Express

The first step in choosing a color for any room is to consider the purpose of the room, who will be using it, and how you want to feel when you're in it.

Kitchens are a great place to start. Do you envision your kitchen as the true heart of your home, where family and friends will gather as you cook? If so, you might want to consider warm colors like terra cotta, red clay, and peach—even gold tones will help warm up and welcome all who enter. But if you're more of a carry-out and warm-up kind of diner, then something more subtle and relaxing may better suit you, like a combination of grays, greens, and blues.

It's best to work with multiple hues to avoid bringing out the worst in an all-over color. Yellow, for example, is lovely in certain shades and quantities. But go big or bold with it, and you might regret it. Almost all colors look better when there are others around them to play off of and with.

And be sure to consider how specific colors make you feel. Does orange make you feel productive like you can do anything? Then consider it as one of the colors to feature—on the walls or in the décor—of your home office or craft room. Are you a "planty" person who likes to be surrounded by green creatures who filter the air and occasionally bloom? Make your plant collection the stand-out element in a room of blues and greens with pops of pink and white.

And how about your bedroom? Do you want to wake up to lots of light accentuated with energetic pops of color? Or would you prefer to fall asleep in a luxe environment that mimics the night itself: midnight blue walls with amethyst accents?

Whatever the feeling you seek to evoke, you can succeed with paint, and the Reagan Homes team can guide you through the process, ensuring your expectations are met.

Know Your Whites (and How to Choose the Right One)

Did you know there are more than 900 interior whites currently available on the market? They come with names like Cloud 9, Snow Day, White Dove, Snow Leopard, Honeymilk, and Lily of the Valley. In fact, Benjamin Moore alone offers more than 150 shades of white! They are described with words that include modern, crisp, soulful, soothing, natural, ethereal, soft, timeless, flattering, bright, reflective, body, glowing, sparkling, character, classic, balanced, radiant, chic, and serene.

It's not hard to get overwhelmed by the options. But there are a handful of things to know about shades of white that can help you choose the perfect white for you—one that complements your room and décor and that you'll be happy with for years to come.

Undertone

All whites will have an undertone or a cast to them that will impact the appearance of anything placed near them and affect the mood and feel of a space. Most white paints will have undertones that appear bluish, greenish, reddish, or yellowish—even grayish whites will have either a cool or warm undertone. I suggest that if you're having a hard time identifying the undertone of a specific shade of white, hold the white paint chip against a sheet of white paper. The undertone should pop.

Room Contents

What colors are present in your furnishings and décor pieces, such as art or pillows? This is a terrific and easy way to narrow down your white selections. If the colors in your room give off a warmer feeling, the white you choose should also be warmer. More tonal greens, blues, and violets? You'll probably want to go with a cooler white. If your décor is neutral, go with a warmer white.

Lighting

You've probably already seen this phenomenon in action, but the look, feel, and nuance of any paint color can change dramatically in various lighting conditions, and white is no exception. In homes (or rooms) with an excess of natural light (lucky you!), pure whites look the best and change the least. More heavily pigmented whites are a great option in rooms that rely more on artificial light.

Put White Paints to the Test

Ideally, every paint should be tested out in the home before you commit to brushing or rolling it onto multiple walls. Because, let's face it, that tiny 2-inch square chip isn't super helpful in assessing what an entire wall will look like when painted and as light moves about a room. Our Reagan Homes team has worked with enough families to have their own favorites and can make recommendations for any room and purpose.

How Color Impacts the Feeling of Room Size

A friend of ours recently decided it was time to update her dining room. Every dining room in every home she had owned was always some shade of red; she'd heard red stimulates both appetite and good dinner conversation. Her current dining room was a cool, deep berry red.

But it was starting to look worn, dated, and tired. She was ready for a change. With the help of the Reagan Homes team, she selected a gray so light, so silvery, it was almost white. She was suspicious on many levels. She'd always considered gray to not even be a color, and as an artist, she lived for color.

But up it went, and when the room was finished? Even our friend admitted it seemed not only like a new room but like an entirely different house. The biggest difference? The light gray made that dining room feel lighter, bigger, and airier. And yet, all that changed was the color of the walls.

Paint can impact our perceptions of the size of a space.

In very general terms, colors that are cooler and lighter appear to recede in the distance. Walls painted in a light color feel farther away. And a single color allows one's eyes to move continuously, also making a space feel larger than it is.

Meanwhile, darker or warmer colors generally feel closer in depth and distance, which might be right for spaces you want to feel cozier or more intimate, like a family room, an entertainment space, or a bedroom.

Ceilings Don't Have to be White

Speaking of colors influencing our perceptions, did you know that ceilings don't have to be white? It's true, and it seems we've all just been conditioned to think that ceilings have to be white. Of course, the vast majority of ceilings are white, and that's just fine.

But the Reagan Homes team wants you to know that there are instances in which painting a ceiling a color other than white might work for you and your decorating goals. When it comes to ceiling paint, you can go white, the same color as your walls, lighter or darker than your walls, or with a contrasting color. Each choice delivers specific results.

You may want to stick with white in rooms that already offer an abundance of color— like a living room with fabric-covered furniture, area rugs, pillows, wood accents, and electronics. White keeps it clean and simple. The same is true for high-traffic areas, like kitchens and entryways.

Painting your ceiling a darker color is a hot trend that you'll see in almost any home decorating magazine that you pick up. As long as your ceilings are of at least an average height and the room has plenty of natural light, a dark color can be a modern, chic, and inviting option. Our team suggests this for a beautiful dining room look.

If you want to make a small room feel bigger and for your furniture and décor in that room to stand out, try a color a step or two lighter than your wall color. Your space will feel lighter, brighter, and larger while delivering personality.

A contrasting color on your ceiling can be a tricky look to pull off. When done right, it draws the eye up and brings attention to items of interest in the room, like artwork or collections. Since this ceiling option has the potential to make a statement—not in the best way—you want to work with the professionals to ensure the work is done right and achieves the desired effect.

You might also want to work with professionals if you're considering a ceiling the same color as your walls. It can be a compelling look done with a neutral color, making your décor the center of attention. But it can also come off as dull or cave-like too.

Accent Walls

Everything old, as the saying goes, is new again. Once a staple of interior design, the accent wall disappeared from the scene for many years. But it's back, and it's another way to draw attention to a room or a specific part of a room.

Pulling the color of your accent wall from among the rest of your room's décor—especially from a focal point or item you'd like to draw attention to—is a practical and stylish approach.

Accent walls can work in any room, but dining rooms, living rooms, and bedrooms are among the most popular. In terms of choosing colors, there are no hard and fast rules. That said, much of the guidance we've already discussed—evoking a feeling with color and choosing a ceiling color, in particular—are highly relevant here, too. A few shades up or down on the color card or a contrasting color—both are doable.

But there are other options as well. An accent wall doesn't need just to be painted. Depending on your space, this is your chance to try something new and express your style. A glittery paint or one with metallic flecks looks gorgeous on a dining room wall behind a credenza or buffet. And a wall assembled from pieces of reclaimed wood can really set off a headboard. A stone wall in a living or family room is another option, as is a lovely, modern wallpaper.

Accent walls are indeed back, and they aren't going anywhere soon.

Trim Color Versus Wall Color

Like ceilings, many of us only know white trim—white baseboards, crown molding, chair and picture rails, wainscoting, mantels and pillars, and door and window casings.

But what if you thought of your trim as the frame of a painting instead of as something to dust occasionally and paint periodically? Look around you now. How many of the frames hanging on your walls are white? A few, perhaps, but probably not all.

This can be true of your home's interior trim. It enhances and defines boundaries. It marks transitions. And it also influences the perceived shape and size of a room and can be used to highlight specific features. A few examples:

- <u>Highlight an Architectural Feature</u>: Draw attention to a mantel, pillar, or archway by painting it a color that contrasts with your wall color. A color of similar intensity to the wall color will best draw the eye to the feature.

- <u>Crown Molding</u>: To raise your roof and make ceilings appear to be higher than they are, paint crown or other ceiling molding a color darker than your ceiling. This draws the eye up and results in a perception of expansiveness.

- <u>Old World Style</u>: If you've ever visited a historic home or site, you may have noticed an unexpected, contrasting trim color, often in classic colonial colors such as barn red, gray-blue, or mustard yellow. Not only may such trim be period appropriate for your renovation or remodel, but it's also a solid choice for warming up the feel of or introducing old-world charm into your custom home.

How to Create Flow in Open Floor Plans

Open floor plan homes are more popular than ever. Yet developing a color palette for open floor plan homes seems to cause much anxiety for homeowners. We field questions on the topic regularly. Clients want to know if they are limited to a single color for the whole house or per floor. If they go with multiple colors, how can the transition between rooms be delineated?

Of course, you can use multiple paint colors in your open floor plan home! The key to choosing paint colors for such a home is to stick with a limited palette of 3 to 5 colors (a white, two neutrals, and two supporting colors is a good rule of thumb) that are harmonious and work together without competing. A common thread through all of your selected colors will maximize impact and provide continuity and cohesiveness. Common threads might be a single color family, various concentrations of the same color, or similar tone (all muted colors or all brights, for example).

For transitions, let your home's architecture guide you. Corners, flooring changes, angles, and increases and decreases in dimensions will dictate the points where your color changes will occur.

Painting your home—and choosing the perfect colors—should be easy, and it should be fun. With experienced professionals like Dave Reagan and his Reagan Homes team by your side, it can be. Dave and his team have helped hundreds of homeowners make all the right paint color decisions for more than 30 years. They're here for you, eager to help regardless of the size or style of the project.

Paint can enhance a home, create or influence a mood or feeling, and help homeowners express their sense of style.

To learn more, call the Reagan Homes team at (860) 962-6250
to learn more or visit www.ReaganHomes.com
to schedule a complimentary, no-obligation consultation.

HOW AN ACCENT WALL CAN
HELP YOUR ROOM'S AESTHETIC

You most likely know that accent walls have been a trend for the last decade. This decorative choice can have a different impact on the room depending on how you decide to style it. Whether you're going for something bold, neutral, or even a textured wallpaper of some kind, accent walls add a little pop of personality to your decor.

You might be wondering how something so simple can change the whole aesthetic of the room you're in, but you'd be surprised how significantly it can impact the overall decor.

Go Bold

The rest of your decor might consist of neutrals like black, white, and gray, which means a bold accent wall in a funky color like teal, yellow, or red can break up the monotony of the room. If you're going to go bold with the color of your accent wall, you'll want a lot of neutrals to help balance the rest of the room. That doesn't mean you have to shy away from putting items of that accent color throughout the rest of the room, but you should use them in moderation.

Black and white rooms can benefit from a splash of red, green, or deep blue. Doing so will add a touch of modern elegance that works well with metallic accents and minimalist furniture. Whereas you'll get an entirely different aesthetic with light woods, cream walls, and a bright yellow, teal, or green accent. That style can give off an air of whimsy and brightness that makes the space look bigger and filled with more natural light.

Neutrals

Not every accent wall has to be bright and bold to make a statement. A simple neutral wall in a white, brown, gray, or even just a lighter more mellow color can change the aesthetic into something calming and serene. If your home is already quite busy with expressive prints and creative decor, a neutral wall can help calm down some of that noise and help tie your room together.

Decorating is all about balance, so it is important to have neutrals to balance out your bolds and vice versa. A calming neutral wall can settle out even the busiest of rooms without over complicating them.

Creative

If you're not digging the thought of neutrals or a bold color, you may be enticed by a funky pattern or textured wallpaper. Unleash your creativity on the accent wall by putting up interesting prints to give the room a modern or abstract spin. Patterns and prints can do a multitude of things for your space as they can drastically alter the aesthetics depending on what you pair them with.

You can also use a different material such as reclaimed wood or stone for an interesting accent wall. Perhaps you want to draw more attention or a fireplace or another feature of your home with an accent wall.

What Else?

At Reagan Homes, we relish your creativity. We want your home to embody you and your family in every aspect. Whether that's through simplistic design or modern innovation, we're here to make your home a dream home.

As part of your new custom home or existing home renovation/remodel we are happy to guide you in choosing the right accent wall for your home and style. We have a team of interior designers to help.

To learn more, call the Reagan Homes team at (860) 962-6250
to learn more or visit www.ReaganHomes.com
to schedule a complimentary, no-obligation consultation.

WINDOW TREATMENT OPTIONS

We all love natural light and how it can change the atmosphere of our homes in such a simple yet significant way. Natural light can make rooms feel bigger, help decor shine, and, overall, leave your home feeling fresh and inviting. However, you may not want the same amount of sunlight in every room or at every time of day.

Luckily, there exist numerous window treatment options you can have installed to change the amount of sunlight you let into each room. Each of these treatments can be customized to suit the aesthetic of each room in your home.

Let's look at a few options.

Shades

Shades are a reasonably affordable option that can be customized to match or complement any aesthetic. Shade styles, including contemporary and traditional, are available to customize every aspect and every room of your home. Shades tend to be a popular option because they are affordable, easy to install, offer insulating benefits, and are easily customized.

Roman Shades

Roman shades are a stylish option if you're looking for shades but want something more than a basic design. Roman shades are more traditional and have been a popular stylistic choice for many years. They can be made from thicker or thinner fabrics, depending on how much light you want to filter through, and the type and weight of the fabric can be varied for insulating purposes.

Roman shades come as a single bolt of fabric that covers a window in its entirety. Then, when raised, the fabric will form a charming accordion-folded look that adds a little bit of visual interest to your window. They can also be modified so they won't be as bulky when you have them raised. These shades won't provide as much insulation as other styles, but that, again, can be modified.

Roller Shades

This style of shade has become increasingly popular in recent years. They are practical and aesthetically pleasing as they deliver an effortless look that is ideal for the modern home. Roller shades roll up rather than pleat or accordion and can be manually operated or fixed with a motorized component, so they roll up at the touch of a button.

Some roller shades can be customized in different colors or have decorations added to make them more attractive. They are great for privacy and keeping out excess sunlight. If you want shades that are more suited for keeping out a lot of light, you can get roller shades customized for that as well.

Pleated Shades

Pleated shades have a crimped look and can be made from many types of fabric. They are easily compressed at the top of the window and can be corded or cordless, depending on your preferences. The colors and designs available vary, and because pleated shades are very thin, they can be made from highly affordable materials.

The only significant issue with pleated shades is that they aren't particularly good insulators. Unfortunately, the material's thinness doesn't help block much light either, so these are optimal for rooms that require less shading.

Honeycomb or Cellular Shades

Honeycomb—or cellular—shades are one of the top shades when it comes to functionality and quality. They are similar to pleated shades but provide a higher level of privacy while blocking more light. The fabric is thick but doesn't take up much space when the shades' honeycomb-shaped cells are in the open position. The honeycomb construction also makes these shades ideal for insulating purposes as air and heat are trapped easily by their functionality.

They aren't necessarily the most aesthetically pleasing shades you could opt for, but they are practical and functional enough to have earned themselves a spot in many modern households. You can even customize them, so they function as blackout shades to ensure your beauty sleep isn't interrupted by the sun.

Solar Shades

Solar shades have become popular in the last few years because they offer the ability to have some shade in your room without obstructing the view. While solar shades don't eliminate the light that enters a room through a window, they can reduce the amount of sunlight and heat that enter. Solar shades are the perfect option for minimizing heat and excessive light while retaining the simplicity and beauty of your room.

Solar shades also protect your furniture from fading and sun damage. With their simple design, they won't detract from the rest of your decor. While they aren't the most attractive from the outside, they are easy to install and incredibly effective.

Woven Wood or Bamboo Shades

These shades are not only budget-friendly but can add a little bit of interest to your room's decor. Whether your style is modern or more traditional, they will suit either design style. They are earthy and natural with a touch of modern elegance, and you don't have to worry about them detracting or clashing with the rest of your décor.

Made from renewable and recycled resources, you can feel good about your carbon footprint. This shade style provides good ventilation and allows the right amount of sunlight to enter the room when you want it. They also offer plenty of privacy, so you don't have to worry about nosy neighbors.

Blinds

Blinds are slatted window treatments that can be adjusted or tilted to filter the light and heat entering your room. They may be made from a variety of materials depending on your individual needs and tastes. A rod or a cord on the exterior edge of the blind will allow you to adjust them. They are incredibly versatile, and you will typically match your decor.

Venetian Blinds

Venetian blinds are typically wood, aluminum, or plastic blinds threaded together with lift cords to fold the blinds when they open. Also available in cordless varieties, Venetian blinds can be lifted with another device or even a remote control. They offer just the right amount of light filtering and can be adjusted to your specific needs. Their design prevents them from getting tangled or coming off a track. They are inexpensive and different materials can be used to complement your look.

Pleated Blinds

Pleated blinds are what you probably think of when you think of window blinds in general. They feature a classic look with thin veins and are usually drawn up using a cord. They may also be corded or cordless, and a variety of design types make them unique to each home. You can choose from wood, vinyl, or even fabric pleated shades to customize these window treatments.

Vertical Blinds

Vertical blinds are a standard option for large windows and sliding doors. They use vertical slats rather than horizontal slats, making them easy to open using a rod or cord to adjust the slats into your desired position. They are relatively low maintenance and don't collect dust the way horizontal blinds do. Vertical blinds will need an occasional dusting or wipe down, but not as frequently as other blinds.

Vertical blinds are typically made of an inexpensive vinyl material or materials that mimic wood. Vertical blinds operate in a sliding track, so there is less opportunity for them to snag or tangle. The shape of the veins can be changed to alter your room's appearance, or you can pick out different designs and colors to better suit your aesthetic.

Draperies and Curtains

Drapes and curtains are timeless classics when it comes to window treatments. Not only can they change or add to any room's aesthetic, they can also significantly modify the amount of light allowed in. They are an excellent option for insulating as they can help prevent air or heat from leaking out your window seams by blocking them.

Ripple-Fold Drapes

These drapes have a curved fold on the track or rod that makes them look like rippling waves. This style is elegant but simple and thus is a standard option for dining rooms and master bedrooms. The rippling effect makes the curtains look more voluminous and softer, so they are neat and orderly while at the same time sleek and charming.

They aren't difficult to maintain and don't sag or brush the floor, so you don't have to worry about the bottom of your them collecting dust or dirt.

Tailored Pleat

These drapes are pinned in a specific pattern to give them a pleated look at the top that then flows out in clean and defined lines. It is an elegant look and doesn't distract the eye with busy patterns unless you choose a bold fabric. The tailored pleats give the curtains a more purposeful look and give any room a gentle, elegant touch

With various patterns, fabrics, and colors to choose from, you can genuinely make the pleated drapery look customized to you.

Pinch Pleat

If you've ever made a pie, you're likely familiar with a pinch pleat pattern. The top of the curtain will look just like the pinch pleats of a pie crust when you're sealing it up for baking. Similar to the tailored pleat, the pinch pleat is more casual and rustic. The tailored pleat is a modern take on the pinch pleat, as the pinch pleat is timeless.

The pinch pleat design is lovely, and you won't be disappointed pairing it with the decor in your living or dining room.

Grommet Curtains

Grommet curtains have become a popular option for people who don't want to deal with complicated curtain rings. Grommet curtains are pressed at the top with grommets allowing them to be slid onto a curtain rod easily. While you can see the metal of the grommets, many manufacturers make them in decorative metal tones that add a touch of modern elegance.

If you're looking for a simple and low-maintenance solution, grommet curtains may be a great option.

Inverted Pleat

The inverted pleat is a spin on tailored or pinch-pleat drapes and lends a sophisticated and thoughtful aesthetic to any room in the home. The pleat itself is hidden—or invisible. What you do see is the fold of the fabric, a clean line, and a smart look. This curtain design would be aesthetically pleasing in an office or a sitting room, as it is simple but sophisticated.

These drapes are typically made with heavier fabrics as heavier fabrics hold and define the pleats better. They can, however, be made with lighter-weight fabrics as well.

Goblet Curtains

This curtain style is named for the look the cinching at the top of each. With goblet curtains, the fabric is bent into a goblet shape before tapering at the "stem." Goblet curtains are more traditional or old-fashioned, but they still have their place in some modern homes. This is especially true if you're a fan of timeless accents. You can make a statement in your home with goblet drapes if they are made with a bold pattern or even a solid-colored fabric.

Cubicle Curtains

Cubicle curtains are unique because you don't typically see them in residential settings. Cubicle curtains are more often used in hospitals and offices. They have been making a bit of a statement, though, as dividing curtains in bedrooms or for reading nooks. They are a great choice for smaller spaces that you want to divide into clearly defined areas. They are also available in a variety of styles.

Rod-Pocket Curtains

These curtains are for those of you who don't want to see a potentially unwieldy curtain rod. There is a tube-like pocket at the top of each curtain. You slide the curtain rod through the pocket, which hides the rod from view. These pockets may include a variety of different designs, so you're sure to find one that's right for you. If you want to go for something a little fancier, you might choose a curtain with a goblet, ripple, tailored, pinch, or inverted-style rod pocket. Either way, these curtains are exceptionally easy to install and manage.

Sheers

If you're looking for something that will help keep a little bit of the light and heat from the sun out of the room while still providing lots of natural light, a sheer curtain is a great option. You can get sheers in chiffon, lace, or another light-weight fabric, depending on the style you're seeking. There are so many different options to choose from to keep your room bright without being overbearing.

How Reagan Homes Can Help You

We know how important it is that every room in your home has the right amount of light. Whether you need blackout curtains or sheers, our trusted design team can help you find precisely the best options for your home. Our skilled and experienced team will make your dreams for a unique home that reflects your personality and interests a reality.

To learn more, call the Reagan Homes team at (860) 962-6250 to learn more or visit www.ReaganHomes.com to schedule a complimentary, no-obligation consultation.

PART 4:

REMODELING/ RENOVATING YOUR EXISTING HOME

10 PITFALLS TO AVOID WHEN RENOVATING YOUR EXISTING HOME

The home you call your own is much more than a residence. It should be the place where you make memories, spend time with loved ones, and find a sense of peace and tranquility away from the outside world.

At Reagan Homes, we understand what it takes to design and build properties that cater to your customized needs. We're proud to be the premier Connecticut-based design- build firm that serves New London and Middlesex counties with a one-of-a-kind approach to designing your dream home.

While our team is well versed in starting a project from scratch and handling any hurdles that arise along the way, we also know what it takes to complete a masterful remodel. Clients come to us when they're ready to turn their design dreams into a reality—and we're always happy to help! A home remodel is typically not a small project to take on, but it doesn't have to be overwhelming when you're well prepared for the journey.

Take a look at the top 10 pitfalls to avoid when remodeling your existing home and when you are ready, schedule your no-obligation initial consultation.

Failing to Consider Design Help

Far too often, homeowners who are looking to remodel their existing residence fall into the trap of thinking that they can split the job amongst various contractors to save money. In reality, this couldn't be further from the truth!

Working with a single design and build company makes the remodeling process comprehensive and will likely save you thousands of dollars along the way. At Reagan Homes, we employ a full team of designers, surveyors, landscape designers, architects, and structural engineers—we've got everything you need to get the project done right, just the way you envision it. Furthermore, if you want help with your vision, we can help guide you in that area as well.

You don't want to waste time trying to figure out how to make changes along the way … that's both costly and time-consuming. Instead, join us and our team of professionals who will be able to understand your vision and who will be committed to staying on track to achieve it.

To guarantee a superior level of client satisfaction, the team at Reagan Homes creates 2D floor plans and 3D renderings before we start any remodeling work. This provides you a chance to thoroughly visualize your ideas and make necessary changes before construction begins.

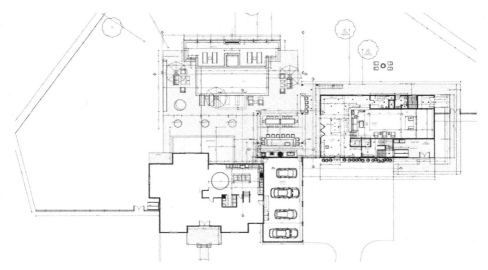

Sample 2D plan of backyard renovation with an additional 3,500 sq feet of living space addition.

Sample 3D rendering of backyard renovation with an additional 3,500 sq feet of living space addition.

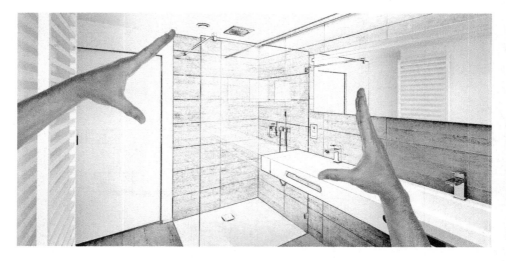

Not Living in the Home for at Least Three Months

Some homeowners get so anxious to get a remodel underway that they overlook one important step–living in the home first! While an amazing remodel is exciting, people who haven't taken the opportunity to spend quality time in a space may end up overlooking some essential areas that they will regret later on.

In general, it's always a good idea to spend a minimum of three months in a home before you start a remodeling project. This will help you to fully understand the functionality of the property and identify areas in which enhancements would be helpful.

Now, there are instances when living in the home certainly does not make sense and a teardown is more practical. At Reagan Homes, we can help you with this decision making process even before you put the offer in on an existing home.

Ignoring Your Home's Original Architectural Style

Fully remodeling a property will usually require some big changes, but aesthetically, clients who completely ignore the original architectural style of their existing home are usually in for some serious disappointment. Simply adding to a property without first considering the design flow can lead to a contrast in styles that is far from satisfactory.

Reagan Homes is proud to be a design-build company that prioritizes the original architecture of homes we are remodeling or renovating. We're enthusiastic about the changes we make through our innovative designs, but we also understand how to weave new features in seamlessly, so they never conflict with your home's unique style.

Being Too Trendy

A quality design-build company knows that trendy styles are fun in the moment, but trends rarely stand the test of time. When it comes to remodeling your existing home, sticking with designs and concepts that stand the test of time is generally a better way to go.

Often, the bolder remodeling and finish selections are, the more quickly the aesthetic will likely go out of style. At Reagan Homes, our team takes the time to guide you through the decision-making process to ensure that the color palettes and finishes you've selected will look amazing and remain timeless.

Choosing Your Contractor On Price Alone

When it's time to renovate your home, looking exclusively for the lowest price point is a risk that's never worth taking. The homeowners who choose to work with less than legitimate contractors who are willing to cut corners to lower prices tend to cost homeowners more in the long run.

Rest assured, Reagan Homes is the design-build company that has the experience and impeccable reputation you can count on and that you deserve. We are your professional partner in the remodeling process and are upfront and transparent about pricing. We help you avoid hidden fees related to things like permit acquisition and debris removal, too!

Working with a National Company

There are plenty of national companies and franchises out there that make a lot of promises. However, when it comes to customizing your home working with Reagan Homes as a local trusted contractor makes more sense.

As a local design-build company, we already have the area-specific relationships in place to get quality subcontractors on board your project. Our teams know about local land conditions, neighborhood and ton restrictions, and climate conditions that may affect the materials you choose. We have extensive experience in acquiring permits and getting approvals on workflows, thanks to more than 30 years of working relationships that we have established.

When you opt to use Reagan Homes for your remodeling needs, you can expect to receive not only a detailed timeline, but an accurate one, as well. We know what it's going to take to get the job done in your town because we have most likely successfully completed one, if not many, previously.

Working with an Inexperienced Contractor

Remodeling your home is a great opportunity to get creative with interior and exterior design prospects, but it's not the time to take a chance on an inexperienced contractor. An extensive remodel or renovation requires considerable experience and confidence. When it comes to facing structural and design hurdles that will inevitably come up along the way, you'll want a team of true professionals like the Reagan Homes team in your corner.

Don't risk the success or safety of a remodeling project by opting to work with a contractor that just doesn't have the experience to deliver up the results you desire. Instead, choose a contractor, like Reagan Homes, that has years of successful remodels to their name. We can guide you through the process with ease and reliability.

Ignoring Your Gut

There are times when you just know something is wrong or right. When you're looking at contractors to partner with for the remodeling of your home, trusting your gut is key - ignoring your instincts can be disastrous.

It's important to do your research before you sign on any dotted line. The contractor you work with should be committed to providing clear, honest, and easy communication from day one.

You should also expect your contractor to be a partner who will guide you through the process, offering up advice after listening to your insight and wishes. Trust your gut when it comes to your contractor, and never hesitate to ask for references before making your big decision.

Neglecting Curb Appeal or Outdoor Living

Some homeowners who are excited and ready to remodel their properties become laser-focused on the interior living space. However, ignoring the outside of your home can be a huge mistake!

When it comes to the curb appeal of a home, landscaping definitely sets the tone. It provides the first impression that guests get of a property. To that end, Reagan Homes is happy to serve clients with a team of landscape architects who are dedicated to creating outdoor designs that will flow well into the new interior spaces that you create.

When you're remodeling, it's also the perfect time to consider adding value to your backyard through outdoor living spaces and fun features like pools or outdoor kitchens. Not only do these additions boost the resale value of a home, but they can also create an enhanced style of living.

Failing to Explore a Multitude Of Financing Options

Remodeling your home is a unique and exciting opportunity. Homeowners inevitably look to make changes that make their home life more efficient and pleasing In the midst of all of the fun, however, it can be easy to jump into a project without exploring all of the available financing options, options with the potential to make the process even easier.

Even if you can pay for the entire project upfront, take the time to consider other options, such as a home equity line of credit or a loan, which can sometimes lead to savings on the overall costs of the project. Currently, home equity financing rates are extremely low, and you may be better off conserving your cash for investments and leveraging your home equity to help finance your project. Perhaps you are also renovating with resale in mind. If so, financing options can help you to maintain flexibility in the marketplace.

Your renovation is a vision that's just waiting to be made a reality ... and there is no reason to wait. We can't wait to hear from you and learn more about your remodeling wish list!

To learn more, call the Reagan Homes team at (860) 962-6250
to learn more or visit www.ReaganHomes.com
to schedule a complimentary, no-obligation consultation.

REMODELING IDEAS
TO INCREASE THE VALUE AND
FUNCTION OF YOUR HOME

One of the smartest things you can do as a homeowner is to invest in your home with additions, remodels and upgrades. You will enjoy a home that is better suited for your current needs and you can command a higher price when it's time to sell.

Home remodeling can be extremely valuable, and we realize every situation is different. At Reagan Homes, we help guide you through the decision-making process in terms of your lifestyle, what you desire, and the costs involved.

We realize many factors go into your decision, such as:

- How long you plan to be in the home.
- Whether or not you really love the location of your home.
- Town permitting laws that may hinder the expansion you may want to make.
- The lifespan of your appliances.
- Changes in your life or family since you originally moved into your home; for example, maybe you have been blessed with an addition to the family, or perhaps you want to add an in-law apartment.
- Your current financial situation.

We work with some clients who know and understand that their desired remodel may not be the best financial decision, but based on their personal situations, their goals, and their lifestyle, they decide to move forward anyway.

For example, installing an in-ground swimming pool in a house that is most likely going to be sold in less than five years may not be a great financial decision but some families may choose to enjoy it with their kids, friends, and family is worth the investment. They may take fewer vacations and enjoy their time at home more.

Regardless of your situation, you most likely have a budget you want to keep to. We help guide you in the design and materials selections throughout the entire remodeling process to help you stay within budget.

To help you make a cost-effective home remodel, we have come up with some remodeling ideas that typically are more cost effective and deliver greater resale value if and when you decide to sell.

Your Kitchen

The kitchen is often referred to as the heart of the home. People tend to congregate in the kitchen whether it's just with your immediate family or a group you are entertaining. A relaxed, spacious kitchen will help give a warm ambiance to your home.

The National Kitchen & Bath Association states that cabinets and faucets are typically the first items in the kitchen to become outdated. While you can reface cabinets, typically the cost to reface them would allow you to get new cabinets. With new cabinets, you have the opportunity to change the layout of your kitchen. With a new layout, perhaps you will have room for a bump out or addition to add more living space.

With new cabinets, will come new countertops. Currently, homeowners are trending towards quartz because quartz tends to become dated as other options. There are some mid-range priced quartzes that look like marble but come with a much lower price tag than marble. Choosing a material that is more timeless (or that looks like a more timeless material), typically leads to a better ROI when the time comes to sell.

Granite tends to be a popular choice as well. With granite, there are different finishes that give different looks and feels, including:

- <u>Polished:</u> (the most common granite finish) glossy and almost mirror-like.

- <u>Honed:</u> a matte finish without any gloss or reflection qualities.

- <u>Leathered:</u> takes the honed finish and adds texture with subtle dimples to provide a more sophisticated look.

- <u>Caressed:</u> takes the leathered finish and adds gloss.

- <u>Brush Hammered:</u> provides a naturally weathered look with a slightly textured finish, which often lightens the color of the stone.

- <u>Flamed:</u> a rougher surface with a natural and faded appearance; often muted in color.

When it comes to flooring, you want to make sure your flooring can stand up to spills, drops, and so on. If you have young children, pets, or plan to remain in your home for years, having non-slip floors is important for safety. Porcelain tile, hardwood, engineered hardwood, cork, and limestone are all great choices for kitchen flooring. Luxury vinyl tile is also a great option that can look like hard-wood, It generally has a cork underlayment that is naturally resistant to odor-causing mildew and mold. Luxury vinyl offers a softer, warmer, and a quieter floor.

For backsplashes, ceramic tile is usually the most affordable option and is available in many colors, sizes, and patterns. Glass tile is a little more expensive than ceramic tile, but it can add visual interest to your backsplash. Both glass and ceramic are easy to clean and maintain. A more expensive option is stone or marble, both of which requires more maintenance and regular sealing. With the appropriate sealing, wood can also be a great option for a kitchen backsplash. There are other options, from metallics to wallpaper to mirrors and more.

Additionally, something as simple as choosing a higher-end faucet can help add value and make your kitchen look more custom.

As you can see, there are many choices when it comes to remodeling or renovating your kitchen. We are eager to help you plan and price out your kitchen remodel, which can help increase the value of your home.

Finish Your Basement

Yes, a dark seemingly uninhabitable basement can be made to integrate with the rest of your home. Finishing your existing basement saves you from new foundation and exterior siding expenses that typically come with an addition.

Often, we can easily transform a basement into an extra bedroom, a bar room, exercise room, office, a home theater, or a recreation room.

We can typically hide lally columns and make them part of the design for your basement remodel, as well.

We help guide all of our clients in terms of how to best layout your finished basement.

Additional Living Space

Perhaps you want to add an additional bedroom, a remarkable master suite, an in-law apartment, a recreational room, or some other form of additional living space.

At Reagan Homes, we listen to your wishes and desires. Then, we look at how to best layout your addition. Furthermore, because of our experience in working with the municipalities throughout New London and Middlesex counties, we can guide you in the better direction for what you can and can't do based on your town's regulations.

If we need a survey, we have surveyors who can do the job. Our team of interior designers will make 2D plans and 3D renderings with different options for you to review. We will even help you with different colors and material finishes within the renderings. Once you are happy with the layout, we will then work with a structural engineer or architect if needed.

We take care of all the permits and insurances needed.

By thoroughly planning upfront, we are able to avoid more significant changes throughout the process. That being said, we are flexible and we can provide solutions should challenges arise.

> To learn more, call the Reagan Homes team at (860) 962-6250
> to learn more or visit www.ReaganHomes.com
> to schedule a complimentary, no-obligation consultation.

Work on the Landscape Design

While people overlook the landscaping of their homes, a good landscape design can contribute as much as five percent to the value of your home. Take a long critical look at your front yard. Does it have a curb appeal? If you're not satisfied with what you see, chances are a buyer won't be either. It doesn't matter how beautiful the interior of a home is if it doesn't look appealing on the outside—it's a total turn-off. First impressions matter.

We can help figure out what landscape design is best for your front yard based on your style and the space you have. Laying out a line of colorful trees and plants in your front yard can be very attractive if you love nature and greenery.

Incorporate a curving pathway, throw in a nice bench, add a few lights in the right places, and you'll have an environment many will fall in love with at first sight. Updating your landscape does not always mean you have to spend a lot. The most basic gardening job, if done right, is enough to make an excellent first impression.

Outdoor Living

While the kitchen is often a place people congregate, many of our clients also want an outdoor space in which to spend time with family and friends. From a firepit to a pool and hot tub to an outdoor kitchen and more, we have extensive experience with the amenities that can turn your backyard into a resort-like space. We can also add more simple areas in which you can enjoy time with your loved ones.

We will look at your floor plan and how to add outdoor living space that functions well, flows with a great layout, and is built efficiently to help save your hard-earned money.

Always Combine Beauty with Function

The trick to making the right improvements to add value to your home is to look for projects that offer a double impact. You should look to achieve a blend of aesthetic and functional upgrades, and if you do, you're likely to get it right. That being said, there are many questions, options, and decisions to be made throughout the remodeling process.

At Reagan Homes, we are eager and grateful to have the opportunity to help make your dreams a reality at your current home.

SIMPLE HOME IMPROVEMENT IDEAS YOU DON'T NEED REAGAN HOMES FOR

Not every remodeling project requires you to hire Reagan Homes. Below is a list of simple and budget-friendly ideas to improve your home's environment.

Repaint Your Mailbox

The mailbox is one of the first introductions someone gets when they come to your home. The mailbox might like a small thing, but repainting, or changing your mailbox, might just be the glow up you need in your home.

Install New House Numbers

Some homes don't even have a house number. Adding or sprucing up your house numbers can help make your home feel more inviting. With more and more packages coming to your home, your delivery people will be grateful that you have upgraded your numbers.

Repaint the Interior of Your Home

Changing a room's color can be an easy upgrade on your way to giving a room a new look and feel.

Repaint Or Replace Your Front Door

Changing the look of the entryway can help improve the overall look of your home.

Add An Accent Wall

Changing the color of one wall in a room can make a focal point, such as a fireplace, pop.

Change Up Your Landscaping

Investing in some new landscaping can certainly increase the curb appeal of your home and soften the entrance to your home.

Add Exterior Lighting

Adding simple landscape lighting can help highlight your home.

Rearrange Furniture

Changing the placement of furniture can improve the flow of your room.

Replace Furniture

Replacing or adding furniture to your living space can give your room a new look.

Add or Replace an Area Rug

Changing out or adding an area rug can add color to your room.

Change Out Cabinet or Door Hardware

Swapping out cabinet or door hardware can give a fresh, updated look to your home.

Give Your Home a Deep Cleaning

From power washing the outside to cleaning the windows inside and out, a deep cleaning can help thoroughly spruce up your home's appearance.

For the above home improvement ideas, you certainly do not need to call Reagan Homes. However, if you want to explore the idea of a more involved remodel or renovation of your existing home, or perhaps you are considering building a new custom home, call Reagan Homes at (860) 962-6250 today for more information, or click here to schedule a complimentary, no-obligation consultation.

PART 5:

LAND EVALUATION

Since 1987, Reagan Homes has been a Connecticut homebuilding icon for residents of New London and Middlesex counties. While our company has built its reputation of excellence on custom-built homes, we understand the many details that must be in place to make the homebuilding process a successful one.

Building a dream home is always an exciting journey, but selecting the right land for that home is just as important. We're committed to helping our clients navigate each and every decision with ease.

Our team of experts do not shy away from a challenge. Instead, we embrace any obstacles that we face. We use many years of experience to find solutions that work for our clients at every turn.

In this chapter, we'll look at seven key issues you need to keep an eye on when you're on the hunt for the ideal plot of land on which to build your dream home.

Never Assume That Land Will Be Easy to Find

These days, it's easy to fall into thinking that everything—including land for a new home—is readily available at the touch of a button.

When it comes to selecting land to build on, listings on well-known platforms can be helpful, but they may not have the most up-to-date information. We have built many great relationships with Realtors all along the Connecticut shoreline so we can work in tandem with them to help you find the prime location at a reasonable price.

Real estate professionals who specialize in land sales often have access to listings that have yet to hit the market. They can also pull records on any restrictions on the land and any survey activity that has been done on the property. This gives potential buyers the chance to see land the minute it hits the market while also providing the right information, so buyers can know that the land they're looking at will fit their purposes.

Additionally, many of our clients work with us directly. We have great knowledge of existing land available as well as other existing properties with homes on them that may work as a teardown so you can build your dream residence. In fact, we have helped clients take multiple pieces of property, tear down multiple existing homes and make one bigger piece of property.

Whether you are or aren't working with a Realtor, we can help. We welcome the opportunity to learn about your dream home and your desired location.

Don't Make an Offer on Land Before Understanding the Zoning Requirements

Setting your eyes on that dream lot is an exciting moment, but it's important not to let those emotions blind you to the reality of zoning laws and requirements that are already in place.

One of the most disappointing scenarios that buyers encounter is finding out the land they love isn't zoned for residential use.

Some lots are specifically set aside by zoning commissions for agricultural or industrial purposes. Even if the land you find is zoned for residential use, prospective buyers will need to make sure that the building plans they have in mind correspond with the setback restrictions linked to the lot.

Setbacks are rules related to how close to the property line a residence footprint can sit. Homeowners with a very clear vision of the dimensions of their dream home will want to be sure these setback parameters fit their ideals before signing the dotted line.

Other typical issues that may cause restrictions to the building requirements of a piece of property include:

- Neighborhood homeowners' association rules .
- The presence of wetlands on the property.
- The size you want your home to be in relation to the size of your property.

These issues and many more could prohibit you from building in your desired location. Rest assured, we work with and have great relationships with all municipalities in New London and Middlesex counties in Connecticut. We are more than happy to help guide you in the right direction as you look for a suitable property as well as throughout the entire homebuilding process.

Take Land Preparation Into Account

Much will need to be done to get the ground ready to build a quality home. Before our customers put building plans into place, we make it a priority to work with them to carefully evaluate the land they're interested in. Our goal is to not only help buyers understand the cost of land preparation, but the effort that will go into it, which may include anything from leveling and grading to clearing existing trees and brush.

Potential buyers will also want to consider their building timeline. Those with a stricter timeframe to work with shouldn't consider land options that will require significant work before building even begins. Instead, they need to focus their attention on land that is close to or already leveled for building projects. We are eager to hear about your timeline and see how we can help find you the land you desire.

Loans Aren't Always a One-Size-Fits-All Solution for Land Purchases

Most potential buyers looking at land for their new home expect to take out a loan for the purchase. What many people don't realize ahead of time is that land loans are not a one-size-fits-all solution to financing. Depending on the size of your lot and its location, you may qualify for various types of land loans.

People who are looking at vacant land with no existing infrastructure will likely need to take out a land loan. These loans can differ from traditional financing used to secure a home that's already built. They may require a larger down payment or have a different interest rate than traditional financing options.

The cost of construction loans should also be taken into consideration. Clients who choose to work with Reagan Homes can count on a comprehensive purchase-to build experience. We have built strong relationships with many local banks and loan officers. Our team will guide you through the process of financing so you can budget accordingly.

Consider the Necessary Permits

Permits that will need to be in place to build successfully on the land should be taken into careful consideration before you buy a lot. When it's discovered a permit is missing, construction can be significantly delayed or halted completely.

Our teams will be the ones to pull the necessary permits, but it can be helpful to know upfront what it will take to get the permits you'll need for the location that you choose.

Don't Forget to Ask About the Utilities

Once you've found that inspiring piece of land to build your future home on, ask about how utilities will be linked. Questions regarding natural gas access, sewer setup, and water lines should be a priority so that you can set realistic expectations, but also stick to your intended budget. When it comes to considerations for utilities, you'll want to ask about several things. These include electricity, natural gas, sewer or septic viability, access to water, and telecommunications. Determining whether a private or public company will handle a home's water supply is something you'll want to know before you ever consider breaking ground. If you're looking at land that's a bit off the beaten path, it's important to check on internet and phone access options, too.

While these details can seem trivial, unexpected surprises are costly. It can be stressful to learn that you'll need to install a septic tank or run extensive power lines to a new home after you've already bought the land that you plan to build on. We are here to help you with all of this before you even put an offer in on a piece of property.

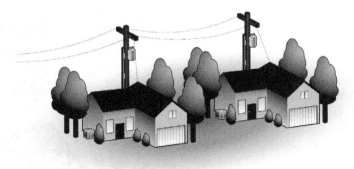

Make It a Priority to Ask About Natural Hazards

All of the preparation and research in the world doesn't negate the fact that Mother Nature just does what she wants. When you find a piece of land that you might want to build on, it's important to take any potential natural hazards into mind.

Checking to see if the land sits in a flood zone is a key to determining if and how a home could be built in the area. You'll also want to have soil testing done to see if the ground is appropriate for building. Soil tests can also allow you to determine if you'll be able to install a septic tank on the property if city sewer access is not available on the build site.

Asking about the natural hazards that are linked to the land you're considering can offer good insight into the types of insurance policies that you may need to have in place on the home you build. Many companies can provide quotes upfront for flood insurance if your land and building plans will require it.

You can also check on the flood zone status of a piece of property from the FEMA website, which can help you to determine what flooding risk your land is likely to face. Again, we help you with all of this.

When you're ready to begin looking at land for your future home, the team at Reagan Homes is here to help. We're passionate about the work we do to help our clients. We understand that it can be intimidating to think about building rest assured that you have the best professionals in the business on your side.

Our comprehensive approach to land development and custom homebuilding lets us stand out from the competition. From start to finish, our customers can count on a safe, seamless, and successful experience.

There's no reason to wait when you're ready to start your homebuilding journey.

To learn more, call the Reagan Homes team at (860) 962-6250
to learn more or visit www.ReaganHomes.com
to schedule a complimentary, no-obligation consultation.

PART 6:

NEW CUSTOM HOMES

11 THINGS YOU MUST CONSIDER BEFORE BUILDING YOUR NEW HOME

Choosing your builder is a crucial decision. There are many factors that can influence your decision-making process. Think about what's important to you in terms of the initial process, the finished product, and the many milestones in between.

Is it one-stop shopping, ease of communication, and/or confidence in quality and expertise? Perhaps the budget and the timeline are your biggest priorities. This article will help guide you in choosing the right builder for you.

We will listen intently, respond quickly, share our knowledge and expertise, and create a uniquely stunning home that meets your every need.

Obviously, we hope you'll agree, based on all of the elements within this chapter, Reagan Homes is your most logical and best choice for building your new custom home. You should work with a builder that you can trust and who will guide you throughout the building process.

Use this article to help direct you in choosing the right builder for you. When you are ready, schedule your no-obligation initial consultation.

1. Do they offer an all-in-one solution?

You're thinking about building a new home. You have questions, ideas, and many options to consider throughout the process. This can be overwhelming, but with an all-in-one solution, Reagan Homes can guide you through each step of the homebuilding process with a team of experts.

Our Reagan Homes team enlists a comprehensive group of surveyors, interior designers, architects, landscape designers, structural engineers, contractors, craftsmen, and professionals to assist you from concept to completion.

Our team will be with you through all the milestones:

- Site selection
- Customizing your home plan
- Interior finish choices

And we will do it while helping you maximize your budget and build efficiently so you get what you want for the best value. We are there for you with the best service and guidance to help you build the home of your dreams.

2. Do they have land available?

One of the most critical decisions you will be faced with in building your new home is where it will be located. You will want to choose a community that suits your needs and that can also accommodate your desired home plan.

Often, Reagan Homes has approved building lots throughout New London and Middlesex counties, building lots with beautiful custom home packages available. We can also help evaluate your independent lot purchase for feasibility and site work estimates before you buy.

We also have extensive relationships with multiple Realtors to give you options on land that may not even be on the market yet. Furthermore, we know of situations in which a teardown may make the most sense based on your lifestyle and home layout plans. Ultimately, we are here to guide you in the process of finding the right land for your dream home.

3. Do they communicate well?

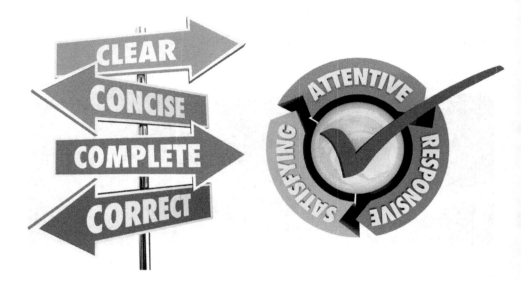

Building a new home encompasses a lot of decisions. From big decisions to small decisions, the need to communicate is paramount to the process. From the initial consultation to project completion, it's important to have a contractor who listens to your needs and provides solutions.

At Reagan Homes, we listen to your ideas, needs and desires. We translate those into your dream home environment. Moreover, we welcome your questions throughout the process. We strive to have a 24 to 48 hour response time, so you're never left to worry if your concerns are going to be addressed. The details are as important to us as they are to you.

We leverage technology such as zoom for virtual meetings, text messaging, email and tools to help make communication easier for you and save you time.

4. Do they have extensive experience?

Building your new home is a big investment of your most valuable resources: time and money. You want to feel confident that the builder you choose for your custom home is experienced and can be trusted to protect your interests and assets.

Our experience also helps navigate getting your custom home approved with the appropriate townships and municipalities. We have extensive experience in working with all towns in New London and Middlesex counties.

5. Do they have relationships with trusted contractors?

Accountability in the building process goes beyond your general contractor. Every sub-contractor is equally important to the process in terms of communications, quality of work, and timing.

Reagan Homes has an extensive network of trusted contractors, both in-house and outsourced, who specialize in quality workmanship and maintaining construction timelines. Our job sites are clean, safe and organized. We manage the details and coordinate how all the elements of homebuilding come together. We guide you in making the important design choices and help transform your ideas into your dream home.

6. Are they a top-rated builder?

In choosing a builder, your own judgment is critical. Maybe you want additional resources beyond testimonials to help reinforce your confidence in your choice.

Reagan Homes is an A+ rated contractor with the Better Business Bureau. In addition, numerous publications have endorsed Reagan Homes as a premier builder in Connecticut. View the gallery of articles on our website, and choose with confidence.

7. Do they take a consultative and informative approach?

Building your custom home involves a lot of decision-making. You'll face choices pertaining to essentially every function and design element, as well as on how best to prioritize and allocate your budget. This process can seem daunting at times. You need a contractor who welcomes guiding you through your options and the decisions that need to be made.

At Reagan Homes, we will work with you to help ease the stress of the decision making process. We present you with realistic options, taking into consideration what we know about your personal style and your available budget. We keep the process exciting and fun as you make important choices that personalize your home and make it uniquely yours.

8. Do they use the highest quality materials?

Your home may be the biggest investment you will ever make. You want quality products and materials that will stand the test of time and showcase the class and elegance of your new home.

Every Reagan home is appointed with the highest-quality brand-name products in the industry. We partner with high-end manufacturers to bring greater quality and value to your home. From appliances to flooring products to cabinetry to plumbing fixtures to home automation to efficient HVAC systems and more, we're proud to build luxury homes featuring outstanding brands.

9. Do they offer any warranties?

New homes are constructed with a host of new systems: heating, cooling, and plumbing, as well as natural design elements such as wood, stone, metals, and more. Although meticulous care is taken while building your home, inevitably there are times when products themselves fail or there are small issues that need to be resolved post build completion.

Reagan Homes offers a five-year full warranty on products, systems and workmanship. If something goes wrong, we fix it. We listen to the issue, respond quickly and efficiently, and make every effort to minimize disruption to your life. We want you to love everything about your new home. We take pride in and stand behind our quality workmanship. Our relationship with you extends beyond the closing on your home, until you are fully settled and certain that everything not only looks beautiful, but also functions properly.

10. Do they provide a 5-star client experience?

What does a 5-star client experience mean to you? Were you satisfied with your new home? Did the building and purchase processes run smoothly and efficiently? Would you choose the same contractor again if given the choice?

Our goal at Reagan Homes is for you to be completely satisfied, and to say with certainty that you would choose us again. We want you to feel excited to recommend us to a friend without hesitation.

Our community reputation is critically important. Most of our business is generated from word of mouth referrals. We pride ourselves on our professionalism, attentiveness, timely responsiveness, knowledge, and competency.

We strive for nothing less than your 100% satisfaction in your new custom home and throughout our process.

11. Do they have extensive financing experience?

Building a new home costs money. Even if you can pay cash for your entire new custom home you may want to take advantage of securing financing for your project. You may have a period of time where you are paying for your existing home or rental and also for your new home as construction progresses. You might not understand how construction loans work, if you can afford dual payments, and how to manage the paperwork.

Our team at Reagan Homes has an extensive knowledge of the dynamics of new home financing. We have great relationships with local and national lenders. We are here to help you when it comes to making your new custom home as affordable as possible.

We can explain the construction loan process, and help you succeed at financing your new home. We can assist you in figuring out how to manage your payments during the time of transition. We provide you with valuable resources and an understanding of how to best manage your financial situation to your advantage.

We hope that our philosophy and approach in constructing quality custom homes are in alignment with what you are looking for in a custom home builder. We take a great deal of pride in the beautiful gallery of finished homes in the Reagan Homes portfolio, as well as the qualified professionals on our team and the trusted reputation we've earned in the community.

We would love the opportunity to work with you to create the custom home of your dreams. Together, we can design the perfect space for you and your family. You provide the imagination and the wish list that suits you, and we will provide the knowledge and expertise to translate it into the custom home you've always wanted.

We invite you to start with a no-obligation conversation about your unique situation, and you can decide from there if Reagan Homes is the best fit for you. We also invite you to view our gallery of completed homes, drive by some of our custom homes in the local community, and speak directly to past clients regarding their experience during and after the building process. We look forward to hearing from you soon and to helping you make your dream home a reality.

To learn more, call the Reagan Homes team at (860) 962-6250
to learn more or visit www.ReaganHomes.com
to schedule a complimentary, no-obligation consultation.

5 REASONS TO BUILD
A CUSTOM HOME

When building a new custom home, you have total control over how you want it designed and the features that you want your home to have. There are obviously many decisions and choices in building your custom home. We have built a great team throughout our 30 years building custom homes in Middlesex and New London counties. We are here to guide you every step of the way, from design to fruition.

Here are the top five reasons you should strongly consider building a custom home.

Suitable for Now and for the Future

One of the main reasons people move into a new home is because their family is growing, and they need a bigger space to accommodate this growth. When you opt for a custom home, you can build a home that fits your present and your future needs—with enough room for now and later.

Suits Your Lifestyle

At Reagan Homes, we help guide you in infusing your taste and personal style into the planning, design, and construction of your new home. For example, if you desire an open floor plan or want an outdoor kitchen to expand your living space outdoors, our team of designers will not only design 2D plans, but we will also provide 3D renderings so you can better visualize your lifestyle in your new home.

Just Where You Want It

Building a custom home lets you choose the exact location in which you want to live. If you have a neighborhood in mind, we can help guide you to available land or potential teardowns so you can live where you want. We have extensive experience in building waterfront homes should you want a custom home right on the water or with water views.

Within Your Budget

Over the last 30 years we have built hundreds of homes along the Connecticut shoreline. After listening to your desires and needs, we will provide you an estimate to build your custom home. Within your estimate will be ample allowances to help you be on budget. Furthermore, because of our extensive experience we can provide alternatives to help you stay within your budget.

Quality Finish and Environment

Our team of interior and landscape designers will help guide you in choosing the finishes that will suit your taste. Our team of highly skilled craftsmen will ensure your home is built with the utmost quality. We stand behind our custom homes with a 5-year warranty.

Moreover, a majority of our new clients are from word of mouth referrals. That being said, our reputation precedes us and should give you confidence that your new custom home will come with the best quality.

Building a custom home is one of the best decisions you could ever make. It's highly personalized and built in the location you want to match your desired lifestyle. At Reagan homes, our designers will sit with you to understand your requirements and give you insights to help you build your dream home.

*To learn more, call the Reagan Homes team at (860) 962-6250
to learn more or visit www.ReaganHomes.com
to schedule a complimentary, no-obligation consultation.*

OVERVIEW OF THE NEW CUSTOM HOME CONSTRUCTION PROCESS

The following is an outline of the new custom home construction process (assuming we have helped you evaluate the land, and obtain the proper zoning and building permits).

Planning and Design

During this stage of the process, we are designing your floor, architectural, and structural plans. Once we have a design, we will obtain the proper building permits with your town.

Clearing The Site

To prepare your land for your new custom dream home, we may need to clear trees, level the land, and remove rocks or other land formations so we can dig the foundation.

Laying The Foundation

First, your foundation will be mapped out with temporary barriers acting as a template for where we will dig and pour your home's foundation. Once we have laid out the boundaries for the foundation, we will begin excavating. Your foundation may require more excavation time if your plan includes a basement.

Any dirt excavated will be set aside for later use. We will put in the footings. Then, it's time to pour the concrete for the foundation. The concrete will then need time to set-up fully and cure. Once all of the concrete is cured, there will be an initial inspection to ensure the foundation is safe and properly set.

Framing

Once the foundation is set and cured, we will begin framing the house. This entails the basic framing or building of floors, walls, and the roof. Framing is essentially a physical representation of the home's layout. Framing brings the blueprint plans to life. Sometimes we will use trusses,which are built offsite, for the roof framing.

Also referred to as your home's skeleton frame, once completed, the sheathing and protective layers will be applied to bulk the structure for further building. The sheathing ensures water and other elements cannot penetrate the frame and that mold or rot won't be an issue.

Once the skeleton is complete and everything has been sheathed, we will start adding siding and roofing, and install the windows and exterior doors. Our goal is to ensure your home is weather-tight.

Plumbing, Electrical and HVAC Rough-In

Next, comes the rough-in of your major mechanicals.

Insulation and Finishing Drywall

You're going to want your home to be energy efficient, which means it needs proper insulation to keep it cool during the summer and warm during winter. Many different types of insulation are available to choose from, including fiberglass, foam, and concrete.

Once the insulation has been finished, we will install the drywall. During this time, your home will start to look more like a finished home with walls instead of cross beams. Exterior details intended to make your home stand out, such as stone or brickwork, will also be wrapped up.

Installations

Your interior doors, trim, and flooring will all be added next. Cabinets, appliances, finished lighting and plumbing fixtures will follow.

Once all of these installations have been completed, we will install your driveway and finish sealing and painting everything. In the final steps in building your custom home we will grow grass or install sod and landscaping. While there are inspections throughout, there is a final inspection to ensure everything has been done correctly and that the home meets occupancy guidelines so you can obtain a certificate of occupancy from the town. We will also complete any punch list items. Our goal throughout the process—and your finished dream home—will exceed your expectations.

WHEN DOES A
MODULAR HOME MAKE SENSE?

Modular homes have been a big trend over the last decade. They are stylish, modern, and have a bit of a charming edge to them that draws in those seeking to buy or build their own homes. Not only are they stylish, but they are wonderful space savers that can fit well into any neighborhood setting.

Some builders may seek them out because they are affordable and owners can save money on square footage and while also saving time on the building process. But why else might you want to invest in a modular home?

Speed of Construction Is Crucial

If you're looking to get yourself into a home fast and you want to have it built from the ground up, a modular design may very well help you get your house built in half the time. Modular homes typically feature easy designs that most modern builders can finish quickly. Most are factory built, and your construction team assembles them and adds your customizations to make your house into a home.

The build time for a modular home is also reduced due to the lack of inspections required with modular designs. The factory usually completes the inspections before the homes are shipped to the consumer. The ease of assembly and the already pre-checked materials make modular homes an ideal choice for those looking to save time and be in their new home in less than 30 weeks.

When Customization Isn't As Important As Cost

While most prepackaged modular homes tend to be similar to one another, this can be something of a blessing. Modular homes tend to be cost-effective because they don't take long to build, and they are all very similar in construction. You do have to pay for the land you're building on, to have it landscaped, gas set up, concrete poured, and other necessities. However, the costs are still less than what you'd likely spend to buy a house already built or to build a custom home.

Customization can always come later through the addition of exterior and interior accents that suit your aesthetic. You may also customize after building by hiring painters or other designers to help you express who you are.

Quality of Indoor Construction

Because these kits are put together in batches, they are all constructed the same. As a result, you can rest assured your model will be of high quality as the designers want each home to rise to a certain standard. They are factory built, leaving little room for error. Each is inspected and checked before it shipped, so you can be confident that the quality will be up to the standards you expect.

Energy Efficient

Because they are manufactured, modular homes reduce waste materials, which in turn improves energy-efficiency. Many modular homes on the market are also built from recycled materials, so waste is even further reduced. As for power, many modern modular homes are outfitted with solar panels or use LED and CFL lighting, so the lights will last much longer and be much more efficient than traditional lighting sources.

Modular homes are also well insulated, so your heating and ventilation won't leak out of spaces around doors and windows and waste money.

Selling Land

Because you have to purchase the land before assembling a modular home, you'll find that when the time comes to sell your modular home, you'll have an easy time of it. Modular homes are incredibly popular now, and if you can strike a good enough deal on the land and house, buyers will snap it up without the need on your part to compromise much on an asking price.

How Reagan Homes Can Help

Reagan Homes is the premier home builder in Southeastern Connecticut. Dave and his team can take on any challenge when it comes to home building, and putting together your perfect modular home is just another one of our skill sets. We can help you through the entire process of getting your modular home placed, constructed, and moved into.

PART 7:

WATERFRONT HOMES

5 MISTAKES TO AVOID WHEN BUILDING OR RENOVATING YOUR WATERFRONT HOME

When it comes to building or renovating your waterfront home, there are many variables to consider before construction begins. Without the proper planning you may lose out on potential living space–or even worse, you may not be able to build or renovate your waterfront property at all.

You have to be very careful of your flood elevations, v-zones, a-zones, x-zones, the FEMA regulations, engineering, flood regulations, deed restrictions, covenants, association regulations, wind loads, view easements, insurance availability, and so much more. Regulations are constantly changing as well.

Not only is this very complex for the inexperienced, you can often receive incorrect information (even from town, state or federal governments). You may also need approvals from multiple governments.

Furthermore, costs can also vary significantly. For example, depending on which zone your structure sits on, you may have to use engineered pilings, steel beams or girders. Rest assured, we are here to help you throughout the entire process.

Read this important chapter and when you are ready, schedule your o-obligation initial consultation with Reagan Homes.

MISTAKE #1: Not Knowing Your Zoning Regulations

There are different zones and different regulations and building guidelines for each type of zone in a town or municipality. There are also instances in which a single piece of land may fall within multiple zones.

Knowing where the zones are on the property is critical to not only mitigate costs but also allow you to have more living space. There are ways we can help you in your design to help save you money. For example, instead of attaching a deck to the home, we can have the deck be freestanding and sit just one inch away from the house. With the deck in the V-zone, and the house out of the V-zone, you will save significant money and encounter fewer restrictions.

Another example: We had a home that was originally built in the V-zone. We tore down the house and moved the home back toward the road a few feet. Now the home is out of the V-zone, and our client was able to build a bigger home with fewer restrictions. If the home had remained in the V-zone—two even just a portion of it--our client would have had only been able to have two levels.

Furthermore, the client saved on insurance, and the house did not have to be built in steel. We have even been involved in scenarios in which we had to push back on flood managers because they were interpreting the regulations incorrectly. In short, we are here to help you navigate the regulations.

MISTAKE #2: Not Looking at the Placement of Home

The placement of your home on a lot is always critical, especially with a waterfront home. For example, sometimes we can angle the home to get it out of the V-zone, which saves on building costs and frequently allows you to have more living space.

Depending on the placement of your home, often you can have a full basement, which means your utilities need not be located either on the first floor or in the attic.

MISTAKE #3: Not Looking at Multiple Options for a Garage

Often you cannot have a garage with a waterfront home. There can, however, be ways around that. Perhaps you can have a drive under the garage with waterproof elevators. In this scenario, we could build with steel piers so water can rush underneath and go back into the ocean.

MISTAKE #4: Not Looking at Surrounding Properties

Depending on your waterfront lot and desired square footage, you may or may not be able to build your dream home.

That being said, for some previous clients, we have been able to contact surrounding property owners and help our clients to purchase those properties. Those homes can then be torn down and combined into a single bigger lot. This may allow for a bigger home for you, while allowing us to place the home farther from the water, potentially out of the V-zone to save on building expenses while delivering more square footage.

MISTAKE #5: Not Utilizing 3D Renderings

One of the most common reasons why people want a waterfront home is for the views. Obviously the placement of your home will impact your views. We utilize 3D renderings to help you visualize the actual views you will have based on how the house is situated on the lot.

Even where you place windows and the types of windows you use will affect your views. By utilizing 3D renderings you can see your options and make a more informed decision when it comes to how you will layout and build your waterfront home.

Your waterfront home is a vision that's just waiting to be made a reality; there is no reason to wait. We can't wait to hear from you and learn more about the home you want to build or renovate on the water.

PART 8:

LUXURY LIVING

SIMPLIFY YOUR LIFE WITH HOME AUTOMATION FROM REAGAN HOMES

Regan Homes provides inspired solutions for automating your home, providing you with increased safety, security, and peace of mind while also saving you money on monthly bills.

We've all done it at least once and probably several times. You're in the car on the way to work. Or, even worse, on the way to the airport for a flight for a business trip or a long-awaited vacation. And you get that little tickle in your brain.

Did I lock the front door? Did I close the garage door? Did I turn the coffeemaker off? Did my daughter unplug her flat iron?

It's always something, right? But what do you do? Do you turn around and go home to deal with the what-ifs? Do you try to forget about it and assume your home is safe and secure? Do you call a neighbor to check it out? And wait, does that neighbor even have a key?

It doesn't have to be stressful. You can be assured your home is safe, you can save time, and you can save money. With smart home automation.

Reagan Homes and its team of experts have helped families up and down the Connecticut shore automate their homes, whether as a part of new home construction or the remodeling or renovation of an existing home.

Do you own a robotic vacuum? Or Amazon's Alexa device? If so, you're a part of the 90% of Americans who are already on the home automation bandwagon. But did you know that aside from simplifying your day, installing smart home systems and technology can save you upward of 30 minutes a day and as much as $2000 a year in household bills? If such facts sound appealing to you and you haven't yet put much thought into automating your home, perhaps now is the time to do so.

According to the Reagan Homes team, the absolute best smart home technologies to include in your new build or renovation project are systems that address energy management, home security, and lighting. Such systems are generally internet-connected, making it easy to control essential features of your home (and, by extension, your life) from your smartphone, tablet, or laptop.

Energy Management

Heating and cooling, especially while you are away from home, can be vexing and expensive. Maybe you've tried one of those thermostats you can schedule? Those buggy, complicated, and decidedly non-intuitive devices that hooked into your existing HVAC system and that you controlled through a panel on your wall? Those devices that were so difficult to use that they were barely worth your time or energy? Yeah. Today's smart technology energy management systems are nothing like that. With installation by Reagan Homes, today's advanced (and easy to use) systems ensure your home will always be comfortable and that you'll save money.

Home Security

More families than ever are opting in for automated security systems, which allow you to both manage and monitor alarms, cameras, door locks, and smoke and carbon monoxide detectors right from your phone. No longer will you have to turn your car around or cross your fingers and hope for the best.

Lighting

Automating your lighting is another avenue to saving money—and your sanity. Do you have family members who turn lights on in every room they enter? And yet it never occurs to them to turn them off? A smart home lighting system allows you to turn them off with a click of a virtual switch on your phone. Or perhaps you like to turn on outdoor lights at night for added security. No need to go back downstairs to flip the switches. Now you can do so from your tablet—in bed. Reagan Homes can install a system for you that allows you to set lighting timers and control motion detectors as well.

Additional Home Automation Options

As the market for such systems and devices grows, so do the innovations. Today you can buy smart appliances—including washers and dryers that connect to your wireless network and alert you to maintenance or repair needs and refrigerators that can help you keep on top of your shopping list.

Smart outlets also connect to your wireless network and are a favorite of the Reagan Homes team. Turn off that coffeemaker or hair appliance by shutting off the outlet, again, right from your phone.

Voice-controlled assistants (like Alexa or Google Assistant) and whole-home entertainment systems make life easy and streamline our daily schedules. They can also connect to our other automation systems and provide another means for controlling, for example, our thermostats and lights.

Clearly, the benefits of home automation are significant, from savings and safety to comfort and peace of mind. Whether you just want to dip your toes into automation or you're ready to do all the automation, you'll need an experienced, professional partner to lead the way. Reagan Homes would be happy to help.

To learn more, call the Reagan Homes team at (860) 962-6250
to learn more or visit www.ReaganHomes.com
to schedule a complimentary, no-obligation consultation.

SIMPLIFY YOUR LIFE WITH HOME AUTOMATION FROM REAGAN HOMES

Many homeowners are leaning toward Sonos as a whole-home music system. What's there not to love about the smart wireless multi-room audio? After all, it offers a unique way to enjoy your audio system. Let's go into the specifics, and you will see why you should consider opting for Sonos as your whole home audio system.

Features of Sonos:

Limitless Music Library

One of the most impressive features of Sonos as a whole-house audio system is its expensive streaming library. With Sonos, there is no limit to the songs you can listen to. You not only get to play songs from your playlist, but you can also stream music online and do it from any room in your home.

Simultaneous Playing

Another fantastic feature of Sonos is that it lets you play different music from different rooms. Imagine enjoying your favorite country music uninterrupted while your teen daughter rocks to pop music in her room and your teenage son listens to his favorite rap album. Different premium sounds can be streamed around your home. Nobody has to disturb the other.

Ease of Control

Sonos provides a way to manage your home audio with zero hassle. Once you install Sonos as your full home sound system, the rest is easy. You don't really need technical know-how to operate it. This audio system is designed with an intuitive app that lets you play–or stream–and control your music from your smartphone, tablet, or computer. Easy peasy, right?

Merging of Old and New Systems

You don't have to discard your existing audio system. You can integrate your new setup into your existing home automation system. A Sonos connect amp lets you convert your speakers into a music streaming device. It doesn't require much. Just attach the amplifier, and you can start streaming music to your room.

No Call Disturbance

Most wireless speaker systems are designed to stream music through Bluetooth connection. This means that your music gets to pause whenever a text or phone call comes into your phone. Not with Sonos. With Sonos, you can enjoy an uninterrupted music experience. Because it is designed to stream music through a wireless internet connection, the music keeps playing regardless of the notifications your phone receives.

Wireless System

Most full-home sound systems are set up with a lot of wires. Imagine how messy the display of wires can be. Not to think of the stress of dealing with so many wires and making sure they are plugged correctly. Sonos, on the other hand, has a wireless control system. It is controlled through an app that allows you to play music from your phone. This means considerably fewer wires and, subsequently, less mess.

Customizable For Any Home

Whether your home is very big or small, you can get a Sonos system that suits it. From Play:1 to Play:5, Sonos comes in a wide array of options that can fit into your needs. The team at Reagan Homes are well equipped to size up your home and determine what Sonos system is the right fit for your space. And if in the future you wish to expand the system, you can get it done.

Is It Worth The Money?

Maybe you're considering Sonos as an audio solution for your home, but you've checked online, and the price seems to scare you off. You doubt it's going to be worth it. Let's go on a short trip to revisit history. Sonos came about as a brand in 2005 at a time when home audio was wired systems with separate amplifiers, loudspeakers, and of course, cables. There were three major problems with the pre-existing systems:

- Audio can't stream across multiple rooms simultaneously - even the same stream
- They came in large components that occupied space
- They were designed with many cables that can be messy

Sonos as a company sought to solve these problems, and with every product release, they did. Following its success in the market, other brands such as Apple have developed their own multi-room audio systems. Most of them have actually priced their products higher than Sonos. Compared to its competitors, Sonos multi-room audio is designed to match every home's listening requirements, no matter how out of the box it might seem. But at the same time, it is not the most expensive on the market. There are even newly introduced speakers like the Play 1 that are more affordable.

Sonos as a brand offers a distinguishing level of usability, sound quality, and longevity. These three qualities make any Sonos system worth every penny. Sonos might not be suitable for people who are after cheap bluetooth speakers. But if you're looking for a blend of quality sound, convenience, and wireless functionality, Sonos is just for you.

How to Choose The Right Sonos Speakers for You

There is a wide variety of Sonos speakers, from the Move to the Beam. And recently, the company introduced more updated speakers. Our team of A/V experts at Reagan Homes is equipped to help you determine which Sonos set best suits your lifestyle needs.

With the right set of professionals, there is so much you can achieve with Sonos. There are a ton of ways you can configure your Sonos system. For example, you can configure yours to fill every room with music once you press a button. Sonos offers a distinguished level of home audio system. Get the right pick, and you'll be glad you did.

If you're looking to install whole home audio or upgrade your existing audio system to Sonos, please consider talking with the experienced Reagan Homes team. Having been in the business of building custom homes and renovating and remodeling existing homes all around Connecticut for over 30 years, Reagan Homes is undoubtedly your best go-to.

*To learn more, call the Reagan Homes team at (860) 962-6250
to learn more or visit www.ReaganHomes.com
to schedule a complimentary, no-obligation consultation.*

YOUR HOME THEATER DESIGN SIMPLIFIED

As streaming services continue to dominate home entertainment, more and more people see home theaters as a necessary investment. When movies could only be seen using film reels and giant projectors that required a certified operator, the home theater was the signature of a Hollywood mogul. But now, because of great advancement in technology, the home theater can be a wonderful addition to any home.

Whether you're building a new home or renovating an existing structure, incorporating plans for a home theater is easy and will increase the value of your home while also providing your family with a place to gather and watch the big game or binge your favorite TV shows.

What makes for a good home theater isn't necessarily cost, but planning. A home theater needs to be properly designed for the space available. In a renovation, the room available will dictate the type of screen, surround sound, and furniture you will be able to have in your home theater. If you are building a new home, the home theater should be designed with considerations for the type of equipment and furniture you have in mind.

Below we will discuss things to consider when designing your home theater. Keep in mind, we guide through this process as part of your renovation or new custom home.

Room Shape and Configuration

The size of your home theater is its most important design aspect. It will determine the size of the screen you can use and the configuration of the furniture.

The shape of your home theater is also important to consider. Furniture configuration and viewing angles will be dictated by this shape and must be kept in mind when designing a new home theater or converting an existing room. Public movie theaters are rectangular for a reason, so that the audience's attention is focused on the screen. The rectangle shape also helps the theater fit as many seats as they can in the available space. While you typically won't be maximizing the number of seats in your home theater, you will want to be able to arrange as many seats as is necessary with the proper viewing angles for the screen.

For a true "theater" feel, your baseline is a room that is 20' x 15' with high ceilings. A room this size will provide natural ambiance and true immersion in the film or sporting event being viewed. The room should be centrally located in the home and should have as few windows as possible—preferably none to prevent sound and light issues.

Finally, we mentioned "viewing distance" a few times. The typical rule for viewing distance is: take the length of the TV and double it and that gives you the minimum distance it should be viewed. Screens are different because they do not project light, they reflect it. The recommended viewing distance of a screen is roughly one-third larger than the size; so for a screen that is 100" the minimum viewing distance is 133".

Acoustic Treatment

A common misconception about home theaters is that they need to be "soundproofed." Ambient noise coming in is less likely in a private home than ambient noise bouncing around the theater itself. That's why your choice for walls, ceilings, and floors is important.

The ceiling of your home theater should be high to help with its overall aesthetic. The walls and ceiling do not need to be soundproofed, but they do need acoustic treatments that will absorb sound waves and prevent sound from bouncing around the room. The floor of your home theater should be carpeted wall-to-wall for the same reason.

Speakers should be inconspicuously placed and arranged by a professional to get the most out of the equipment and your experience. There are many options for equipment that will fit into any budget. We will cover that in the next section.

Different Types of Equipment

Now that you have your home theater space designed properly for viewing and sound, it is time to choose your equipment. Depending on your budget and your expectations, there is a wide range of options available.

Projectors

Projectors have come a long way from the early days of home theaters. Now they are available in HD and 4K and they offer a picture that is as crisp and clear as a TV. You do not need to buy the most expensive projector to get the best quality picture. Choose the projector that fits your screen and your budget. As a Reagan Homes client, our A/V team will help you choose the projector that makes the most sense for you.

TVs

One of the advantages of having a screen in your home theater used to be the size of the picture, but now they make televisions as large as some projection screens. An 85" TV may be a better fit for your home theater space than a projection screen. Just remember what we said about viewing distance. Always keep the proper viewing distance and angles in mind when you are making decisions about equipment and furniture.

Surround Sound

No home theater is truly wireless because each component needs a power source, but many surround sound speakers are now wireless and can be controlled with an app on your phone. We will be able to advise you on the correct speaker configuration for your home theater space and help ensure you buy equipment that fits in your space so you don't have speakers that are too powerful for the available area because it could ruin your experience.

Hire an Experienced Contractor

Whether you are building a new home or renovating an existing structure, hiring an experienced contractor will help get the most benefit from your home theater design.

If you end up choosing Reagan Homes for your remodel/renovation or new custom home we will be able to design and build the proper home theater space with the correct equipment so you and your family will get the most enjoyment out of your investment.

To learn more, call the Reagan Homes team at (860) 962-6250
to learn more or visit www.ReaganHomes.com
to schedule a complimentary, no-obligation consultation.

YOUR WINE STORAGE SHOULD BE AS PERSONAL AS YOUR WINE COLLECTION

Regan Homes provides inspired solutions for the preservation and enjoyment of wine.

According to a 2016 study (from the Wine Institute), the average American drinks more than three gallons of wine each year. That's a significant increase from just 20 years earlier. As a result, people who are considering building a new home (especially an upscale, luxury home), as well as those who are considering renovating an existing home, are asking for wine cellars—or, as is true in many instances, wine rooms.

Whether red or white, a hundred bottles or a thousand bottles, collector or consumer, building a wine cellar is a specialized project that requires a team of experts like those at Reagan Homes.

In the company's 30 years, its team has proven it can create any wine cellar atmosphere and functionality an enthusiast craves.

Sure, you want to show off your collection. But you're also protecting an investment when you build a specific area dedicated to storing your wine. Much creative and technical expertise goes into spaces tasked with the proper storage and aging of wine.

The experts at Reagan Homes bring to life their clients' vision through a collaborative and consultative approach.

If a wine space is something you are considering, you should give plenty of thought to how it will be used. To help meet your expectations, determine and work within your budget, and get the best out of your working relationship with your builder or contractor, That's the No. 1 issue that will inform planning and design. Will it be used only for storage? Or will tastings be held inside?

Perhaps you'll use it for entertaining on a grander scale. Imagine, for example, hosting dinner parties or even casual tasting events for friends in your wine cellar or wine room.

While basements are still popular (and strategic locations) for wine cellars, homeowners aren't limited to basements. Enthusiasts have converted closets, spaces under staircases, and areas more traditionally attached or linked to primary living spaces. No matter where you decide to locate your wine space, having a wine space will increase your home's value.

Regardless of size or style—sleek or classic, modern or traditional, stone or glass—building this type of amenity into any home requires ingenuity to incorporate the necessary mechanical equipment into a space that should also be breathtakingly beautiful. (Wine cellars and rooms with stone walls are particularly on-trend now. We also see a trend toward more sleek and sophisticated styles.)

Reagan Homes succeeds in delivering world-class custom wine cellars that exceed client expectations. State-of-the-art products and materials in cooling, construction, finishes, lighting, and racking are sourced from trusted partners, and installers offer unparalleled levels of craftsmanship and service.

It all adds up to wine storage and entertaining solutions to suit any taste.

To learn more, call the Reagan Homes team at (860) 962-6250 to learn more or visit www.ReaganHomes.com to schedule a complimentary, no-obligation consultation.

CIGAR SMOKER? WHAT YOU NEED TO KNOW ABOUT ADDING A WALK-IN HUMIDOR TO YOUR HOME.

Regan Homes provides beautiful yet practical solutions for cigar connoisseurs.

If you're a cigar connoisseur who has outgrown your stand-alone electric humidor and are looking to incorporate an impressive wow factor in your new custom home or as a part of a renovation or remodel of your existing home, a walk-in humidor is the way to go!

Walk-in humidors can be built in a variety of shapes and sizes and frequently resemble walk-in closets. They are designed to maintain a specific level of humidity that prevents your collection from getting too dry (in which your cigars will crack and be rendered useless) or too moist (which can cause mold).

Think of an at-home humidor as similar in purpose to a wine cellar. Both keep your investment—your passion—safe and sound while simultaneously impressing friends and acquaintances.

Both also require specific climates and technical features.

When professionals, like our Reagan Homes team, build your walk-in humidor, you can rest assured that your smokes will remain fresh and moist and that they will mellow and improve as they age.

What Does a Walk-In Humidor Entail?

To appropriately store and age cigars requires careful maintenance and specific conditions, including temperature and humidity. They may be simple structures without much in the way of design, or they may feature many special, artisanal touches. Typically, they run the gamut from the size of a closet to a divided or even a full room. Spaces without windows (light exposure can damage cigars) and near the center of the home (or in the basement) are typically the best options. The larger the space, the greater the cost to build and maintain.

Once you've decided on a location, sealing and lining, flooring, ventilation, shelving, and mechanicals are all further considerations.

Reagan Homes can add value and practicality to your project and make a daunting proposition easy with their vast experience building custom walk-in humidors. Their team is well-versed in how properly to seal your humidor to keep heat and light out and humidity in. They also know which system of humidification is best based on the size of your space. And they're on top of the trends and can explain the difference between Spanish cedar and okoumé for shelving, the purpose of a hygrometer, and why your walk-in humidor needs a ceiling fan.

Private walk-in humidors are the pride and joy of serious collectors. While once thought of as only for the wealthy and privileged, today—with the help of Reagan Homes—anyone can enjoy the benefits of their own private walk-in humidor.

To learn more, call the Reagan Homes team at (860) 962-6250
to learn more or visit www.ReaganHomes.com
to schedule a complimentary, no-obligation consultation.

THE CASE FOR
AN INDOOR POOL

You can have early morning laps, private swim lessons, and relaxing evenings poolside–365 days a year. The last resort you vacationed at has one. So does the high-end gym (or health spa) in your town. Your kids' school probably has one. And it seems like you can't throw a stone in Florida without hitting a home that has one. What are we talking about?

Indoor pools.

So why can't you have one? Or can you?

The mere idea of it feels dreamy. You can easily envision yourself doing laps early in the morning before the rest of the family has woken. Or late in the evening after a long, stressful day of work. So relaxing. The kids could have private swim lessons right at home. And can you imagine a better birthday party venue for your little ones?

It turns out that if you want an indoor pool badly enough, you can have one. It isn't the easiest, nor is it inexpensive to add a private indoor pool–your own indoor pool!–to your custom home plans or existing home. But it can be done, and there are plenty of reasons why you might want to. There's also a lot to consider and really think about before pulling the trigger.

If you are seriously considering adding an indoor pool, the first thing to do is discuss the subject with a reliable, experienced builder/installer who has done this before. Someone experienced can share in greater detail the process, the pitfalls, and so much more that you'd likely never think to ask on your own. Our Reagan Homes team are such builders, with over 30 years of experience building, renovating, and remodeling homes–many with indoor pools–throughout the southeastern Connecticut region.

What to Consider

The ability to control every aspect of the pool's environment is one of the biggest draws of the indoor pool. You can swim 365 days a year without having to clean up leaves or other outdoor debris. You can swim when it's dark outside, and you can even include skylights, lots of sliding glass doors and panels, or even a retractable roof if you want to. Perhaps you want your indoor pool area to have amenities such as changing rooms, exercise facilities, a sauna or steam room, showers, or a wet bar. Your imagination (and your budget!) are the only limits.

But it's also many of these same features that add cost and potential maintenance issues later on. First and foremost, you cannot have an indoor pool without its own HVAC system.

Consistent humidity and temperature levels are critical to comfort, air quality, and maintenance and upkeep costs. These systems are so crucial that, in many cases, they are the most expensive aspects of the entire pool-building process. An appropriate HVAC set-up also helps control evaporation.

Indoor pool owners should also invest in the best quality automatic pool cover they can afford, as this is the most effective means of reducing monthly energy costs.

Deck drainage is another consideration not to be overlooked, since puddling and wet decking can cause evaporation and increase humidity. Radiant flooring is also recommended as another way to address standing water and increase comfort.

And don't forget about a pool heater and lighting.

Indoor pools also have the potential to cause mold growth and freeze/thaw damage behind walls if structural framing isn't adequately addressed.

And then there is the matter of space? Do you have enough? For the pool, decking, and amenities you choose, and an equipment room? The most common sizes for indoor pools are 8' x 15', 12' by 24', and 30' by 50'. Additional space for decking, amenities, and equipment and mechanicals needs to be added to those size estimates.

It should also be noted that while an outdoor in-ground pool can be built and then enclosed and/or attached to a home at a future point, this is not recommended. For the cost, it would be better to start all over with new, indoor pool construction. Doing it right the first time and ensuring your plan includes all you want it to is more efficient and less costly in the long run.

Once you've considered the above factors and their costs, it's time to begin thinking about the kind of pool you want.

Types of Indoor Pools

Like outdoor pools, indoor pools are made of three types of materials: fiberglass, concrete or gunite, or vinyl liner.

Fiberglass

Fiberglass pools are a popular option. They are low maintenance and easy to clean, and manufacturers estimate owners spend as much as75% less time and money maintaining fiberglass pools than other pool types. Since they are manufactured shells, they are easy to install, and installation can be completed in a matter of a few days. They are also durable and attractive.

They do cost more, however, than vinyl liner pools, and they are not customizable in size or shape.

Concrete/Gunite

On the other hand, concrete pools are entirely customizable, which is their most significant advantage. They are also durable, and many consider them to be the most attractive option. But they require more hands-on maintenance; algae and mold growth can be a terrible problem because of the porous nature of concrete. Because of this concern, more chemicals are necessary to maintain concrete, which adds to both short- and long-term costs. Concrete pools also have longer-term maintenance requirements, including periodic acid washing and replastering. Due to the custom nature of every concrete pool, installation can take quite a bit of time. Also, a concrete pool's surface is abrasive and can be uncomfortable underfoot.

Vinyl Liner

This is the most affordable pool option, which makes it quite popular. Shapes and sizes can be customized (although customization adds to the cost). The biggest drawback to a vinyl liner pool is the frequency with which the liner needs to be replaced—once every 5 to 9 years. Over a lifetime, liner replacement costs can mean owners pay more than they would have if they had gone with a different option. While easy to clean and more comfortable underfoot than a concrete pool, this pool type does require more cleaning and maintenance than a fiberglass pool.

That's your basic indoor pool primer in a nutshell. (Did you know the technical term for an indoor pool is a natatorium?) If you can imagine an indoor pool as a part of your lifestyle and you have the budget for it but want to talk it over a little more or have questions, remember: we have decades of experience working on projects like this. And we would welcome the opportunity to share our knowledge with you and ensure the pool choices you make are the very best ones for you and your family.

TENNIS LOVER?

Have you considered adding a tennis court to your new home or as a part of a remodel or renovation?

Imagine what it could be like to have your own tennis court right there at home. You could play anytime you want—after work, early in the morning, and even late into the evening. The exercise tennis provides—for you and your family—is unrivaled. And if you have children, tennis is perfect for teaching them commitment, focus, and sportsmanship.

Adding a court to your custom home plan or your existing home as part of a renovation project isn't as unusual or unlikely as you may think. In fact, the Reagan Homes team, specializing in building and renovation projects throughout southeast Connecticut, has helped dozens of families achieve their tennis dreams by building residential tennis courts to meet every need. There are, of course, many factors to consider before you run out and buy a new racket.

Factors to Consider

Municipal zoning laws and homeowners' association rules may preclude you outright from adding a tennis court to your property. Even if allowed, specific regulations or restrictions may dictate fencing types and heights and lighting options (if lighting is permitted). Court size and surfacing may also be dictated. The first step is determining if you legally can install a court and the parameters for doing so. With more than 30 years of building experience in the region, Dave Reagan and his team are likely in the know about zoning and HOA requirements. But even if they aren't experts in the laws and bylaws of your specific town or subdivision, they'll get answers.

It's also critical to know before you get too far into such a project that you have the physical space to accommodate a tennis court. The minimum play area for a home doubles tennis court is 78 feet by 36 feet. For singles play, the recommended court size is 78 feet by 27 feet. Both of these recommendations come from the International Tennis Federation.

These court sizes do not include service area or sideline space, which will add approximately 14 feet to your court's width and 21 feet to the length. Depending on the geography of your court's anticipated location, you may also need to factor in additional square footage for drainage.

Ideally, you will also know which type of tennis court surface you would like before you begin such a project, as your court type will impact longevity, maintenance, and cost. Your options include:

- Grass: A classic that unfortunately requires a lot of expensive and time-consuming maintenance; may be unplayable in certain weather conditions.

- Clay: A less expensive option than some others in terms of construction, but one comes with time-consuming maintenance needs.

- Har-Tru: Often referred to as a clay court, Har-Tru courts are actually made of crushed stone. Har-Tru is an excellent option: porous, quick-drying, easy to maintain, cooler, and easier on players' joints.

- Asphalt or Concrete: The most popular option, a layer of acrylic or other cushioning material is typically added over the top of an asphalt or concrete base. While maintenance needs are relatively light—these courts can be pressure washed—they may require repainting and anti-algae treatments somewhat regularly.

Play on each of these courts—the way the ball moves and bounces—and the comfort players will experience differs significantly, as may installation requirements.

Your tennis court will require a fence—to keep balls in and for privacy. Chain-link fencing is an easy and relatively affordable option. But you'll also have to decide on windscreens (definitely recommended), backboards, and rebounders.

If you want and can have a lighted court, your lighting system and layout should be decided upon as early as possible since poles will need to be sunk into the ground during construction.

Estimating Costs

As you can see, many variables go into the cost of building a residential tennis court. In total, the following expenses may be included in the cost of your at-home tennis court:

- Backboards
- Excavation and construction
- Fencing and installation
- Lighting
- Maintenance
- Net system
- Permits
- Seating
- Storage (such as a shed)
- Surfacing materials
- Windscreens

If you decide to move forward with the installation of a private tennis court—whether as a part of your new, custom home or as an addition to an existing home—you are sure to be rewarded with years of enjoyment.

For the best results, be sure to work with an expert team, like Dave Reagan and the Reagan Homes team. Experienced builders and installers can help ensure that you've covered all your bases and made the best decisions for yourself, your family, and your property. A tennis court can enhance your lifestyle, increase your property values, and provide years of entertainment.

*To learn more, call the Reagan Homes team at (860) 962-6250
to learn more or visit www.ReaganHomes.com
to schedule a complimentary, no-obligation consultation.*

"BASKETBALL IS LIKE POETRY IN MOTION"

Serious players and fans deserve to have their own at-home basketball court.

It's a little-known fact, but shooting hoops can be a fantastic way to deal with stress. The rhythmic sound of the ball as you dribble against hardwood or asphalt. The whoosh as it soars through the net. Both help you think clearly, relaxing the mind and body. And, of course, basketball is just plain fun. If you have kids, all the better. Nothing like a rollicking game of HORSE after dinner to bring the family together. Or maybe your high school athlete could benefit from some extra playing time. And if that practice could happen at home—in your driveway, backyard, or even in indoor court—well, how cool would that be?

If you are a basketball player or fan or want to instill a love for the game in your children, you can have your own hoop or court at home, and it can be as simple or elaborate as you want. At-home basketball is just a part of a growing trend toward bringing fitness and recreation home. The experienced team at Reagan Homes has plenty of experience in constructing pools, tennis courts, golf simulators, and more for their custom home clients. The team also works with clients who are renovating or remodeling existing homes up and down the southeastern Connecticut shore.

If a basketball hoop or court is something you're interested in, read on to learn about the available space you'll need, the decisions that need to be made concerning products and quality, and more.

Outdoor Hoops and Courts

The considerations for playing basketball outdoors at home include court surfacing, hoop, rim, and backboard types, and backboard supports.

Space is perhaps the most critical element to consider if you're thinking about adding a court to your home. While a regulation NBA court is 50 feet by 94 feet, the average backyard court is 60 feet by 90 feet. A half-court is also an option and would measure 30 feet by 50 feet. Of course, if you're looking just to shoot around, a driveway hoop is a simple option.

Several playing surfaces are available and chosen based on the location of the court and personal preference.

Asphalt, for example, is the No. 1 most common outdoor surface. It is inexpensive and stands up well to potentially harsh weather conditions. It will, however, break down over time. Asphalt is prone to chipping and cracking and may require repair or resurfacing occasionally. It can also be hard to fall on, contributing to cuts, scrapes, and other injuries.

Multi-purpose plastic flooring has also become popular for outdoor basketball (and indoor basketball, too) and delivers excellent traction and safety as well as reliable bounce. It's a perfect option if you have room in your backyard for your playing area, as such flooring adapts easily for soccer, street hockey, tennis, and volleyball as well. Multi-purpose flooring consists of a smooth concrete slab topped with modular snap-together polypropylene plastic tiles. The tiles come in numerous colors, stand up well against the elements, and are less hard on the body.

High-end advanced multi-purpose flooring is another option. Such options typically consist of a layer of rubber sandwiched between the concrete slab and plastic tiles. This system offers better shock absorption, increased sound dampening, and enhanced durability and moisture resistance.

As for the hoop itself, three main options exist—in-ground, portable, and wall-mounted. If you plan to live in your home for the foreseeable future, an in-ground hoop, one that is set in concrete and properly leveled, might be the right choice for you. It's more stable and secure and recommended for players who are serious about the game.

Portable hoops are currently the most popular option, and they are easy to transport and install. They typically require that the base of the hoop be filled with sand or water to ensure stability. The primary drawback to portables is that they are more prone to movement and vibrations (both of which can negatively impact performance) than in-ground or wall-mounted hoops.

Portables have also taken a bite out of the market for wall-mounted hoops due to their ease and convenience. But don't count wall-mounted hoops out. They are more stable (since they are attached to a building) and are an excellent choice for driveway courts.

Rims are another critical element of your outdoor basketball court. Most include a breakaway mechanism to relieve tension and minimize the risk of breaking the backboard when the ball is dunked. Rim options include standard, exposed spring breakaway rims, and enclosed spring breakaway rims.

Standard rims have fallen somewhat out of favor with the introduction to the market of breakaway rims. Unfortunately, standard rims tend to bend, break, or warp over time, especially with dunking. If you anticipate a lot of training or playing with only lay-ups and regular shots, a standard rim may be an option to consider.

Most of the rims sold today are of the exposed spring variety. That doesn't necessarily mean they are the best option for everyone, though. In humid climates, the exposed springs may rust, and this rim style frequently results in play that is too bouncy. Repeated dunking will still wear down the mechanism.

Enclosed spring rims are the top shelf of basketball rims. At the higher-end, you'll have a set-up similar to those in professional arenas because of the design and quality materials that go into these rims. And the enclosed springs are much less exposed to the elements, thus extending this style of rim's overall lifespan.

There are also three main options for backboards: acrylic, polycarbonate, and tempered glass.

A quality, durable acrylic backboard is a middle-tier product that delivers more bounce than polycarbonate, which is an appropriate choice for a simple recreational driveway hoop. Polycarbonate backboards are constructed of rigid plastic. While polycarbonates hold up well against the elements, play performance is less impressive, with less bounce and less forceful returns.

Tempered glass is the choice for serious players, used in gyms throughout the country, and contributes to the best possible gameplay. Still, tempered glass is glass, and a glass backboard is more likely to break than one made of polycarbonate or acrylic plastic.

Backboards come in multiple sizes and shapes, too. While most are square, fan-shaped backboards are also available. Square-shaped blackboards are available in sizes between 42 inches and 72 inches (which is regulation). Regardless of the materials a backboard is made of, choosing one that includes padding is the safest option.

You might also consider a hoop that is easily adjustable for height (handle and crank models are a breeze to adjust). Most hoops adjust from 7.5 to 10 feet (which is regulation).

Indoor Hoops and Courts

If you can swing an indoor court, it's an option worth considering. An indoor court can grow and adapt to the needs of your family, allow you to control myriad aspects of the basketball-playing environment, and allow for play 365 days a year.

Generally speaking, you have all the same options as an outdoor hoop, except flooring.

Hardwood is an excellent option, but not for outdoor playing. Most hardwood basketball courts are made of maple and are easily damaged by exposure to sun, rain, and other weather conditions.

It seems that most indoor hoops are wall-mounted. If you opt to go with an indoor court and wall-mounted hoops, you should add edge padding to your backboard. Padding protects against injuries, including sprains and fractures, that could otherwise result from forceful confrontations with the backboard.

With a home basketball hoop or court, you can provide your family with an excellent option for exercise and fitness and teach your children the ins and out of not only the game but sportsmanship in general. If you're a lover of the game, don't you deserve the best b-ball experience possible?

If you'd like to learn more or chat with someone who has experience constructing and installing home basketball courts, remember: The Reagan Homes team has decades of experience working on projects like this. They'd love the opportunity to share their knowledge with you and ensure that, whether indoor or outdoor, the choices you make for your home basketball court are the very best ones for you and your family.

To learn more, call the Reagan Homes team at (860) 962-6250
to learn more or visit www.ReaganHomes.com
to schedule a complimentary, no-obligation consultation.

YOU CAN PLAY EVERY DAY

How would you like to play St. Andrews today, Pebble Beach on Wednesday, and the PGA National Course on Saturday? With your own in-home golf simulator, you can!

If you're serious about your golf game, you can have a golf simulator added to your new custom home or an existing home, and you don't have to be Rory McIlroy or Dustin Johnson to enjoy this technology. You can choose from various options that come with as many or few bells and whistles as you want. Most golf simulators are, um, pricey. But for anyone really into the game, a simulator is worth the money; you'll enjoy countless hours of practice and pleasure.

Creating the space or "studio" for your simulator and installing the gear is something with which my team and I have plenty of experience. For more than 30 years, Dave has been working with homeowners to build their dream homes and retrofit existing homes to achieve the same goal.

Due to increased interest and access, the market for home golf simulators is bigger than ever before, and golfers should be able to find an appropriate match at almost any budget, from $1,000 to $70,000.

Overview

If possible, most golfers prefer to have a permanent dedicated space for their simulator set-up. (Although many enjoy the flexibility, versatility, and lower costs associated with portable models.) Space is the only essential that needs to be met before one begins choosing components. You will need a space that measures at least 12 feet long by 12 feet wide. The minimum ceiling height for most systems is 9 feet. A good rule of thumb is to grab your driver and take it to the room or space you're considering using. Take a few slow backswings to see if your club hits the ceiling. If so, you'll need to find a spot with more clearance. If not, you're ready to research the options and start making decisions.

Your golf studio will need the following items: a golf simulator or a launch monitor with golf simulation, a computer or iPad to run your simulation software, a golf mat, a simulator screen, and a projector. Some people prefer to use a golf net rather than a screen and projector, which is a valid option. Some manufacturers offer kits that include all these items, making the buying and set-up almost effortless. The bottom line is that there is no cookie-cutter solution for choosing a simulator; yours can be custom built to suit your needs and meet your desires.

And rest assured, it's unlikely you'll ever get bored with or tired of the selection of courses you can play; most simulators offer more than enough famous courses to keep your interest, and several offer software updates that add new courses regularly. Some even allow you to create your courses, both from scratch and by mixing and matching holes from various courses.

Let's take a quick look at the various elements that will make up your golf space:

Mats

Available at multiple price points, your hitting mat is something you should not cut corners on. More expensive to manufacture than you might expect, mats are truly essential to your experience. A top-quality, premium mat will last longer and help prevent injuries. Costs vary from $300 to almost $1,000.

Strong, reliable, and built to last, Fairway Series Golf Mat from Shop Indoor Golf is an excellent mid-priced product.

TrueStrike Golf Hitting Mats, meanwhile, are frequently named a top premium pick for their realistic feel and silicone gel insert.

Projectors

With projectors, it's important to recognize that you get what you pay for! Lower-priced options are likely to frustrate with longevity, quality, and usability issues. The Optoma EH412ST Golf Simulator Projector, however, is an excellent option that will impress with a bright image and vivid color. This projector is multi-functional, renders HD content perfectly, comes with a powerful built-in speaker, and features an auto shut-off for energy savings.

Golf Simulator and/or Launch Monitor

So what exactly is the difference between these, and do you need just one or both? First of all, every simulator is also a launch monitor, but the reverse is not true. With a simulator, you hit a ball, and the simulator simulates how your shot plays out on a screen, projector, or laptop. The launch monitor, either built into the simulator or separately, determines the distance of your shot, virtual or otherwise. Some might opt for a launch monitor only for the sake of convenience; launch monitors are more portable and easier to pack and store. Launch monitors are quite accurate, with high-end versions expected to be accurate within about 5 yards. Mid-range models are accurate within approximately 10 yards. Simulators will deliver similar accuracy.

If you think a launch monitor alone might be for you, be sure to check out the SkyTrak Golf Launch Monitor, the first and only one of a few launch monitors that is also a simulator. The SkyTrak is as accurate as top-of-the-line commercial quality monitors at a far more consumer-friendly price. It measures, among other data points, total distance, clubhead speed, sidespin, roll distance, and angle of descent. The SkyTrak Golf Launch Monitor is one of the best investments you can make in your game, and it is a highly enjoyable tool.

If you want the virtual experience of seeing your ball soar and land on the 17th hole at Pebble Beach in addition to obtaining your stats and data points, The Golf Club is sure to please. The high-definition graphics—the very best available—are stunning, and the software includes an astonishing 92,000+ golf courses. Incredible details, like player apparel and mowing patterns, are the icing on the cake.

Screen

An impact screen or net is necessary to prevent damage to your walls from errant balls. You may even wish to put netting around your impact screen for the best possible coverage. Rain or Shine Golf's SwingBay Golf Simulator Screen & Enclosure includes both features in one package. It's big, solidly made, and attractive. It measures a whopping 7'3" tall and 9'8" wide, blacks out external light, and was developed to withstand balls moving at as much as 250 miles per hour!

All-in-One Packages

As previously mentioned, many companies also make packages available that include all of the required elements. The absolute best of the best (with a price that's at the top of the range) is the Golfzon Vision Premium, chosen by Golf Digest as Best Golf Simulator three years in a row. The Vision Premium includes the following benefits and features:

- Multi-surface hitting mats
- High-definition projector
- Moving swing plate
- Smart auto tee-up
- Online community so you never have to "play" alone
- Swing replay
- 190 world-class course simulations with no-added-cost updates
- Live online festivals and events
- Junior tee-box (perfect for teaching your children the game)
- Up to six players at a time
- 72-hour maximum build-out time

Golfzon makes the bestselling golf simulators in the world. And according to Golf Digest, among the package's biggest draws is that "While most simulators have a stationary, one-surface mat, Vision Premium boasts a moving platform, which provides uphill, sidehill, [and] downhill lies along with three hitting surfaces (fairway, rough, sand)." It's a luxury golf experience at home.

With a home golf simulator, you can play golf regardless of the weather, improve your game, and entertain friends and family. If you're a lover of the game, don't you deserve the most enjoyable simulated golf experience possible?

If you'd like to learn more or chat with someone who has experience constructing and installing in-home golf spaces, remember: Our team has decades of experience working on projects like this. We'd love the opportunity to share their knowledge with you and ensure that the choices you make for your golf simulator are the very best ones for you and your family.

To learn more, call the Reagan Homes team at (860) 962-6250
to learn more or visit www.ReaganHomes.com
to schedule a complimentary, no-obligation consultation.

PART 9:

OUTDOOR LIVING

USING FIRE TO ADD BEAUTY
TO YOUR LANDSCAPE

There is something so comforting about gathering with your friends and family in a space with the beauty and warmth of a roaring fire. Whether that's toasting off ingredients for s'mores around a fire pit, or livening up a pool party with fire bowls, a fire element can take your landscape to the next level. It also gives you as a homeowner plenty of creative liberty over your space in a new and exciting way.

It can be tricky to choose what suits your needs best with so many options available. But each piece can add a charming aspect to your landscape with a simple touch.

Fire Pits

A popular choice for outdoor entertaining is the ever-useful fire pit. It provides a place for leisure where you and your guests can gather around and enjoy the warmth and comfort of the fire. They also provide an interesting focal point for any parties or family gatherings you might have.

They can be used as a place to talk and tell stories, or you can have your own campfire cookout right in your backyard. They come in a variety of forms that vary in style and shape so they will suit the aesthetic of your backyard. It can be constructed with stonework, metal, a mixture of both, or even marble.

Fire Bowls

A fire bowl is ideal for nearby a pool as it is less of a center point for gathering and works more as a place for casual warming. Once you've been swimming all day and a chill starts to settle in they can be hugely beneficial. They also add a gentle, warm ambiance while you're grilling or enjoying the pool.

With this little added element you can change the atmosphere of your backyard entirely. Not only does it add function, but charm as well. They can be made of ceramic, stone, tile, metal, and other common materials.

Fire Tables

The appeal of a fire table has everything to do with function. It isn't just somewhere you gather to sit and talk, but where you can have your meals and entertain in a comfortable and unique way. These can either run on natural gas or propane and have a multitude of sleek and modern styles to suit the aesthetic needs of your landscape.

Imagine all of the evenings you will spend with friends or family enjoying a meal around the warmth and ambiance of a proper fire.

Woodburning

There are many options to consider if you're wanting to go the route of a wood burning piece in your backyard. There are wood-burning stoves, fireplaces, and of course the trusty fire pit that can add a rustic charm to any home. There are even portable wood burning appliances such as the SoloStove or Breo which can help your fire be virtually smokeless. The scent and the crackling of a wood fire can be very enticing for you, your family and guests.

How Reagan Homes Can Help

Regardless of what exactly you're looking for to liven up the landscape of your backyard, we know how to help. Our expertise is making a simple house into a home by adding your creativity into the mix. Reagan Homes is the premier home builder, consultant, and renovator in New London and Middlesex counties. It is our passion and our mission to provide our clients with homes that will serve them, their families, and their children for years to come.

As part of your new custom home or existing home renovation/remodel, we are happy to guide you in selecting the fire pieces to beautify your landscape.

To learn more, call the Reagan Homes team at (860) 962-6250
to learn more or visit www.ReaganHomes.com
to schedule a complimentary, no-obligation consultation.

ADD A SWIMMING POOL
TO YOUR CUSTOM HOME OR
REMODEL RENOVATION

Reagan Homes provides inspired solutions for the addition of a swimming pool to your outside living and entertainment area.

Perhaps you've always had this dream, this image in your head, of what life would be like for you and your family if you had a backyard pool. From pool-side birthday parties to cookouts to cocktail parties, many people in Connecticut share that same vision.

Reagan Homes and its team of experienced experts have helped families up and down the shore add this summertime amenity to their homes, whether they are new construction or as part of a remodeling/renovation project of an existing home.

In addition to the good times you are sure to have with a pool, they also provide leisure, luxury, and a healthier lifestyle for many. Swimming also happens to be one of the most popular outdoor activities in the country. Swimming improves flexibility, can help with weight loss, and can improve your muscle strength and tone.

And let's not discount the mental health benefits of swimming. Biologists and mental health professionals suggest that people "feel better when they interact with water." According to marine biologist Wallace J. Nichols, interacting with water can put us in a "mildly meditative state characterized by calm, peacefulness, unity, and a sense of general happiness and satisfaction with life."

Today's swimming pools often have an adjacent tanning ledge where you can have chaise lounges right within about 12" of water. Or maybe you want to have a hot tub as part of the pool or separate from the pool so you can enjoy the hot tub all year round, even in the colder winters we experience in New England.

There are many options you can add on to customize your backyard swimming oasis. For example, typically with rectangular shaped pools you could have an auto cover on your pool to help retain heat and allow you to cover and uncover your pool with a click of a button. An autocover also adds additional safety to your pool. You can add special lighting, water or fire features to enhance your pool area even more.

Make no mistake about it, adding a pool to your custom new home or existing home is not a decision to be taken lightly or without considerable forethought. Pool ownership has exploded over the last 50 years, and approximately 10.4 million households in the U.S. have them. But custom, in-ground pools are not inexpensive. Depending on the style, materials, and your personal specifications, in-ground pools can cost anywhere from $30,000 to $100,000 or more.

From gunite to fiberglass to vinyl liner pools, we have experience in working with the best pool contractors in Connecticut. Our team can discuss the advantages and disadvantages of each type of pool with you as well as the myriad of options that come with building your new pool. We also can incorporate an outdoor kitchen, dining area and ample patio space for your outdoor environment.

While once rectangular and kidney-shaped pools dominated, today there's no limit to the possibilities. If you can imagine it, it can be constructed. From saltwater to natural to chlorinated pools, we have relationships with the best pool contractors in Connecticut.

Even if your yard is small or irregularly shaped—or if you desire something that is truly one of a kind—Reagan Homes can help bring unlimited fun to your life and your home, both inside and of course outside.

Overall, we can help you determine if a pool is right for you and help design and build the pool of your dreams as part of your new custom home or existing home renovation.

*To learn more, call the Reagan Homes team at (860) 962-6250
to learn more or visit www.ReaganHomes.com
to schedule a complimentary, no-obligation consultation.*

OUTDOOR KITCHEN OPTIONS

Cooking is quite literally what keeps human beings going, and the great outdoors is known to enhance your living, so if you add them together, you're sure to be getting an awesome experience.

Outdoor kitchens are in vogue these days, and why wouldn't they be? They combine so many things that make life worthwhile, and you'll be open to more benefits so long as you learn how to do it the right way.

Our team of experts are here to guide you in what types of appliances you can have for excellent outdoor kitchen experience.

Here are some of the appliances you should consider adding to your outdoor kitchen.

Possible Appliances

Grill

The grill is one of the most popular and, frankly, vital items all outdoor kitchens need. The grill has been respected for decades, and rightly so. Grills come in different shapes and sizes, so before choosing one, you should assess whether it will be a comfortable fit for your backyard. Grills are super useful for an array of cooking styles.

Smoker

Smokers are super popular at the moment, but they're also versatile. They imbue meat and fish with a better taste, and they have become staples of many outdoor kitchens. It's worth noting that cooking with a smoker allows you to create food that has a hickory or barbecue flavor that cannot be achieved when you are simply cooking on a grill. That's just the tip of the iceberg of possibilities.

Refrigerator

Refrigerators come in different shapes and sizes, and you should consider the quantity of food and beverages you anticipate storing in your outdoor refrigerator. Don't hesitate to go for high quality as that's the longest-lasting legacy of a fridge.

EVO Grill

An EVO Grill is also a fantastic addition to your outdoor kitchen that you should consider. The EVO has been described as the future of grilling. EVOs may run on propane or natural gas. Some of the best things about EVO Grills are the electronic push-button ignition and the ability to control the temperature with remarkable ease.

Green Egg

Next on the list is the highly versatile Green Egg, which is easy to use, quality is assured, and it is incredibly durable, making it a staple of outdoor kitchens for years to come.

Kegerator

A Kegerator is a refrigerator that has been designed to store and dispense beer, coffees, teas or wine.

Ice Maker

You most likely will need ice for drinks when having a backyard cookout or gathering. In less than 10 minutes, an outdoor ice maker can produce ice for a couple of drinks and a little under an hour to get enough ice to fill a bucket.

Power Burner

Everything in an outdoor kitchen needs to be able to help minimize time and but maximize the experience. That's why you need a burner of some sort, preferably a power burner. A power burner helps produce a controlled flame by mixing a fuel gas such as acetylene, natural gas, or propane with an oxidizer such as the ambient air or provided oxygen, allowing for ignition and combustion. A power burner can get the work done of boiling water in record time compared to a traditional side burner.

Hood

A hood may be necessary over your grill in your outdoor kitchen if your outdoor kitchen is in a covered environment. You don't want to smoke out your guests. A hood can help provide proper ventilation.

Pizza Oven

Now it's easy to make pizza yourself in the comfort of the gentle breeze outside your back door. A pizza oven can heat up as high as 900°F. Your pizza will be ready quickly and cooked to perfection in your outdoor kitchen.

Warming Drawer

If you're looking for something to hold and warm your dishes while you're preparing additional food, then a quality warming drawer might be another terrific addition to your outdoor kitchen.

Warming drawers allow you to cook multiple dishes simultaneously, and the best part is that everything will come out at the proper temperatures all at once.

Sink

Having a sink as part of your outdoor kitchen to clean and prep foods is helpful.

Factors You Should Consider

Location

In an ideal scenario, your outdoor kitchen will not be very far from your indoor kitchen so you can carry things from the inside to the outside efficiently. You may also require less appliances if your outdoor kitchen is closer to your indoor kitchen.

The Stations

All the stations in your outdoor kitchen are vital. We can help you map out space for areas to prep, cook, serve, and clean.

Outdoor Dining

It's necessary to add outdoor dining furniture to your list of considerations for setting up your outdoor kitchen and living space.

Entertainment

Unlike in an indoor kitchen, entertainment may be something to consider when setting up a proper outdoor kitchen space. From music to movies to sporting events investing in an outdoor TV or built-in speakers can help make your outdoor space even more enjoyable.

If you are interested in an outdoor kitchen as part of your existing home renovation or new custom home, we are here to help design and build your amazing outdoor living space.

To learn more, call the Reagan Homes team at (860) 962-6250 to learn more or visit www.ReaganHomes.com to schedule a complimentary, no-obligation consultation.

ARE OUTDOOR TVS WORTH THE COST AND EFFORT?

Reagan Homes can help you create the outdoor living space of your dreams as part of your existing home renovation or new custom home.

Family movie nights under the stars.

Summertime sleepovers and birthday parties.

Football season games and cookouts.

Netflix and chilling with a beer and a burger after a long day at work.

These are just a few of the reasons you might consider adding a television to your outside entertainment area.

The team at Reagan Homes fields plenty of questions about this very subject, such as:

- Is it practical to have a TV outdoors?
- How can I keep an outdoor TV safe from theft and the elements?
- Do I need to buy a special television for outdoor use?

The fact that watching television outside on your patio is becoming a more popular trend shouldn't be a surprise. As our outdoor living spaces continue to become extensions of our indoor spaces, it's a natural progression. And Reagan Homes has helped dozens of families—both those building new custom homes and those doing significant renovations and remodels—to live their best possible lives outside in the fresh air and sunshine.

Do I need to buy a special TV for outdoor use? Or will any old set work?

It seems like every year, television manufacturers are adding new bells and whistles to their products. And the prices for sets are, more often than not, astonishingly low. OLED, 4K, HDR. There's a whole alphabet out there to learn about.

Of course, there are televisions explicitly made for use outdoors. While they might not come with all of the perks of some of today's indoor televisions, they are made to meet specific criteria, and if you can swing the higher prices that come with outdoor sets, it's likely worthwhile to do so.

Outdoor televisions feature screens that are brighter than traditional TVs to ensure that people can watch even in the lightest and brightest of conditions. They likely also come with anti-glare and anti-reflective screens to combat often harsh natural light.

Outdoor televisions are also waterproof. They need to be in light of the unique conditions—including cold days, hot days, dust, insects, rain, salt air, and snow—they could come in contact with.

Surprisingly though many don't include speakers. You'll most likely require a separate soundbar and speakers for your outdoor living room if it's to include a television.

Can you use a regular TV meant for indoors if you really want to? You can, and doing so is a much more economical approach, but you'll have to keep your expectations a bit lower as it may be more challenging to see the screen well, especially in direct sunlight.

And you'll need to compensate for an indoor TV's lack of weatherproofing by adding a weatherproof case or cabinet. Humidity and evening dew can wreak havoc on the electronics of an indoor TV which will certainly shorten the lifespan of your indoor TV even if it is under a covered porch or veranda.

What About Security?

First of all, a dedicated outdoor television, whether produced for outdoor use or not, should be securely bolted to a wall or similar surface. Doing so will prevent it from being stolen but also from falling or being knocked over.

And for a variety of reasons, your outdoor entertainment area should be as hidden as possible from prying eyes. If you have a home security system that includes outdoor camera monitoring, it's worthwhile to have one set up to help secure this area and help deter someone from swiping your TV.

All in all, investing in your outdoor living space by adding a television is likely to bring hour upon hour of family entertainment. As for what kind of TV you use and what the area looks like, well, you're only limited by your imagination.

Reagan Homes has the experience to guide you through the process and ensure your outdoor viewing meets your needs and exceeds your expectations. We have a team of A/V experts to help.

To learn more, call the Reagan Homes team at (860) 962-6250
to learn more or visit www.ReaganHomes.com
to schedule a complimentary, no-obligation consultation.

COVER YOUR LUXURY OUTDOOR LIVING AREA WITH A POWERED OR NON-POWERED PERGOLA

Installing a pergola certainly raises the bar for your outdoor living area. Beyond beautiful aesthetics, an outdoor living space with a pergola serves as a breathable cover of shade. From more traditional pergolas to even pergolas that feature louvers that open and close with a remote control, there are many choices available.

Generally speaking, pergolas improve the overall outdoor appeal of your home and create a more comfortable environment. Today, you can choose from many types of pergolas.

Different pergolas come with specific pros, cons, and uses. So, make sure to get the pergola that caters to your needs.

Keeping that in mind, let's take a look at the benefits, uses, and design ideas of installing a pergola to your outdoor living space:

Best Design Ideas and Uses:
Learn to Make the Most Out of Your Pergola

You can install a pergola in virtually any outdoor living space. For instance, you can add a pergola alongside a balcony deck, pool deck, outdoor eating area, and even a fire pit. With more outdoor settings you can have more options to enjoy different types of pergolas.

Apart from the aesthetic beauty of the pergolas, they come in various functions and features. For example, most homeowners choose to install a pergola to create added space for verandas and increase the flow of open air while providing some shade.

If you enjoy gardening, installing a pergola can create more vertical space into your garden. You can practically create a beautiful garden up in the air and hang your favorite plants and flowers. Plus, you can design and restructure the ceiling boards of pergolas for even more visual appeal.

Curtain Call

You can install a bohemian or culture-specific curtain with mounted beams in your pergola. You can tie the curtains to let in the sunshine and airflow for a more private and romantic outdoor living space. After that, you can add wood chairs and potted plants to add more beauty to your outdoor setting.

Side Curtains

Invoke elegant charm by installing a pergola with light white or gray curtains to one or both sides. If you want more privacy, you can get a thicker material with a variety of bold colors. Just make sure your curtain material matches your specific needs.

Slide and Sleek

Another way to modernize your outdoor space setting is through the installation of wood-based pergola with sleek lines. You can make the roof cover retractable to control exactly how much moonlight or sunlight you want to pass in the pergola.

Modern Minimalist

Create a modern outdoor look with pergola essentials such as shade, seating, and privacy. In fact, the minimalist approach often appeals more to homeowners than heavily designed and structured pergola designs.

Geometric Screens

If you want to stay away from the usual pergola designs, you can opt for more imaginative and creative geometric-style roof and screens in your pergola.

Garden Pod

If you want to take the privacy to the next level, install a corner-style garden pod pergola. It is essentially a pergola-based traditional box that fits in a mid-size or small backyard.

Understand the Power of Powered Pergola First

A motorized or powered pergola with the help of a louvered roof can expand your outdoor living space. Your roof louvers can rotate at 120 degrees, which means you can control exactly how much shade, sunlight, and flow of air you want in the space with a single click of a button. Similarly, you can count on an automatic rain sensor to close your louvers at the start of any rain.

As much as the traditional approach to pergolas matter, the modern powered pergolas are in a league and class of their own. It may come as a surprise to you, but powered pergolas can withstand harsh weather conditions, speedy winds, and mountainous snow loads. Plus, you can enhance your powered pergola with more add-ons such as heaters, screens, lighting, gutter systems, and more.

Powered Pergolas: What are the Main Benefits?

Here are the essential benefits of installing a pergola to your outdoor living space:

Improved Home Value

Whether you want to install an outdoor pergola to your backyard, pool area, or garden, it will add more value to your home. Outdoor living was already popular, but during the pandemic crisis, people now want to make their backyard, pool area, and garden more spacious, comfortable, and beautiful.

A pergola offers a heightened sense of relaxation in a finished outdoor setting. It combines the architectural beauty of your home and nature to create a unique look. In time you view the addition of pergola as an investment.

Increased Privacy and Protection

You can't enjoy outdoor space without shades that offer privacy and protection. In fact, most people avoid spending more time in outdoor space because of the lack of privacy. Your pergola, however, serves as your own private dome. It offers you a personal space to create and think freely.

You can opt for a drape-style pergola to create even more privacy. You can also get a cabana-style pergola for minimalist appeal and still maintain privacy.

Serves as an Another Home Extension

One of the highlights of installing a pergola is that it extends the usability and flow of your outdoor space. Whether you select a free-standing or attached pergola, it will create a separate outdoor extension with your home. When you have a dedicated defined space, you can use a pergola for outdoor entertainment and create seamless home-to-pergola outdoor transitions.

The Ultimate Outdoor Space Upgrade

A pergola can turn your traditional and rustic outdoor space into a modern getaway. Once you figure out the details to install a new pergola into your backyard, it would represent a far better and bigger upgrade than an uncovered outdoor patio. The newest pergola designs include modern, classic, and contemporary options. You can try a combination of pergola designs to create the outdoor living space of your dreams.

You can get a pergola in metal or wood structure without having to worry about constant maintenance. But even a simple pergola has the power to transform your entire outdoor living space. Despite build quality and structure, the benefits outweigh the limitations.

So, if you've been reluctant about installing a new pergola into your outdoor space, now might be the perfect time to add one. The modern pergola options allow you to expand on top of your old school pergola designs. Whether it's the absence of latticed walls or louvered roof, you should be able to find what you're looking for.

Living with a pergola is an experience you deserve to enjoy.

If you want to incorporate any type of pergola into your remodel/renovation or new custom home, Reagan Homes is eager to guide you through the process and options.

To learn more, call the Reagan Homes team at (860) 962-6250 to learn more or visit www.ReaganHomes.com to schedule a complimentary, no-obligation consultation.

UPSCALE ADDITIONS
TO YOUR OUTDOOR KITCHEN

Cabinets for Your Outdoor Kitchen

If you want the best—backed by a lifetime warranty—then you want Werever Outdoor Cabinets for your outdoor kitchen.

According to the National Kitchen and Bath Association, of all the 2020 "quarantine home improvement projects" completed, 76% were outdoor kitchens.

Increasing one's home value while also enjoying every possible moment outside is a trend that isn't likely to go away anytime soon. From outdoor TVs to spectacular fire pits to upscale commercial ovens and grills and custom swimming pools, outdoors is the place to be and a natural extension of the trend toward blurring the lines between indoors and out.

Dave Reagan and his team of designers, builders, and installers have decades' worth of the kind of experience you need if such a project is on your home improvement list or it's something you'd like to add to that custom dream house you're planning to build.

And while the Reagan Homes team can advise and answer questions about any part of creating an outdoor oasis, they strongly suggest you don't overlook the importance of the cabinetry that will form the bones of your outdoor kitchen. There are plenty of options available, but the cabinets Reagan Homes recommends more than any other— the cabinetry they trust the most—is Werever Outdoor Cabinets.

Werever cabinets are built in the USA to last a lifetime and are backed by a lifetime warranty. The company's weatherproof line of HDPE (UV-stabilized High-Density Polyethylene) is virtually indestructible and available in 12 colors and five wood-grain options. The colors are solid and go all the way through the boards and will never fade. They will look as good at year 10 as they do on day one.

Werever cabinets are also available in eight door styles, and custom design is an option They are the superior cabinetry product intended for outdoor use and can be found in outdoor kitchens, boats, greenhouses, parks, and zoos.

And yet, many builders and designers may not be in the know about Werever. They might still recommend stainless steel for your outdoor kitchen or other outdoor cabinet needs. But not even stainless steel can compare. In potentially challenging climates and under the most difficult environmental conditions, Werever Outdoor Cabinets will come out on top every time.

Before you consider stainless steel, you should know about the following:

- They are not inexpensive.
- They don't offer much in aesthetics and customization is mostly nonexistent.
- More is required for maintenance than with Werever Cabinets.
- Stainless is susceptible to corrosion and pitting.
- Edges are sharp and potentially dangerous.
- Stainless may dent and scratch.
- Stainless cabinets are noisy.
- When you factor in the labor required to maintain stainless steel, you most likely are not saving much money in comparison to Werever cabinets.

Werever Cabinets are a far superior product engineered specifically for outdoor use and backed by that lifetime warranty. They are super-easy to clean, stain-resistant, and impervious to the elements, insects, and critters. They don't heat up in the sun the way other materials do, and they'll never fade or become chalky. They won't be negatively affected by rain or snow the way wood would be. And they will never fall prey to mold, they'll never warp, and you'll be thrilled by their long-term performance.

You'll find the superior products from Werever Outdoor Cabinets anywhere you find luxury outdoor kitchens, from Montana to Massachusetts, California to the Carolinas, and Colorado to the shoreline of Connecticut - where we have the most experience.

If you're planning for a new outdoor kitchen as part of our new custom home or existing home renovation and are interested in using Werever Outdoor Cabinets, please consider talking with our experienced Reagan Homes team.

Reagan Homes has been building custom homes and renovating and remodeling existing homes up and down the Connecticut shore for more than 30 years.

HOW CAN AN EVO GRILL ENHANCE YOUR OUTDOOR KITCHEN?

From cooking pizza to hibachi to cooking breakfast to searing and grilling steaks is an EVO grill is an extremely versatile and stylish addition to your outdoor kitchen.

The team of builders, designers, and installers at Reagan Homes love working on outdoor kitchens as part of your existing home renovation or new custom home.

First and foremost, the EVO Grill is American made and built to last a lifetime. While many utilize the EVO grill in addition to a traditional grill, you may find yourself using the EVO grill even more often than your traditional grill.

While technically, you might be able to do more than just grill with your retrofitted Traeger or Weber, the EVO (available in four models) is built for cooking both directly and indirectly. With an EVO, you can grill, sauté, sear, stir-fry, and toast. You can also boil, braise, fry, and poach. You can even roast, smoke, steam, and warm. The EVO offers exceptional heat control, and you'll never have to deal with hot spots. You'll have even, consistent heat between 225°F to 550°F.

The EVO is a commercial quality flat-top grill on which you can cook anything you can cook in an indoor kitchen, only outside. Each EVO cooktop is a single piece of pre-seasoned steel and is naturally non-stick. The EVO is also ridiculously easy to clean.

The key to the EVO's superiority is in its single-piece, flanged, stainless steel cook surface. Its two burners function independently, and each EVO Grill comes with removable steel drip pans and spillover trays. At the end of the day, you can remove them and run them through the dishwasher.

Unlike any other grill out there, the EVO Grill makes your outdoor kitchen a proper kitchen. The Reagan Homes team can help you plan your outdoor kitchen with unique appliances such as the EVO grill, pizza ovens, smokers and more.

A GREEN EGG CAN TAKE YOUR OUTDOOR KITCHEN TO NEW LEVEL

If you're more of a traditionalist and prefer charcoal to gas, the Reagan Homes team suggests a Green Egg Kamado grill might be right for you.

The Green Egg. Even just hearing those words can send a thrill down the spine of the most dedicated grillers and barbecue enthusiasts.

The best known Kamado-style ceramic grill in the U.S., The Green Egg has a substantial cult following and for very good reason.

The Kamado grill concept dates back thousands of years to a time when clay and earthenware cooking dominated in the Far East. Having evolved over the centuries, Kamados landed in their current form only a few decades ago. Today, the leader in the world of Kamados, the Big Green Egg, is a ceramic vessel that offers almost unparalleled versatility, even cooking, and efficiency.

It excels as a part of an upscale outdoor kitchen, the likes of which my team and I design, build, and install for new, custom home builds and existing home renovations and remodels.

If you and your family prefer grilling with charcoal—real BBQ, some might say— the Green Egg deserves a place in your outdoor kitchen, a place that will dazzle and impress friends and family alike.

Available in five sizes, there are a handful of reasons, say the Reagan Homes team, that the Green Egg deserves all the exceptional reviews and the cult-status it maintains.

Versatility is the most significant benefit of this grill. Sure, it grills and smokes, but you can cook just about anything on it that you would otherwise cook on a grill or in an oven. From a low-and-slow pork roast to seared steaks to pizza and even apple pie, you'll be impressed by the Green Egg's performance.

It's also exceptionally easy to use, which cannot be said of all outdoor kitchen appliances and definitely not of all charcoal grills. A Green Egg is ready to cook in only 10 minutes after the charcoal is lit, and the Green Egg makes lighting your fire easier than you can even imagine. Temperature control is easy to manage, and the unit's style and construction ensure moisture remains inside, delivering delicious food with every use.

Charcoal grilling is also healthier than many other cooking methods, especially when you use the Big Green Egg's private label lump charcoal. The Egg's special charcoal is manufactured to meet exceptionally high standards and is guaranteed not to include any additives, fillers, nitrates, chemicals, limestone, or petroleum products. It starts faster, burns cleaner, and lasts longer than commercial brands. It can be combined with wood chips to impart your favorite flavors into your meats.

The quality of the Big Green Egg is unrivaled. It's built to last and comes with a lifetime guarantee! Because it's ceramic, it won't rust. Ever. It should genuinely last a lifetime.

So popular has it become that an entire community of like-minded people—Eggheads—has popped up to support the product and each other. They share tips, best practices, and recipes and have created an environment around grilling that is about more than grilling; it's about fun.

Numerous accessories can expand your Green Egg repertoire, some of which are near-necessities and some that are just for fun. Among the necessities are the Nest (the stand your Kamado sits in), the convEGGtor, a ceramic plate that essentially turns the Egg into a convection oven, speeding up cooking times and expanding the possibilities even further, and an Egg cover to help ensure the protection of your investment.

The Green Egg line of Kamado grills is in a class of its own, and once you try one, we think you'll be hooked.

If you're planning for a new outdoor kitchen and are interested in making the Green Egg your anchor, please consider talking with the experienced Reagan Homes team. Reagan Homes has been building custom homes and renovating and remodeling existing homes up and down the Connecticut shore for more than 30 years.

To learn more, call the Reagan Homes team at (860) 962-6250
to learn more or visit www.ReaganHomes.com
to schedule a complimentary, no-obligation consultation.

WHAT'S NEEDED FOR
AN OUTDOOR MOVIE NIGHT?

Watching a movie under the stars is a great way to enjoy a warm summer evening. An outdoor movie night is a creative way to have an intimate yet fun time with friends and family. Imagine lying on a cozy cushion or blanket on a starry night, surrounded by the people you love, watching a thrilling movie while munching on delicious snacks. You get to pick the film, invite who you want, and choose the snacks. A million times better than the overpriced stale popcorn they serve at your local cinema. You can even set up the grill and serve burgers and dogs if you'd like. You and your guests will definitely enjoy your movie under the stars.

The fact is, there's just something magical about outdoor movie nights. Proper planning will allow you to work with the space available at home and make the best of it.

To start with, here are the necessities you'll need to host your own top-quality outdoor movie night.

Equipment

An integral part of your outdoor movie experience is the equipment you use. Getting the electronics in order is step one. Below is a list of the equipment you'll need:

Projector

While moving your TV outside is a possibility, it's not the best option. If you're hoping for a quality experience, invest in a projector. There are options available in every budget range that will work well. The following factors are important when considering a projector for use in outdoor movie viewing:

- Lumens: The lumen rating of a projector determines its brightness output. Projector models with a lumen range between 2,500 to 4,000 work well. The more light a projector outputs, the sooner your movie night can begin. A brighter projector makes it possible to start the movie right after sunset instead of needing to wait an additional 30 minutes for it to get darker.

- Matching Input: The projector you choose must have a connection input that fits your laptop, Apple TV, Blu-ray player, or whichever other media player you opt to use.

- Resolution: It is vital to get a projector with a resolution well-suited for your purposes. A projector with 1080p resolution or a 4K projector is acceptable.

- Size: When buying a projector, keep in mind how big your screen is and how far away the projector will need to be to project to the size of your choice.

Media Player

You will need a disc-based system like a laptop, Apple TV, DVD, or Blu-ray player to play a movie. If you have a good Wi-Fi connection, you can use a streaming device. Whichever video source you opt for, don't overlook sound quality. You don't want to select a media player that will be too complex to connect with a sound system. Streaming devices, like the Fire Stick, connect directly to the HDMI input on your projector and are designed to draw power from the projector's USB to stream movies via Wi-Fi.

Screen

Outdoor screens come in different shapes and sizes. Among the options are inflatables and stand-mounted screens. Your environment will determine the screen size and type you should get. For instance, if you are setting up in a windy area, it is advisable to get screen support anchors to keep your screen in place. You can also easily cut corners with the screen by hanging a white sheet or projecting the movie on a wall of your home. However, with this approach, you sacrifice viewing quality.

Sound System

Usually, projectors come with built-in speakers but don't expect them to provide the deep, rich sound needed for an outdoor movie. Only an external powered speaker system can do that. And the variety of options when it comes to sound systems for outdoor movies is extensive. The key to achieving a robust and high-quality sound is to match your speaker input to your projector. The size of the speaker you will need might depend on the space you have. In some instances, you can also have the audio play through outdoor speakers and/or your landscape speakers.

Suitable Location

Where you set up your outdoor cinema depends on how your home is built and situated and the geography of your yard or property. You should also make sure the location you choose for movie night is sheltered from the wind if possible.

Comfy Seats

An essential element of an outdoor movie night is the seating. So when you're planning yours, pay attention to the seating arrangement. There is a wide array of seating options from which you can choose. Lawn chairs, loungers, bean bags, sling chairs are popular options. If you don't want to stress over seating, however, you can always spread a large blanket over the ground.

Ambiance

If you're going to be inviting people to your home for an open-air movie night, you have to make the experience as enjoyable as it can be. Make the area warm and cozy. Incorporating warm lighting if you can. Hurricane candles create an ambiance that's perfect for watching movies. And if there are trees nearby, you can string lights through them.

Having an outdoor moving night is a great addition to your outdoor living. As part of your existing home renovation or new custom home we can help you determine a potential location where an outdoor movie night would be best suited on your land.

*To learn more, call the Reagan Homes team at (860) 962-6250
to learn more or visit www.ReaganHomes.com
to schedule a complimentary, no-obligation consultation.*

RETRACTABLE SCREENS TO ADD MORE OUTDOOR SPACE

It can be annoying to have the constant glaring sun bearing down on you when you're trying to enjoy a day out on your porch. Pesky insects can also ruin any relaxing afternoon if they are able to roam freely. So how do you shield yourself from the annoyances that lurk outside while still enjoying the fresh air and warmth of the sun?

Retractable screens have become the most popular feature to add to modern homes. It provides the right amount of shade while still allowing fresh air and sunlight to be enjoyed on your porch. The true beauty of a motorized retractable screen is that it can be brought down and put away at will. You can decide how much you want and how long you want it.

They can even provide the illusion of a bit more outdoor space as well, only improving your entertainment options and the aesthetic of your landscape.

How They Improve Outdoor Space

Retractable Screens add an attractive element to your outdoor spaces by allowing natural light in without it becoming too harsh. The sun can heat up your porch too quickly and make it uncomfortable for entertaining. With a retractable screen, it can be raised just enough to give you warmth and light without the brightness ruining yours and your guest's comfort.

They also make your space seem larger. Your outdoor space no longer has to be limited to your front yard or your backyard for entertaining. It allows your porch, covered patio or terrace to become a gathering place that can be opened or closed off at will.

They can be customized easily as well with different shade colors to match your home's siding and color scheme. That way it won't look tacky or out of place with the rest of your house. They can also be placed in areas where you might not expect to have need of them.

Not only can you screen in your porch, but you can add screens to patios, balconies, and even your garage.

Other Benefits

Besides protecting your space from the elements, these screens offer a sense of privacy. Most of them are shaded enough that prying eyes can't peek in on what you're doing and you can still enjoy the breeze. That way you can go about your business without feeling like everyone can see your every move.

This allows those spaces to become more of a part of your home as they can provide protection and privacy with the tinted screen. Your comfort is important and these screens add a feeling of safety while still allowing you to be outdoors. You shouldn't feel like you have to stay inside all the time to read or entertain, and with a retractable screen, you can enjoy a nice breeze without your neighbors prying in on everything you're doing.

Retractable screens can also add a great benefit to your covered outdoor kitchen or covered dining area. Inherently, food attracts insects. With retractable screens you can help keep out those pesky insects while preparing or enjoying an outdoor meal.

What We Can Do For You

At Reagan Homes, we have a skilled team of designers that can help you pick out the right screens for your needs as part of your new custom home or existing home renovation. Whether that's light, medium, or dark shades, we've got you covered and can help you take the next step to broaden your outdoor space. When you're a homeowner, you should be able to use every bit of your home to the fullest, and we can help you accomplish that.

*To learn more, call the Reagan Homes team at (860) 962-6250
to learn more or visit www.ReaganHomes.com
to schedule a complimentary, no-obligation consultation.*

PART 10:

UNDERSTANDING YOUR FINANCING OPTIONS

Perhaps you're thinking about buying property on which to build your dream home, or possibly you already have your little slice of heaven, and now it's time to build.

Or, maybe, you already own a home, a home that you and your family love but it requires renovating or remodeling if it's going to continue to meet your needs in the long run.

With interest rates so low, financing your project makes a lot of financial sense. But do you know what kind of loan? Do you know what options are available?

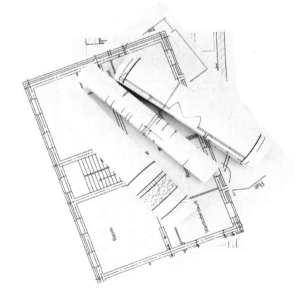

In short, there are likely far more home-financing options available to you than you even realize. If you know and understand your options upfront, you'll be in the best position possible when the time comes to speak and negotiate with lenders.

For more than 30 years, Reagan Homes has helped
individuals and families purchase and finance land,
new home construction, and renovations of existing
homes throughout New London and Middlesex counties. Not only can our team of
experienced and professional builders bring your vision for your dream life to reality,
but we can also guide you in securing financing to make it happen. We have worked
with hundreds of families to determine which financing options are best for them, from
loan type to terms and interest rates.

In this report, we share a bit of our knowledge with you—the basics about the different
loan types available for various projects. We have gleaned this information over the
years through our network of building adjacent industry experts, from mortgage
brokers to financial advisors to bankers and more. We would be thrilled to guide you
toward the best possible options for your unique set of circumstances.

Financing is just one more area in which our vast experience can help you achieve your
goals and help you live in your dream home.

We don't just care about homes. We care about you.

FINANCING OPTIONS
FOR BUYING LAND

If you're looking to finance and buy land, many options exist. But without proper consideration and risk assessment, your real estate transaction could run into complications that can put your entire project in jeopardy. Our team can help you avoid such complications. So, before you move forward and purchase that piece of land, let us help you review the many financing options and choose the one that best meets your needs.

Your financing options may include using your current home's equity, seller financing, or enlisting the help of local lenders. For instance, if you are interested in purchasing rural property, make sure you conduct thorough research to establish whether you're eligible for a USDA loan.

In most cases, financing to buy the property on which you will build the house of your dreams becomes more challenging than simply applying to take out a traditional home mortgage. If the condition of the land is improved, for example, you might pay a lower down payment.

To help you make the right decision, let's take a look at the most popular and the best financing options for buying land.

Seller Financing

Seller financing or owner-financed land is an alternative to conventional bank financing. With seller financing, you will make direct payments to the seller until you pay off the agreed upon purchase price. Buyers typically pay a down payment of at least 10 percent on seller-financed properties.

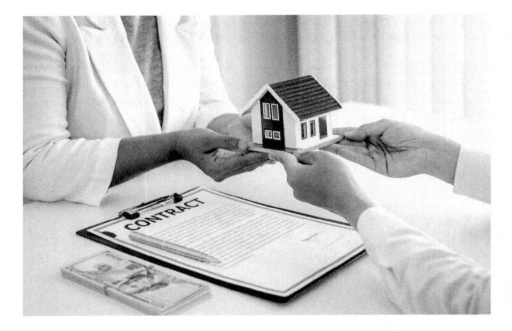

Is seller financing more secure than other options?

The truth is that no matter what financing option you choose, there will always be some risk. Objectively, seller financing can be more advantageous than some federally backed financing options.

Since you're dealing with the seller directly in such arrangements, you typically enjoy a high degree of flexibility on the down payment. Other advantages of seller financing may include no credit checks, a short closing period, low closing costs, minimal paperwork, and of course, a lower down payment.

When you don't have to wait for third-party approvals or dive into an ocean of paperwork, you can expect your borrowing process to be smoother and quicker.

USDA Loan

If the local banks and credit unions don't grant you the funds you need to buy land, you may still be able to secure financing through federal aid. The USDA, or United States Department of Agriculture, offers subsidized loans with favorable terms and minimal requirements. However, keep in mind that the process to get these funds typically takes more time and effort than other financing options.

Institutional Lenders

Local credit unions and institutional lenders can provide funding to secure land. In fact, local credit unions and reputable institutional lenders are known to offer mortgages, credit, and loans with reasonable terms for your home building and land purchase all in one loan.

With this financing option, your creditworthiness is the primary consideration in securing the required funds. To improve your chances with such lenders, you'll need to provide positive financial statements that showcase your assets, stocks, and other equity.

Home Equity Loan or Home Equity Line of Credit

You can use your current home as a source of financing for your next home. Leveraging equity in a property or properties you own is an excellent financing option—if you have the equity. Essentially, an equity loan functions as a second mortgage on your home.

Your first option is to get a standard home equity loan at a fixed rate. Your second option with a home equity loan is to opt for a home equity line of credit or HELOC. It allows you to borrow from a lender as a line of credit instead of a lump sum. With a HELOC, you have the flexibility to pay only interest for a period of time as defined in the terms of the HELOC agreement.

The process and terms of HELOC financing work more or less like a credit card. That means you have to make sure you don't exceed the maximum limit of your line of credit. If you fail to abide by the repayment terms, you might lose the money you've invested in your land altogether.

Borrowing Against Your Taxable Investment Accounts

Depending on your investment portfolio, you may be able to borrow as much as 70 percent of the current asset value of your portfolio, depending on your brokerage. With this type of loan, the application process is usually relatively easy. You can also pay back the loan whenever you want. You can even defer the interest, which is generally a fair interest rate. This allows you to keep your securities working while leveraging the value of your investments. Talk with your financial advisor to see if this option is available to you. Such financing is recommended for short-term loans.

401(K) Loans

With a 401(k) loan, you typically have to sell your securities and pay back the funds you borrow within five years to avoid financial penalties. A 401(k) loan isn't as advantageous as borrowing against the assets in your portfolio because your equities and mutual funds need to be liquidated; thus, your investments are no longer gaining interest (and actually cease to exist). This scenario assumes you are under age 59½.

If you are over the age 59½ you can liquidate your assets within your 401K with no penalty or repayment.

Cash for Land

You can use your current home as a source of financing for your next home. Leveraging equity in a property or properties you own is an excellent financing option—if you have the equity. Essentially, an equity loan functions as a second mortgage on your home.

FINANCING OPTIONS
FOR YOUR NEW CUSTOM HOME

A home construction loan is a short-term financing option that allows you to pay for the total cost of building a home through financing. You can select between a stand-alone and construction-to-permanent loan.

Stand-Alone Construction Loan

With a stand-alone construction loan, you will need a mortgage loan after the completion of construction. It's important to remember that your lender provides the stand-alone construction loan as a means to begin construction. It is necessary to pay interest on this loan throughout the construction process.

A stand-alone construction loan is essentially a home construction loan available only for a specific period. Once the construction process is complete and the house has been built, you will likely need another loan to pay off the first loan.

You can refer to the second loan as an end loan. But the critical thing to know is that you can finance—and refinance—your stand-alone construction loan at the end of the loan term. You may then, if desired, select a traditional financing option, such as a fixed 30-year mortgage, for your end loan.

This loan arrangement requires two closings, which means there's a good chance your end loan will carry a different interest rate than your stand-alone construction loan. With this option, you'll also be paying closing costs twice.

Construction-To-Permanent Loan

A construction-to-permanent loan is a combination of a standard mortgage and a construction loan with one closing. As the loan's name suggests, it saves you the hassle of refinancing following construction completion. In short, the lender adjusts the original adjustable or fixed interest rate.

It is entirely up to you to decide the terms, which generally range from 15 to 30 years. Comparatively, this type of loan is a more flexible and convenient financing option than the stand-alone construction loan. Usually, this type of loan requires at least a 20 percent down payment.

How Exactly Do Home Construction Financing Options Work?

The process of building a new home through a home construction financing option is pretty straightforward. The first step is to choose a piece of land for development. Rest assured that we can and would be happy to help you evaluate any chosen property. We can also work with you to establish a budget for building your new home based on the design and floor plans you desire. We can also work with your lender to establish the payment schedule required to build your new custom home.

Once you secure a home construction loan, the lender will advance the initial payment to us and continue to pay us throughout the construction process at specified intervals determined through collaboration between you, your lender, and us as the builder. The lender follows this schedule to release payments to us until the construction process is complete.

Throughout the construction process and until the completion, you will pay the interest on the original loan. For the sake of simplicity, think of these interest payments as payments for a mortgage with an amortization schedule.

Home Construction Financing Options: Determine Your Eligibility Criteria

- Typically, you will need to make a down payment of 20 to 30 percent of the new construction loan. Some programs allow you to provide as little as 10 percent down (or even less), especially if you are former military and qualify for a VA construction loan.

- Lenders want you to have a positive debt-to-income ratio, and most lenders expect a loan to account for no more than 45 percent of your income.

- You will typically have to provide a credit score of 680 or higher to the lenders to qualify for such a loan.

Alternative Options

Borrowing against your mutual funds and equities in a taxable account is another option. Depending on the specifics of your investment portfolio, you may be able to borrow 70 percent of the current value of your investments (depending on your brokerage). The application process for this type of loan is easy. You will also have the flexibility to pay back the loan whenever you want. You can even defer the interest which is generally at a fair interest rate. Opting in on such a loan allows you to keep your securities working for you while you are at the same time leveraging the value of your investments. Speak with your financial advisor to learn if this option is available to you. Loans like this are usually recommended for short-term loans.

401(K) Loan

With a 401(k) loan, you typically have to sell your securities and pay back the funds you borrow within five years to avoid financial penalties. A 401(k) loan isn't as advantageous as borrowing against the assets in your portfolio because your equities and mutual funds need to be liquidated; thus, your investments are no longer gaining interest (and actually cease to exist). This scenario assumes you are under age 59½.

If you are over the age 59½ you can liquidate your assets within your 401K with no penalty or repayment.

FINANCING OPTIONS FOR YOUR REMODELING OR RENOVATION PROJECT

Cash-Out Refinance

One of the easiest ways to pay for a home remodeling project is through a cash-out refinance. With a cash-out refinance, you leverage whatever equity you have in your home to a typical 80 percent loan-to-value (LTV).

For example, let's say your home is worth $750,000, and you owe $250,000 on your first mortgage. In this example, let's imagine that you also have borrowed $50,000 from your $150,000 home equity line of credit (HELOC). You do not have a second mortgage on your home. In total, you currently owe the bank a total of $300,000 ($250,000 from your first mortgage plus $50,000 HELOC balance). If the bank values your home at $750,000, in essence, you could borrow an additional $300,000 ($750,000 times 80% Loan to Value = $600,000 minus the $300,000 you owe on your first mortgage and HELOC = $300,000 available in equity). In this example, you would use the cash to pay off your home equity line of credit, your first mortgage, and start a new mortgage with a balance of $600,000 and still have $150,000 in equity and $300,000 of cash to put towards your remodel/renovation.

In short, the money you get from a cash-out refinance option comes from your home equity. Furthermore, no specified rules exist concerning how you can (or cannot) spend the funds from a cash-out refinance. That means you can use the funds for multiple home remodeling projects, should you wish.

Home Equity Loan

A home equity loan or HEL is another practical financing option to borrow funds against the accumulated equity in your current home. Equity is calculated by evaluating your home's current value and subtracting your mortgage's unpaid balance and any other outstanding HELOC balances. With a home equity loan, you don't pay off your existing mortgage and start a new mortgage. Instead, you

continue to pay your original mortgage as is, and a second payment to pay off your home equity loan is added. The interest rate on a home equity loan is usually slightly higher than that of your primary mortgage. It is usually a respectable interest rate, though, because you are securing the loan against your home's equity.

Home Equity Line of Credit

You can also finance a remodeling project through a home equity line of credit. A HELOC is very similar to a HEL, but instead of getting all of your financing in a lump sum, you access what you need when you need it. With a HELOC, you only pay interest when you withdraw money from your line of credit.

This financing option works similarly to a standard credit card. You can borrow an amount up to a pre-approved limit. When you pay back that amount, you can borrow it again. Another difference between a HELOC and a home equity loan is that a HELOC comes with an adjustable interest rate. The interest rate associated with your unpaid HELOC balance can increase or decrease throughout the loan term. But you only pay interest on the amount you borrow as opposed to the entire line of credit. As a borrower, you'll have more freedom to use a portion of the credit for one or more remodeling projects. This process will typically also lower your payments as well as the interest rate. Usually, there is a time when you don't even have to pay down the principal; you pay the interest only. Then, at a predefined time, the credit line converts to a loan for which you must pay principal and interest.

FHA 203(K) Rehab Loan

If you are purchasing a new property, you can combine your mortgage and renovation costs into one loan. With this type of loan, you are not applying for two separate loans, and you will need to pay closing costs only once. An FHA 203(k) Rehab Loan is an excellent option if you buy an older home that requires significant updating or improvement.

FHA 203(k) Rehab loans are backed by the government, allowing you to provide a lower down payment and still be approved with a lower credit score. In fact, with FHA 203(k) Rehab loan, your down payment can be as low as 3.5 percent, and you can still be approved with a credit score as low as 620. This type of loan does not require you to be a first-time buyer.

In short, the money you get from a cash-out refinance option comes from your home equity. Furthermore, no specified rules exist concerning how you can (or cannot) spend the funds from a cash-out refinance. That means you can use the funds for multiple home remodeling projects, should you wish.

Renovation Construction Loan

Some lenders offer programs to use your home's future value to help finance your renovation project. For example, let's say your home is worth $500,000 and you owe $400,000. You're already at an 80 percent loan-to-value ratio, which means that qualifying for a HELOC or HEL is going to be challenging. We can work with you to submit plans to your lender

and estimate your home's future value after the completion of renovations. The lender will finance a portion of the renovation based on the future value instead of the current value before the renovations.

Personal Loan

A personal loan is an unsecured loan that provides homeowners the opportunity to remodel their homes. Since personal loans are not secured, it is unnecessary to use your current home as collateral.

The process for obtaining a personal loan is usually relatively straightforward. A personal loan can come with a fixed or adjustable interest rate. A personal loan's interest rate is generally higher than traditional home equity loans due to its unsecured nature. If you have an excellent credit history, you may still be able to obtain a personal loan at a reasonable interest rate. On average, you will have to pay back a personal loan within five years. We have relationships with local and national financial institutions which can help you obtain a personal loan for your renovation project.

No Interest Credit Cards and Remodeling Specific Loans

If you have good credit, you might be able to qualify for one or more 0 percent interest credit cards. You might also be able to benefit from a manufacturer's financing program for a portion of your remodel or renovation project. For example, if you add a pool to your existing home, financing programs specifically for pools may be available to you. As another

example, sometimes cabinet companies will offer special financing when you purchase their products. Some of these programs are interest-free, while others are not. The application process for manufacturer financing is straightforward, and approvals are typically based on your credit score, income, and debt-to-income ratio.

BORROWING AGAINST YOUR TAXABLE INVESTMENT ACCOUNTS

Borrowing against your mutual funds and equities in a taxable account is another option. Depending on the specifics of your investment portfolio, you may be able to borrow 70 percent of the current value of your investments (depending on your brokerage). The application process for this type of loan is easy. You will also have the flexibility to pay back the loan whenever you want. You can even defer the interest which is generally at a fair interest rate. Opting in on such a loan allows you to keep your securities working for you while you are at the same time leveraging the value of your investments. Speak with your financial advisor to learn if this option is available to you. Loans like this are usually recommended for short-term loans.

To learn more, call the Reagan Homes team at (860) 962-6250 to learn more or visit www.ReaganHomes.com to schedule a complimentary, no-obligation consultation.

401(K) Loan

With a 401(k) loan, you typically have to sell your securities and pay back the funds you borrow within five years to avoid financial penalties. A 401(k) loan isn't as advantageous as borrowing against the assets in your portfolio because your equities and mutual funds need to be liquidated; thus, your investments are no longer gaining interest (and actually cease to exist). This scenario assumes you are under age 59½.

If you are over 59½, you can use your 401(k) money without penalty for any reason.

Our team can guide you in the financing options to buy the best land with suitable terms and conditions. We can also help you with the construction financing for your new custom home or financing for your existing home renovation.

Comparing multiple financing options is a safety net to make the decision that will secure your investment for years to come. The right approach would be to have a predetermined plan of action and seek out tax, loan, and real estate experts' guidance to make the right decision. Each family's situation is different, and some loan options may be better for your unique circumstances than others. Again, we are happy to help you start the process and point in the right direction based on your unique situation.

PART 11:

WE LOVE TO EXCEED OUR CLIENTS' EXPECTATIONS

YOU CAN LIVE IN
YOUR DREAM HOME!

At Reagan Homes, we'll build your new home or renovate your existing home like it's our own.

Reagan Homes is CT's design-build company committed to efficiently building your dream home by constructing your new custom home or renovating your existing home.

Life is too short to live in an environment you are not thrilled with. Save time, avoid frustration and save significant money when you entrust Reagan Homes to build your new custom home or renovate your existing home.

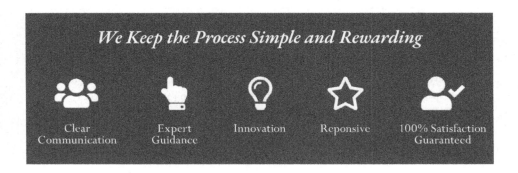

We Keep the Process Simple and Rewarding

Clear Communication   Expert Guidance   Innovation   Reponsive   100% Satisfaction Guaranteed

CLIENT SUCCESS STORIES

"

"We recently built a house with Reagan Homes. We were completely satisfied with the project from start to finish. This was the first home we ever built and we were nervous about how the process would go. The people at Reagan Homes made it so smooth and simple, and they alleviated our stress."

~ Jon and Pegg

★★★★★

"

"It was great working with Dave and his team. We are so proud of our home! He took our plans through the historical commission process and 4 months later, we moved in." *~ Anastasios I.*

★★★★★

"

"I have only praise for Dave. He always makes sure we're happy, he's easy to work with and he's easy to contact through email, phone or text. Plus Dave's been very accommodating. He didn't mind that we wanted to use our own tile man and Dave helped us fix an existing garage on the property. Now I can't wait to move in!" *~ Sarah*

★★★★★

"

"What impressed us most was Dave's consistent approach to "keep the customer satisfied" and resourceful solutions to problems. We are very pleased with our new home and would recommend Reagan Home to anyone considering building a home." *~ Dave and Lori*

★★★★★

"

"We have used Reagan Homes for numerous renovations at multiple homes we have lived in over the years. We can always count on Dave and his team to help guide us through the design process, permitting process and every step of the remodeling process. We couldn't imagine working with any other contractor other than Reagan Homes." *~ Jennifer and James*

★★★★★

We would love you to be our next success story!

HOW WE CAN HELP YOU

Land Evaluation

Design

New Custom Homes

Waterfront Homes

Renovating Your Existing Your Home

Financing

A lot of people feel like building a new custom home or renovating their existing home is not possible. At Reagan Homes, we understand that nearly every family can afford their dream home. Really what you are investing in is bringing family and friends together to create priceless memories that will last a lifetime.

4 SIMPLE STEPS
TO YOUR DREAM HOME!

1.
Consultation

2.
Design
& Budget

3.
Build or
Remodel

4.
Enjoy Your
Dream Home!

We don't just care about homes.
We care about you.

 100+ successful new custom homes and renovations.

$ Each client saves an average over 25% with Reagan Homes.

✓ More than 30 years of experience & community relationships.

Schedule your complimentary,
no-obligation consultation.

www.ReaganHomes.com
(860) 962-6250

Made in the USA
Las Vegas, NV
20 December 2021

39015965R00174